Florence Morse Kingsley

Prisoners of the Sea

A Romance of the 17th Century

Florence Morse Kingsley

Prisoners of the Sea
A Romance of the 17th Century

ISBN/EAN: 9783744675833

Printed in Europe, USA, Canada, Australia, Japan

Cover: Foto ©Thomas Meinert / pixelio.de

More available books at **www.hansebooks.com**

Prisoners of the Sea

A Romance of the Seventeenth Century

By Florence Morse Kingsley

Author of "Titus,"
"Stephen" and "Paul"

❁

Philadelphia:
DAVID McKAY, Publisher
1897

CONTENTS

(iii)

CONTENTS

PRISONERS OF THE SEA

CHAPTER I

ADRIFT

THERE were five persons in the boat, three men and two women. The faces of the women were bowed upon their knees, but the three men stared fixedly at a black shapeless mass which lay rising and falling upon the long Atlantic rollers about an eighth of a mile away. Certain jagged protrusions here and there about the mass and the tangle of broken cordage which streamed out dismally upon the night wind, suggested that this dubious object might once have been a ship. Besides the boat and the low-lying mass of wreckage there was no hint of human presence as far as the eye could reach.

"She's going now!" exclaimed one of the watchers suddenly in a loud husky whisper.

The woman nearest him threw up her head with a sharp cry. As if in answer to the cry the wreck leapt upward convulsively then disappeared amid a sudden fury of boiling surges.

The death struggle of a ship in mid-ocean is an awesome sight, awesome enough if one be safe and sound on the deck of a staunch vessel, but if there be but the flimsy shell of a skiff betwixt the beholder and the eternity of waters beneath, then indeed does the breath come hard, and the puny heartbeat well nigh cease.

For some minutes after the disappearance of the wreck no one of the five persons who had witnessed the catastrophe uttered a sound. With eyes fixed blankly upon the spot where the vessel had gone down each sat as if frozen in his place.

After a time the man in the middle of the boat gave vent to a short sound, half groan, half snort. "Wall, friends!" he ejaculated slowly, "She's gone down, and the crew's gone down—saving the three of us. The tarnal fools, they've gone whar they belong!" His voice died away into a husky whisper. Then he began again in a loud defiant tone, "Yes, gone whar they belong, cap'n and all! God A'mighty kin take care of cowards as 'ull desert their ship and them as is helpless. 'Will you leave the women?' says I to the cap'n. 'Let'em go to heaven, and be damned to you, sir!' he yells in my ear and jumps into the boat after the others. I heard their death scream a cable's length and I laughed to hear it. Yes sir, I did! Didn't I tell'em no boat 'ud live in that boiling hell of water? Didn't I say, 'Stand by the ship and the ship 'ull stand by you?'" The speaker's voice rose to a shrill quavering cry and he sprang to his feet with a wild gesture, but the man behind him laid hold on his seaman's jacket with no gentle hand.

"Come, Winters, sit down, sit down! it won't help matters to tip the boat over."

The man addressed as Winters sat down and seized his oars. "What's your further orders, sir?" he growled without turning his head.

"My orders?" repeated the other meditatively.

"We had best eat something, I suppose. After that—
Yes, decidedly we must eat. Cato, hand up some food
for the women."

This last remark was addressed to the third man of
the party—a negro, who sat flat upon the bottom of
the boat, surrounded by a heap of miscellaneous articles.

The old sailor shook his head slowly. "A bad business," he muttered to himself. "I wish the women
was safe out of it. Thank God they ain't the cryin'
kind—neither mother nor daughter." He leaned forward and addressed himself to the silent figures in the
stern in what was meant to be a soothing and concilia-
tory tone. "Be you feelin' much scairt now, ma'am?
Feelin' scairt won't help us any, if you'll excuse me for
sayin' so. Jack Winters wasn't built to be drowned, I
reckon. I've had a heap of luck in shipwrecks and
that's a fact." The speaker paused and laid a cautious
forefinger on the bowed shoulder nearest him. "Mebbe
she's asleep."

"No, I am not asleep," said a sweet clear voice, the
English words spoken slowly and with a decided foreign
accent. "But I—ah, what will become of us?"

"Wall, now, that I can't rightly tell you, miss; but
Lord love ye, ma'am, there's land in these here parts
and there's vessels—in course there's vessels! wa'n't
our ship here a spell ago? to-morrow, mebbe, 'ull see
us on the way to Ameriky with a better ship under us
than *The White Gull* with all her feathers on."

The old man faltered a little as if his confident words
had choked him in the utterance. The other woman had
raised her head and was regarding him earnestly. "You
hear what this good man is saying, Madeline; there is
yet hope that we may be saved."

3

"Hope!" roared the sailor, "in course there's hope! Who says there ain't? While there's life, there's hope, my hearties!—I mean ma'am. Young Baillot here knows every word I've said is Gospel truth, there *is* land and there *is* vessels, mebbe not ten miles distant; more'n that the sea's calm as a milkpan, we've water aboard and—What'd you say, sir?"

"That we must eat now, and then take what rest we may till morning. We may need all our strength to reach the land you speak of, Winters." The young man stepped cautiously past the sailor as he spoke, and silently proffered a cup of water and a basin filled with sea biscuit to the two women.

The girl laid her hand impulsively upon his arm. "Tell me, monsieur," she began, then stopped abruptly. "I forget—" she faltered drawing back. "But the English, I know it so little—is it possible that we have any chance of safety? You also are a sailor and a brave man—ah, how brave, since you did not abandon us to our fate in the storm; tell us shall we be safe?"

"We are in no present danger," replied the young man looking down into the dark eyes which were lifted appealingly to his. "As for to-morrow, who can say. We are in God's hands." He said these words in the French language.

"You are then—one of us?" It was the older woman who spoke.

"I am a Huguenot, madame."

At this avowal the girl gave a little cry of joy and surprise, but the other only bowed her head.

"We are in God's hands," she repeated gravely.

4

CHAPTER II

TOWARDS midnight the fog which had for some hours been creeping about the horizon closed in upon them, bringing with it a cold penetrating drizzle, while the wind freshened so considerably that an occasional dash of spray broke completely over the boat.

"It's turned a nasty night, sir, and no mistake," observed Winters, buttoning his jacket tightly about him. "There'll be precious little sleep for the crew of this craft to-night."

The old sailor had apparently recovered his spirits by this time, and handled his oars with as much unconcern as if he were in charge of a pleasure excursion. "Here you, Cato!" he bawled. "Catch on to that saucepan and heave some of this water overboard; we'll be swamped if we ain't keerful."

Hours passed, the boat wrapped in a smother of fog and night, lashed by the keen whips of the flying crests, laboriously climbed the long sides of the crinkling hills of green water which thrust themselves forward with monotonous regularity out of the darkness, only to feel her way into the yawning valleys between with irresolute pauses and sudden shivers as if she were minded to give up the unequal struggle.

"The water's about my ankles," growled Winters at length. "Quit rowing, mate, and bear a hand with the bailing. I can hold her up to the sea."

5

"May I not bail?" cried a clear voice from the stern. "I am chilled and stiff with inaction. I must do something to help."

"Let her be!" roared Winters, as the young Huguenot began a remonstrance. "She'll be better astir, and with something to limber her up a bit. Give her the panikin from under the bench, and God help the poor lass to be nimble with it."

The regular sound of the basin as it struck the bottom of the boat showed that the girl had set about her task with vigor.

"Bravo, miss!" cried Winters at length. "Hold hard, and rest awhile, the water's gone down a good bit since you began to ply that panikin. The dawn's at hand now, and please God, the breeze'll quiet down."

The old sailor was right; before many minutes a faint gray light began to struggle through the fog which still enveloped them. Cheered by the sight Madeline fell to bailing again, though she was wet to the knees, and the heavy masses of her hair, which had become loosened as she worked, fell all about her shoulders.

"Madeline, child," said her mother anxiously, pushing aside her encumbering wraps, "let me take the basin for awhile. You must rest."

"No, madame," said Baillot decidedly, "forgive me for having yielded to Winters here; mademoiselle should not have undertaken such a task."

"Don't fret yourself about Winters," growled the old sailor, evidently displeased at this speech. "It's not hurt the young lady, and she's done a good stroke of work, which may save us all in the end."

"Indeed you are right, sir!" exclaimed Madeline.

6

"I am quite able to go on with it too," she added stoutly.

"Of that there is no need at present," said Baillot, taking the basin from her reluctant hand. "The boat has ceased to ship water for the present."

An hour later the fog had entirely vanished, and there was nothing to hinder a clear view of the narrow horizon about them, a floor of dancing waves, foam-crested, closed in upon by the cloudless dome of a pale blue sky.

"We're too low in the water to see anything," observed the young man impatiently to Winters, who was standing at his side. "Our circle of vision seems no larger than a dinner plate."

"Ay, a lofty perch on the mast, with a good hull rolling beneath were more to my liking," replied the sailor with a chuckle. "But what make you of yonder speck! My eyes are rheumy for lack of sleep, but thar's something thar."

Baillot looked keenly in the direction to which the old man pointed. At first he could see nothing but the dazzling play of the sunlit waters, but at length he too seemed to make out something which appeared, as the sailor had said, like a speck on the extreme verge of the horizon.

"I see it, Winters," he said at length, "and since we have nothing better to do this morning, let us make for it. What do you think it is?"

"Wall, sir,' said Winters slowly, "you can't find out from me; it may be a rock, it may be a floating mass of wreckage. But as you say, we might as well go that way as any for aught I see."

For some time the two bent vigorously to the oars,

7

then Baillot again stood up to ascertain the position of the distant object. " We have either fallen off a couple of points," he observed, " or our rock is afloat ; it has changed its position since I last looked."

"What is it?" asked Madame de Langres anxiously ; "have you sighted land ?"

"Alas, no, madame," replied the young man. " It can be no object of very great size ; but as our course is one of chance, we have determined to find out what yonder black fleck on the horizon is."

"I can see nothing," said Madame de Langres after a prolonged gaze in the direction which the young man had indicated.

"I can !" cried the young girl, who was standing up and shading her eyes with her hand from the dazzling sunlight, " and it seems to me that it moves about !"

"You are right, miss," exclaimed Winters. "It does move about ! Unless I am mistaken, yonder object is the hull of a vessel. Of a wreck mayhap ; but there may be that about her which we shall find useful."

The two men again fell to their oars, the negro keeping steadily at his work of bailing, for the boat, it appeared, was leaking badly. " I hope to de Lawd," he was muttering, " dat we'll git quit ob dis boat before night. Ol' Cato can't keep up dis yer bailin' much longer."

They were now rapidly nearing the object of their search ; the old sailor was right in his conjecture, it was a hull, apparently that of a small vessel, lying low in the water, and rising and falling on the long ocean swell.

"It has masts !" exclaimed Madeline presently, —"two of them, but I see no sails."

8

At this intelligence the men dropped their oars.

"Ay, masts she has!" cried Winters. "And as delicate as a lady's finger. Yonder's no wreck, but blow me if I can make her out! She's like no craft I ever saw at sea. Give way, man! we'll soon find out what she is."

Half an hour more of hard pulling brought them within hailing distance; and Baillot, standing up in the bow of the boat, and making a trumpet of his hands, shouted:

"Ship, ahoy! Ship, ahoy!"

He paused and waited, but no sign of life appeared about the vessel.

Again rang out the long musical cry across the water: "Ship, ahoy! Ship, ahoy!"

"Can we not go nearer?" cried Madeline, her eyes shining like stars in her excitement. "Surely there can be nothing to harm us!"

The little vessel, with its dark green hull, its slender masts, against which lay the neatly furled sails, its glittering brass work, and the delicate web-like tracery of its rigging, looked like a fairy craft.

The old sailor sat staring at her, his eyes bulging out of his head, his mouth open. "Wall, I'll be everlastingly blowed if I can make her out!" he ejaculated at length. "I've seed her like on the Thames, I'm thinking. 'Tis a pleasure yacht! But how did she come here? Why ain't she blowed to pieces with the hurricane? Whar's the folks what sail her?"

"There must be some one on board," said Madame de Langres, with manifest excitement. "Perhaps they are below."

"*L'Espérance!*" cried Madeline, as she caught sight of the gilded letters which ran about the bow.

9

"*L'Espérance!*" echoed Madame de Langres. "Are we all dreaming? Surely this seems to be too wonderful a thing to belong to the waking world."

"Look, sir!" suddenly exclaimed Winters, catching at the arm of the young Huguenot. "Do you see that?"

He pointed, as he spoke, to the end of a heavy cable which was hanging from the bow. "It's her hawser, sir, and it wasn't cut many hours since!"

CHAPTER III

THE young man caught the end of the rope and swung himself to the deck of the yacht. "I will look below and report," he said, briefly. "Keep clear of her sides, Winters, till I come back!"

With that he disappeared down the companion-way.

He was on deck again within five minutes, and waved his hand reassuringly to the party in the boat.

"There's not a soul on board!" he cried. "*L'Espérance* is a derelict, and ours by right; let us take possession at once. Here, Winters, make the boat fast at both ends; then pass up the ladies."

Winters prepared to obey. A few minutes sufficed to make their frail craft secure; then the old man, planting his sturdy legs far apart, reached out his hands to Madeline. "Come, miss," he said, "I'll take you first."

"But how am I to get up there, sir?" said Madeline, drawing back a little.

"Wall, you can't get aboard as our friend Baillot did just now, can you, miss? So I must just hand you up to the deck, like a precious bit of cargo as you be." And unceremoniously seizing the girl in both his brawny arms, he lifted her to where Baillot was waiting to receive her.

The natural embarrassment which she felt at this novel

mode of conveyance was speedily lost in concern for her mother, who still sat in the boat below.

"Mother," she cried anxiously, "do not fear!"

"I am not afraid," said Madame de Langres, with a quiet smile.

Winters lifted her with surprising gentleness, and in another instant she stood beside her daughter on the deck. Cato followed, scrambling over the side of the vessel as nimbly as a cat, and lastly Winters.

All instinctively looked down at the boat which they had just quitted. It was nearly a third full of water, for the leak had been gaining on them rapidly within the past hour. For a moment no one spoke; then Cato, true to his craft, exclaimed, "We have left our water and biscuits behind; dis yer ship's mighty fine, but what about her victuals?"

No one had thought of that, and Winters paused as he was about to cut the ropes which held the water-logged boat.

"You've got more sense in your woolly pate than I gave you credit for, Cato," he said. "Suppose you do a little exploring on your own account; you'll scent victuals if there be any, I'll warrant me. I'll bring aboard what we had, sir," he continued, "though wet biscuits are sorry eating; but it'll serve us, I reckon. By the token of the fresh-cut hawser, we'll see land afore many days."

With a last look at the sinking boat, the women turned toward the companion-way. They were wet to the skin, and trembling with fatigue.

As they entered the cabin Madeline could not repress a cry of delight. Rich rugs carpeted the floor; costly tapestries covered the walls; while parted curtains of crimson stuff revealed a second cabin, also a marvel of comfort and beauty.

"'Tis nothing less than a fairy craft!" she said, shaking her head solemnly. "What if it dissolve in foam beneath our feet, and leave us luckless wanderers to sink to the ocean caves of the tricksy sprites who created it?"

"Heaven forefend!" said Baillot with a grave smile. "Luckily for us it seems more substantial than the fabric which dreams are made of, though it is quite as strange and hard to believe in. I will send Cato with refreshments of some sort."

The women scarcely had time to look about them, when a light tap sounded on the cabin door. It was Cato bearing a tray laden with silver dishes. "More marvels, Cato?" inquired Madeline.

"De best ting yet, lady!" cried the old negro joyfully. "De Lawd mus' hab put dis yer ship here a purpose for us. Dar's de lubliest cook's galley ye eber see, with ebery kin ob saucepan, an' all shinin' like pure silver. An' dar's victuals fit to make a hungry man's mouf water. I didn't wait to do no fancy cookin' though, jest knocked up somethin' in a hurry, case I knew ye was 'bout starved."

The old negro had been busy setting forth the contents of his tray on a small richly carved table. His task finished, he paused a moment longer to say, "Dey's a makin' ready to get under way. I don' surely know, but I tink dey see lan'. I ain't in no hurry, de Lawd knows when I'll get anodder such kit o' saucepans."

"You had best get back to those same saucepans, Cato, or our hungry crew will be helping themselves," observed Madeline, smiling. At this suggestion the old man vanished at once.

Above stairs all was hurry and excitement. Baillot had climbed into the rigging, and was studying the horizon with a small glass which he had found in the cabin below.

"What do you make, sir?" questioned Winters anxiously. The young man handed him the glass.

"Ay, ay, land! And that not far distant. If this 'ere craft has a nimble foot, as befits so fine a lady, we shall make it afore sunset! We can crowd all sail, sir, in this breeze."

The two set busily to work, and soon every stitch of canvas was set. Baillot sprang to the helm, the sails filled and the graceful hull began to move through the water.

"This is a glorious little craft, sir!" cried Winters. "See the spray fly from beneath her forefoot! But she's not built for bad weather, and that's a brewing for to-morrow. Give me the helm, sir, and get something into your hold."

"Tell Cato to fetch me a biscuit and do you go and eat, Winters," said Baillot, observing the ashen pallor which showed beneath the old man's tan. "You're starving, man!"

"Ay! mate, something's the matter," grumbled the sailor, laying his hand over the pit of his stomach. "I am not the man I was once!"

"You'll sing a different tune after a good meal. Come, begone; and don't show your face on deck in too great a hurry."

Left to himself the young man cast a thoughtful glance about the vessel. He was greatly perplexed by her appearance, though he had said little to any of the company. In a region of the ocean which he knew to be desolate and far from any civilized coast, how was it possible for a yacht fit for the occupancy of some gay queen to be afloat. He was presently aroused from his revery by the sound of a light footfall behind him.

"I have not your permission, monsieur, to appear upon deck," said Madeline demurely, "yet I am here, with my usual boldness, to ask a question."

"Surely, mademoiselle! you did not misunderstand me, when I forbade you to venture onto the slippery, wave-swept deck of the wreck."

"Assuredly not," said the girl dropping her eyelids. "I am not an able seaman, but only a woman, and therefore quite unnecessary and seriously in the way. You did right to rebuke me as severely as you did; 'twas well merited on my part."

"Mademoiselle!" exclaimed the Huguenot, "what can I say to assure you that far from being—"

"You may tell me," interrupted the girl hastily, "whether it is true that we have sighted land : Madame, my mother, sent me to inquire. We are forced," she added haughtily, "into many positions which are distasteful."

The young man bowed with an air as haughty as her own. "I have the pleasure of informing Mademoiselle de Langres, that we have sighted land; if the breeze holds good, we shall reach it before sunset."

"What can it be?" said Madeline easily, apparently quite unmindful of his frigid manner. "I know nothing of our whereabouts, but are we not in the very midst of the ocean?"

"I made instant search for maps and instruments when I first boarded the vessel," replied Baillot, "but I found nothing to throw any light on our position. This vessel is evidently a pleasure craft, intended for the idle amusement of a summer's day; she has drifted from her moorings which cannot be far distant, as the freshly-cut hawser and her perfect condition testify. We shall doubtless find a very prosaic explanation of the mystery when we reach yonder shore," he added with a short laugh. "Perchance the barbaric prince of yonder island has seized this gay craft—but, no, that cannot be." And fixing his eyes on the horizon the young man relapsed into silence.

"The barbaric prince of your imaginings must be a man of learning," observed Madeline quietly, "for see what I found lying on the open lid of an escritoire below!" And she held up a slip of paper on which was inscribed in a peculiar, but perfectly legible hand a fragment of Latin verse. "But I must go below— thank you for the information which will enable my mother to repose more at her ease."

By the middle of the afternoon the shores and promontories of the island—for such it appeared, began to assume distinct proportions. The women had reappeared upon deck, looking greatly refreshed by their hours of repose.

"Would you not like to examine the shore with the glass?" said Baillot, addressing Madame de Langres near whose chair he was standing.

The lady accepted the proffered instrument and gazed long and earnestly at the coast which they were rapidly nearing.

"I see nothing to indicate that the island is in-
16

habited," she said at length, raising her eyes to the young man's serious face. "Nothing but wooded heights, and a desolate reach of shore. Yet I shall be most thankful to once more set foot upon solid ground, even though it be but a savage solitude. Do you see anything more than I have said, daughter?"

"No, mother," said Madeline. "I see nothing but hills covered with trees, and the beach below on which the surf appears to be rolling heavily. How shall we effect a landing?"

"That's what I want to know," said Winters, who had overheard the question. "What say you, sir; shall we skirt the island a bit in search of a bay or creek into which we may safely thrust our little craft? If yon's a desert island we shall want to sail further some fine day, and I've no notion of stubbing my lady's toe on yonder beach; she'd do no more dancing for us, nor for any one else."

"Let us skirt the island by all means," said Baillot. "We shall then have a clearer idea of the character and extent of the coast. We may find it a difficult if not impossible task to land at any point."

"Never fear, sir, we'll find a nook for our beauty to weather the night in. I've no notion of sailing her much further on this cruise."

"We shall see, Winters. I sincerely hope that you are right."

"And I," said Madame de Langres, "hope for the sight of a civilized town on the other side of the island."

"That you won't see, ma'am," said the sailor. "For though I couldn't tell you precisely where we be, I'll bet my head thar's no town within a thousand miles of us."

"Is there no other land in sight?" asked the lady.

"No other, madame," replied Baillot, who was in his turn examining the coast with the aid of the glass.

"Then must not the owner of this wandering butterfly of a vessel dwell on yonder island? It can scarcely have been afloat long."

"If such be not the case, madame," replied the young man, "we shall be forced to adopt old Cato's pious explanation. He declares that the powers above have dropped this little craft from the clouds for our especial benefit."

"That we were providentially guided to it, I do not for a moment doubt," said Madame de Langres with emotion. "The negro's simple trust puts our anxieties to the blush; we should have faith to believe that the same hand which has guided our course amid the darkness and dangers of the past will continue to care for us; life were unbearable else."

CHAPTER IV

THE CHÂTEAU ON THE ISLAND

THE yacht had now approached so near the coast that the low thunder of the surf could be distinctly heard. There was no sign of creek or bay, nor any evidence that the land they were approaching was other than desolate and uninhabited.

Winters looked anxious; the breeze had begun to die away, and the vessel made but little headway. "If we fail to make a landing soon," he said at length, "we shall be forced to put to sea for the night, and I'm blessed if I like the look of yonder bank of clouds!"

"We have still two hours or more of daylight, Winters," said Baillot; "if we are not utterly becalmed, we can make several miles yet before the darkness overtakes us. Rather than risk another night at sea in so frail a vessel, would it not be better to run her ashore and trust to our wits to land our party?"

"Our wits would be of little use in yonder smother of surf," growled the sailor. "We might strike at least fifty feet from dry land, and go to pieces like a bubble."

His sharp eyes were searching the sea and the coast unremittingly as he spoke. "The glass, sir!" he exclaimed suddenly.

"What do you make?"

"I fancied that I caught a gleam of something white through yonder trees, but if I did, 'tis vanished now. My old eyes are of little use of late."

19

"Your eyes did not deceive you this time, mate; for on yonder slope there is assuredly an object which shows white through the surrounding foliage," said Baillot. "But what it is I cannot make out," he added after a more careful survey.

The distant object, whatever it was, was now lost to view as the vessel rounded a little promontory clothed with foliage to the water's edge. Beyond this wooded height a slight indentation occurred in the coast-line, scarcely noticeable by reason of the luxurious vegetation on either side; but slight as it was it did not escape the vigilant eye of Winters.

"Yonder's a creek!" he exclaimed joyfully. "Now if we may but thrust our little craft into its mouth without mishap, we shall soon stand on solid ground!"

As they approached nearer, it became evident that the vessel could proceed with ease through the narrow channel, which, moreover, widened quite unexpectedly as they made their way cautiously along. The shores on either side showed delightful glimpses of verdant meadows, while strange shrubs of tropical appearance crowned with bright-hued blossoms dipped their branches into the glassy water.

The breeze had quite died away, but the little vessel was borne gently onward by the force of the inflowing tide. The sun was setting, and the rich colors of the sky above shone in the silver mirror of the stream. Spicy breaths of perfume greeted the voyagers, and from the woods and thickets sounded the vesper song of myriads of birds. The little party stood close together in the bow of the vessel, scarcely speaking. The scene was inexpressibly delightful to eyes wearied with the desolate monotony of ocean.

" It is as if we had left the earth and all its sorrows behind and were sailing into some heavenly country," sighed Madeline softly.

The stream now diverged suddenly to the left; and as the yacht slowly rounded the wooded point a cry of joy burst from all on board. High on a rocky cliff overhanging the little lagoon, into which the waters of the stream now expanded, stood a castle. Long and low, rather than lofty, solidly built of stone, its windows glowing brilliantly in the sunset light, it seemed to speak of hospitality and comfort to the weary travellers.

"Our bird has flown straight to her nest!" exclaimed Winters, pointing to the wharf which they were approaching. In another moment the little vessel had touched the pier. Baillot jumped from her side, and, seizing a bit of heavy cable which was trailing in the water, he held it up to view. It was the other end of the severed hawser !

"Ay, ay, my beauty, straight to your nest ! Let us make her fast, and perhaps by that time some one from the big house yonder will have spied us. We shall expect a right hearty welcome, since we have brought back so valuable a bit of property."

While the men were busied in securing the yacht to her moorings, the women were anxiously watching the castle. The sunset light had faded now, but no welcome gleam showed along its dark front. Madeline shuddered slightly. " I fear we shall be unwelcome guests in yonder château," she said slowly. " Surely no one would choose such a residence as this unless for some dark reason."

" And all because we see no light in the windows, my child ! It may be—indeed it is quite likely—that the inhabitants of the castle have not perceived our approach," said Madame de Langres cheerfully. "That anyone could refuse to receive us in our present helpless condition I cannot believe."

"Is it your wish, ladies, to scale the heights and assist us in storming yonder inhospitable-looking dwelling? or will you remain here under the guardianship of Cato while Winters and I announce our arrival, and claim our share in the salvage of the vessel?"

Madame de Langres hesitated. "I hardly know—" she began slowly, when Madeline laid a beseeching hand upon her arm.

"Let us remain here, mother," she said, in a low voice. "You are not strong enough to attempt such a climb to-night, and who knows what our reception may be? We are safe for the present—and free!" she added in a still lower tone.

"We will remain if you wish it, my child," said Madame de Langres. "But it will be quite impossible to conceal our presence on the island even should we wish to do so. For my own part, I have no fear of what we shall find awaiting us in the castle, gloomy as it appears."

"We will return as speedily as possible, and shall hope to bring you cheering intelligence," said the young man, as he swung himself over the side of the vessel.

The two women watched them as they climbed the steep embankment, the sound of their voices dropping back in airy echoes on the faint evening breeze; then all was silent save the occasional twitter of a belated bird. A feeling of loneliness and foreboding swept over them as they sat hand in hand in the gathering darkness.

They were presently aroused from their sad thoughts by the voice of Cato from the companion-way:

"Mabbe yo' git no gran' supper in dat castle to-night! 'Pears like yo' better come down stairs and see what I'se got for ye. 'Taint bes' fur ye to sit yer in dis damp anyhow."

"Cato is right, mother dearest," said Madeline. "I have been very thoughtless. Let us go below by all means."

The glowing interior of the little cabin certainly presented a most cheering contrast to the gloom outside. It was lighted by numbers of wax candles in gilded sconces, from which depended fringes of sparkling prisms. In the middle of the cabin was set forth a tempting repast, rendered yet more inviting by the snowy linen, sparkling glass and delicate china with which it was served.

"We are partaking of the hospitality of the castle, whether its lord will receive us or no," commented Madeline. "What right have we to make so free with all these fine things? Would it not be embarrassing if some black-browed pirate should of a sudden burst in upon us?"

"Embarrassing were scarce the word, should such a thing happen, child," said Madame de Langres. "And yet I think that even the black-browed pirate of your fearful imaginings might be tempted to forget his erring ways in sight of such a banquet as Cato has provided."

"Nebber fear, lady," said Cato, who was hovering about the table, bestowing sundry finishing touches upon its arrangement. "Dis craf' belongs to us; didn't yo' hear de cap'n say dat she was a derelic'? Dat

23

means, I take it, dat she was a runaway. We done brought her back, didn't we? and we's got a mighty good right to eberyt'ing we wants in her. Tell you what, lady, if dey don' want us up dere, we'll jest simply derelic' again. I don' want noffin better to do than to cook for you ladies. It's time dey was back a' ready," he added, with an anxious look toward the companion-way.

Madame de Langres glanced up at the clock, which was ticking busily on the wall. "Nine o'clock," she said slowly. "Perhaps they have been detained. They will come soon, I hope," she added, after a pause; "it is not late."

But ten o'clock came—then eleven—twelve—and the two men had not returned.

CHAPTER V

THE CASTELLAN

WE must now turn back a few hours, that we may follow the fortunes of the two men whom we last saw climbing the steep path which led up to the château.

"There's been folks afore us not many hours since," said Winters, pointing to the grass on either side of the path.

"Heaven send that they be of a decent sort and charitably disposed!" quoth Baillot. "'Tis a strange thing to light on a château like the one yonder in this region of the earth. If we lived in the days of black magic, I should say that it must have flown from the neighborhood of Versailles."

"Ay, ay, mighty strange!" echoed Winters. "The place and the little craft yonder are off the same piece; but the yacht has served us rarely, mayhap the castle will do the same."

The rugged path now merged into a tolerably broad and smooth roadway which lay along the base of the steep wall of rock from whose summit frowned the dark mass of irregular buildings; behind the castle a ragged fringe of poplar trees showed black against the greenish hue of the sky, where the first faint stars were beginning to shine. The explorers presently came upon a flight of steps cut deep into the solid rock.

"These steps will take us to the castle gate," said Baillot in a tone of satisfaction; "directly we should come upon a guard, or at all events a porter. These people, whoever they may be, have taken too much pains with their position to leave their posterns unguarded."

"Wall, sir!" growled the old sailor under his breath, "I'm no coward, but blow me if I like the looks of the place! Let's go back to the yacht, and slip away with the ebb tide into the honest ocean. When the sea means mischief it roars it right out, so you can't miss it; you don't have to go sneaking round by any back way to find it out."

"Tut, Winters! would you take those passengers of ours out to sea in yonder cockle-shell, and with a storm brewing? We've seen nothing to frighten us yet, man! Come now, put on a bold front, for I'm going to hail the porter. Hola, above there! Hola!"

But no answer came back from the frowning walls above, save a reverberating echo of his call.

"Hola, above there! Hola!" repeated the young sailor. "Come on, man, I'm going up! Our porter's heavy with wine, and not expecting visitors."

The heavy oaken door at the top of the stair stood ajar, swinging to and fro in the evening breeze. Baillot pushed it open and looked cautiously within, then entered, Winters following at his heels and grumbling audibly.

The place in which the adventurers found themselves was an ordinary paved courtyard, empty save for a fountain which gurgled plaintively in the half light. On three sides of the yard arose the walls of the château, its upper stories resting upon richly carved colonnades beneath whose heavy shadows could be discerned the dim outline of several massive doorways.

Baillot strode boldly up to one of these doors and bestowed a thundering knock upon its oaken panels. Then catching sight of a bell rope hanging near he gave it a lusty pull.

"These folks are either asleep or dead," said Winters after an anxious pause of several minutes.

"Or," interposed the younger man hastily, "there are no people here."

"How do you account for the yacht, sir?" questioned Winters. "And the well-worn track to the water's edge?"

"I can account for nothing," replied Baillot. "It may be, however, that somewhere in this mass of build- ings we shall find human beings, 'tis big enough to house a regiment."

As he spoke he laid his hand upon the door; to his surprise it yielded to his touch, swinging open noise- lessly.

"These must be honest folk," quoth Winters, "since they leave their doors aswing. Shall we go in, sir?"

Baillot hesitated a moment before replying. "'Tis growing late," he said at length, "and our companions will be anxiously awaiting our return—yet so far we have learned nothing; the daylight will serve us for a few minutes longer. Yes, we will go in, and look about us a bit."

By the dim light which streamed in through the open door the two men perceived that they had entered a long and wide corridor, paved with marble, and lighted at the further end by a lofty window of richly-colored glass; on either side of this corridor were numerous doorways, while beyond Baillot thought that he could make out through the gathering gloom the outlines of a winding stairway.

They had scarcely taken more than a passing glance at their surroundings when, with a sound as of rushing garments, a violent gust of wind swept adown the passage-way; in an instant the heavy door swung to with a bang which reverberated in startling echoes through the silence.

"This'll do, sir, for me," cried Winters. "I've no stomach for creeping about old castles in the dark. Who knows what's behind yonder closed doors? Nothing that we can't do without for the present, I'll be bound. Let's get back to the ship and take this 'ere job in hand by daylight!"

"I'm with you, Winters!" said the young man. "There's no reason, as you say, why we should not be satisfied with the shelter afforded us by the yacht for a single night."

"Good Lord, sir, I should say not! She's fit for a king, and the honestest thing there is about this place, I'll warrant." With that the old sailor laid hold of the door and gave a sturdy pull; to his dismay it refused to open. He turned and faced his companion. "What sort of devil's work is this," he demanded fiercely,—"a door swinging open to a touch to let you in, then shutting as fast as the doors of hell on a lost sinner?"

"There's no devil's work about it, Winters," said Baillot calmly. "'Tis plainly enough a spring lock; the door was unlatched when we entered, that unlucky gust of wind closed it, and here we are!"

"Yes, sir, here we are! and a nasty job we may find it to get out," growled the old man, distractedly running his fingers through his grey hair. "This is a dummed sight worse than any shipwreck I was ever in."

"We'll get out somehow, and that's something you can't be sure of in a shipwreck," said the other with a short laugh. "There were several outside entrances; come on!"

The last gleam of daylight had now vanished and the two groped their way cautiously along the walls in the thick darkness.

"What do you say, sir, to trying a window?" asked Winters in a tremendous whisper. "Consarn it all, we can't stay foolin' 'round here much longer!"

Baillot stopped short; his hand had encountered a door sunken deeply into the wall. He opened it without difficulty, and after straining his eyes in the direction of two dim spots in the darkness which he took to be windows, he stepped cautiously forward; to his horror his foot encountered nothing more substantial than the empty air. Clutching wildly at the door to save himself, he fell heavily forward.

"Lord love ye, sir! What's got ye?" exclaimed Winters who was just behind him. "Be you killed!"

Baillot sat up and rubbed his head ruefully. "If I was killed, Winters, what would you expect me to say? No, I'm not dead, nor even hurt, for I've tumbled onto a remarkably soft carpet; but if you're inclined to follow my lead, I advise you to do it in a little different way: I fancy you will find about three steps there."

"Ay, ay, sir, three steps! But now we're here, what next?"

"That's the question. I suppose we might pursue our investigations till morning, and be no wiser than we are now. I confess I'm not so anxious to keep on with them as I was a few minutes since. My ideas have been shaken up like the bits of glass in a kaleidoscope, and they've arranged themselves in a brand-new pattern.''

'' I don't follow you, sir ! but if you mean that a tumble into some tarnal hole in the dark is a thing to be tried but once, I agree with you. We were a pair of lubberly fools not to bring a ship's lantern with us. Beg your pardon, sir, I should have said—''

'' You needn't apologize, Winters. I'm in a sufficiently humble frame of mind. But what do you think we had better do ?''

'' Wall, sir, it's my opinion, since I'm asked, that the best thing for us to do is jest to lay to till daylight. There's nothing to be gained by cruisin' about in the dark, with neither chart nor compass. Let's drop our anchors, sir, and get a bit of sleep; it's precious few hours of it we've had since we left *The White Gull.*''

'' But the women ?''

'' I'll resk 'em, sir ! They've had a good meal of victuals by this time, I'll be bound ; old Cato's on guard, and not a mouse to peep at them.''

'' We're not so sure of that,'' remarked the young man after a pause. '' But I fear it is out of our power to do other than follow your suggestion. It would be worse than folly to risk a broken limb in this place.''

Winters, who had been fumbling about him in the darkness, now tossed some soft object toward his companion, saying as he did so, '' Catch on, cap'n. I've found a nest of cushions here. We'll sleep as sound as the women-folk in yonder craft.''

'' They'll not sleep to-night, you may be sure of that.''

"Wall, I shall," returned the old man calmly, and in another moment his loud snoring showed that he had kept his word.

Baillot lay open-eyed, staring into the blackness for some time longer, but at length, he too, exhausted by excitement and fatigue, fell into a heavy slumber.

How long he slept he could not tell, but he sat up suddenly broad awake and listened intently. There was a slight sound not ten paces off, as if some one were feeling cautiously about in the dark. And now he distinctly heard a long-drawn sigh.

Thoroughly alarmed, he put out his hand and gave his sleeping companion a sound shake.

"Ay, ay, sir!" growled Winters sleepily. "I'll be on deck directly, sir!"

"Hist!" said Baillot in his ear, "there is some one in the room with us!"

The old sailor was awake in an instant. He sat up and listened. "You've been dreaming, sir," he said at length, "and if you've no objections, I'll go to sleep again."

"Hist, man!" repeated Baillot. The sound was unmistakable this time, there was somebody in the room; again came that long-drawn sigh.

"Dang it!" cried Winters with decision. "I'll soon find out what it is! Ahoy there!"

But there was no reply, only a renewal of the soft fumbling sounds.

"Good Lord, sir! What's that?"

Not a yard away two glowing balls of fire hovered low in the darkness. They moved—they were advancing.

Winters gave a smothered yell of fear and buried his head in the cushions.

Baillot whistled slightly. " Come here, come here, good fellow !'' he said coaxingly. A whine of delight followed, and a quick scuffle of small feet across the floor.

"Sit up, Winters, old man ! 'Tis nothing but a dog, and a little fellow at that—a King Charles by his ears. I knew what it was the instant I saw the eyes.''

" "The eyes, sir !'' gasped the old man. " I thought it was the devil himself, all on fire inside !''

The two men composed themselves for a second time, for it was still intensely dark ; the dog nestled between them, manifesting his delight from time to time by gently licking Baillot's hand.

" This little fellow throws almost as much light on our position as though he carried a lantern,'' observed Baillot.

" How's that, sir.''

" Why, don't you see that his presence here indicates that we are not alone on the island ; he must have a master—or mistress.''

" Wall, I wish he'd kep' dark till morning,'' growled the sailor. " Nobody was asking for information from him !'' And with that he rolled over and was soon snoring again.

But there was no more sleep for the young Huguenot. He lay wide awake listening to the wind as it sighed drearily about the casements, and watching eagerly for the first indication of dawn. The little creature at his side nestled closely up to him, shivering now and then as if with cold or fear.

CHAPTER VI

To the two women on board the yacht the night wore drearily away. A prey to a thousand distracting fears and maddening conjectures, neither could sleep. Madeline persuaded her mother to lie down in her berth, but she herself spent most of the night pacing up and down the little cabin.

"Why did we not go with them?" she asked herself a thousand times, "we should at least have known the worst!"

At the first streak of dawn she roused Cato, who had spent the night curled up on a rug outside the door.

"We must go up to the castle at once," she said decidedly, "and see what has become of our companions. Oh, what if we never find them!"

"Lawsy, miss!" said the old negro coaxingly, "you jus' lie down an' res' a little, and let old Cato get yo' some breakfas'. Den I'll go up dere muself. Der ain't no need for you to wear yo'self out climbin'. I'll come right back."

"You will do nothing of the kind," cried Madeline. "We will all go this time, and we will start now. No, I want nothing to eat; it would choke me."

"But yer lady moder, miss," pleaded the old man. "Yo' surely do'n' spect her to start out till she hab some breakfas'?"

3   33

Madeline hesitated. "No," she said at length, "she must have something; but make haste!"

"Madeline!" said the soft voice of her mother, "my child, what ails you? In all our troubles I have not seen you so impatient!"

"Well, mother," sighed the girl penitently, "it must be the uncertainty; only think how dreadful it would be if we never find them; what should we do?"

"Can you not learn, my child, the folly of pursuing so hotly after trouble. Surely, we have had distresses enough without imagining more which may never come to pass. A few hours may see all these clouds dissipated, and our brave friends restored to us in safety. Let us at least hope so till we have better reason to fear the contrary."

"He would never have left us to suffer such anxiety without some terrible reason," declared the girl obstinately.

"Perhaps not," said her mother quietly; "Mr. Winters is a very thoughtful old man."

"Mr. Winters!" echoed Madeline. Then she blushed scarlet. "Here is Cato with the breakfast! Let us make haste, that we may start as soon as possible."

Madame de Langres made no further remonstrance; truth to tell, she was almost as anxious as her daughter.

The slight repast was partaken of in haste and silence. Then the two women arose, and after the somewhat difficult feat of getting from the vessel to the pier had been accomplished under the able generalship of Cato, the little party was fairly under way.

The morning had dawned red and threatening; the wind, as it swept through the trees, had in it the sound of weeping, while the low pile of buildings on the heights above looked not a whit less gloomy and sinister than in the twilight of the preceding evening.

Madeline shuddered as her eye rested upon the dark walls fringed with battlements and bristling with turrets, but she said nothing, only hurried on faster than before.

"Madeline," said her mother breathlessly, "I fear that I cannot walk so rapidly. Can we not stop for a moment?"

"Oh, mother, how thoughtless I am! You ought not to make such an exertion. Return to the yacht with Cato, I beg of you; I will go alone."

Madame de Langres had sunken onto a great stone by the roadside, where she sat for a moment silent and exhausted. Presently she arose. "I am quite ready to go on now, my child. Any further division of our little company is not to be thought of."

By this time they had reached the flight of stone steps which led up to the castle. Without a moment's hesitation Madeline began the ascent; then glancing back, and seeing that her mother was hesitating, she returned.

"Lean on me, mother!" she cried; "we have not far to go now, and this mystery will be solved."

"Bes' wait here, and let me go," said Cato, who had been toiling along in the rear, laden with a large basket.

"What have you in your basket, Cato?" questioned Madeline, for the first time noticing his burden.

"I thought mabbe dey be hungry," returned the old man deprecatingly, "becase dey had no supper las' night."

"I am sure I hope they at least had bread and water, however inhuman their jailors!" cried the girl, raising her eyes defiantly to the castle, which now frowned directly above their heads.

A few more steps brought them to the top of the flight of rock-hewn stairs. Pushing open the door the little party entered the courtyard. They stood for a moment looking timorously about them. Then Cato set down his basket, and proceeded to try door after door.

"Dese folks ain't bery early risers," he remarked, as he rolled his eyes reflectively about. Presently observing an arched opening which had escaped the notice of the explorers the evening before, he picked up his basket. "We'll walk in dis yer way, and see what we fin'."

The arched opening in question proved to be the entrance into an inner courtyard, and the anxious searchers had scarcely entered it when they were startled by the sound of a window going up above their heads, followed by the excited barking of a small dog.

"*Bon jour, mesdames!*" cried the voice of the young Huguenot cheerfully. "A most welcome sight to two prisoners gaunt with famine and perishing with thirst is a rescue party with a basket."

"Are you then prisoners?" questioned Madame de Langres anxiously. "Where are the inhabitants of the castle?"

"Prisoners only of the darkness in league with a breath of wind," replied the young man. Then he briefly related the events of the preceding night, winding up his story with the hope that the ladies had not been unduly anxious over their prolonged absence.

"Not at all, monsieur," said Madeline coldly. "We felt reasonably sure that nothing serious could have befallen two such bold adventurers; but where is Mr. Winters?"

"Here, miss!" replied that redoubtable seaman, popping his head out of the other window. "I've just been rigging up a little tackle to get us out of here." He was busy fastening something to the window-sill as he spoke, and in another moment had descended hand over hand on a rope improvised from various gay fabrics knotted firmly together. "Come on, sir!" he shouted to Baillot. "It's all ship-shape!"

"I must arrange for the safety of our little castellan," said Baillot. "As far as we have learned he is the only inhabitant of the château."

So saying he drew up the rope, and fastening it firmly to the body of the dog, lowered the little creature, despite its frantic struggles and pathetic yelpings, safely to the courtyard below.

"What a little darling!" exclaimed Madeline. "But how thin he is, and how he trembles; I am sure he is starved. Cato, did you not say that you had something to eat in that basket? Do give me something for this poor little fellow."

"Better give him a drink firs', lady," said Cato. "He's terrible thirsty; look at his tongue."

"If there's anything to eat in that basket, you black rascal," put in Winters, "I don't mind looking into it myself; I'll git some bones ready for the dog," he added with a grin.

Baillot in his turn had now descended into the courtyard, and the two hungry men, at the request of Madame de Langres, addressed themselves with vigor to the welcome contents of the basket, which Cato had unpacked and set forth on the stone steps of one of the entrances.

"It is fortunate that Cato was so thoughtful," remarked the lady complacently. "Madeline would have it that you were pining in some dungeon with no better refreshment than bread and water."

"We should have been mighty glad of that last night," said Winters betwixt his mouthfuls. "And so would yonder pup," indicating with a wave of his hand the dog, which was eagerly eating tidbits from the hand of Madeline.

"But do you really think," pursued Madame de Langres, "that the château is deserted? It must at least have been a recent departure, since the dog is alive."

"Now that we have appeased the pangs of hunger, and are once more all together," said Baillot rising, "let us pursue our investigations. It may be that there is someone in one of the wings of this great pile, who is as yet wholly unaware of our presence here."

"Very good, sir, I'm ready to clap on all sail and cruise ahead," said Winters, "but I shall keep the tail of my eye out for spring-doors and such bedevilments!"

"What if we fail to find any one," said Madeline, fondling the pretty head of the spaniel, who in return bestowed upon the slender white hand of his benefactress every token of affection.

"We can then take possession of the château, and await further developments," replied Baillot. "We shall find no reason to complain of our accommodations," he added.

"'Twere more to my mind, sir," said Winters, "to try a cruise in yonder yacht, as soon as the weather sets fair; there's something wrong if we find this place empty; 'tain't natur' for folks to go off in such a hurry."

"Why do we stand here talking about it," cried Madeline impatiently. "Let us find out at once whether the place be empty or no." And she boldly laid hold upon a door near at hand. It opened readily, but the young girl shrank back from the interior, which showed dark and gloomy in contrast to the broad daylight without. In an instant, however, she recovered herself and entered, followed closely by the remainder of the party.

"Belay there, till I fasten this 'ere door open!" said Winters. "The women-folks might not enjoy coming down our outside stairway."

"These seem to be mostly offices and rooms for the accommodation of attendants," said Baillot, throwing open door after door. "Let us ascend this stairway and see what we shall find above."

Accordingly the whole party proceeded up the grand stone staircase, their feet falling noiselessly upon the thick carpet of crimson velvet. Having gained the top, the adventurers found themselves in a high and wide corridor, lighted from above, and hung with pictures; while here and there a cushioned bench, or a chair covered with rich embroidery cast dim reflections upon the polished floor of inlaid wood.

"A picture gallery!" exclaimed Madame de Langres, as the party hurriedly traversed this apartment.

By a sort of common consent, all presently paused before a pair of double doors of white and gold, the entrance being further guarded by heavy draperies of embroidered damask.

"Had we best await the arrival of the lackey, who

39

should by rights be lolling on yonder bench?" questioned Baillot lightly, though with a beating heart.

"See the dog!" exclaimed Madeline.

The little animal had struggled down out of her arms, and was whining and scratching frantically at the threshold.

Baillot laid his hand upon the door, and after a moment's hesitation opened it softly. The spaniel bounded in, barking joyously, then his bark changed to a piteous whine, and returning to Madeline, he crouched at her feet and looked up beseechingly into her face.

The room, at the entrance of which the party still hesitated, was both large and lofty, and as they could see by the light which struggled in through the heavy draperies of lace and damask which shrouded the windows, furnished with great magnificence.

"A pretty snug harbor for somebody!" observed Winters in a hoarse whisper. "Shall we go any further on this tack, sir?"

"There seems to be no one here," said Baillot, and after another hasty survey he entered, the others following.

"See, mother," said Madeline, "the room has been recently occupied!"

She pointed as she spoke to a table upon which stood a tall Venetian vase, containing a magnificent rose, from which the petals were just beginning to drop. Beside the vase was a book, opened and lying face down upon the table as if the reader had deposited it there at some trivial interruption.

The party now moved cautiously toward the open door at the end of the room; they looked in. This was a sleeping apartment, as the lofty canopied bed bore witness; its satin coverlid was turned back, and on the pillow, covered with finest linen and edged with lace, still lingered the faint imprint of the sleeper's head. Over the back of a great arm-chair which was drawn up before the fireplace hung a dressing-gown elaborately embroidered.

"How strange, how very strange this is!" murmured Madame de Langres with an involuntary sigh. "Where can the occupant of this chamber be?"

"Quite possibly upon a hunting party, madame," said Baillot, "accompanied by his household. We have still many rooms to explore, to say nothing of the unknown territory of the island about us."

At this moment Madeline caught sight of Cato; the negro had disappeared for a moment, while the others were occupied in examining the bedchamber. Now he thrust his wooly head in at the door and beckoned violently to the young girl to come out. Wonderingly she obeyed.

"What is it, Cato?" she said.

"Dey tinks der's nobody in dis yer place," he whispered, grasping her arm. "Do you hear dat?"

She listened intently, and presently heard a peal of discordant laughter, followed by the snatch of a French *chanson* sung in a loud tuneless voice.

The young girl turned like a flash, and running back to where the others were standing, cried out,

"There is some one in the next room!"

CHAPTER VII

THE GARDEN OF ROSES

"THERE is some one in the next room!" repeated the young girl. "I heard them singing and laughing— such a horrid inhuman laugh, it must be a mad man!" she added with a shudder.

"To be sure, cap'n," said Cato, who had followed closely, "it do soun' powerful like a crazy man."

"We must attend to this at once, Winters!" said Baillot shortly. "Have you arms?"

"Sartain, sir," replied Winters, stretching out a pair of brawny limbs, "and good strong ones they be, thank God. Let us get after this rascal at once, we'll soon make short work of him."

"Take this, you dunderhead, and come along!" said the Huguenot impatiently, picking up one of the irons from the fireplace as he spoke. "It will serve in place of a better weapon; I have a pistol."

Thus equipped the two men crept cautiously into the corridor, followed by Cato, the women hanging fearfully back, yet not quite daring to remain behind.

Another burst of the screaming laughter greeted them, as they approached a closed door at the end of the passage, followed by a hoarse incoherent murmur.

Baillot laid his ear to the crack of the door, and heard these words muttered in a low, harsh voice. "*Bon jour, monsieur!* Water! Water! Ha, ha!

42

I say, where are you all? Pierre, you pig, fetch me my breakfast!" Then a sort of screech as of inarticulate rage.

The young man straightened himself and turned his grave face toward the others, a faint smile lurking about his mouth. "Another case of quite needless alarm, friends," he said quietly, laying his hand upon the door. "I think we shall find our madman to be a harmless, if not useful member of society."

The women shrank back, but Winters advanced, boldly grasping the iron in both hands.

"You villain! You pig!" shrieked the voice. "My breakfast! My bath! *Bon jour*, ha, ha, ha!"

"Well, I'll be—blamed!" ejaculated the old sailor, staring open-mouthed at a large rose-colored and white parrot, which was dancing impatiently upon its perch, shaking its gilded chain violently. "You're a pretty one to be left in charge of a castle!"

"A pretty one!" screeched the parrot, putting its head on one side knowingly. "A pretty, pretty, pretty Pol-ly!"

"The poor creature hasn't a drop of water, nor a mouthful to eat!" cried Madeline, who had quite recovered from her fright. "No wonder that he screamed!"

"Where is Pierre?" said the bird, regarding her gravely out of its red eyes, as it twisted and turned on its perch.

"Where, indeed?" echoed the girl. "But we must provide for your wants at once, poor Polly."

"Let me go, let me go!" screamed the bird.

"Not a bad suggestion," remarked Baillot. "And since we are likely to be pretty well occupied in attend-

43

ing to our own wants, we will set you at liberty." With
that he unfastened the chain from the leg of the parrot
and opened the window.

The bird flew out with a screech of delight, and was
soon lost to view amid the masses of foliage.

"Oh, mother, see the garden!" exclaimed Madeline, who had stepped out of the long window onto a
stone balcony. "The roses, oh, the roses!"

Madame de Langres looked dreamily at the beautiful
scene which was spread out beneath them, the velvet
lawns, the stone balustrades wreathed with flowering
vines, the fountain throwing up showers of crystal
spray into the bright sunlight, and above all the roses ;
roses everywhere, and of every imaginable color, pink,
white, yellow, deep crimson, banked in stately pha-
lanxes on the terraces, twined in rich profusion about
gleaming statues, and breaking in a many-colored foam
of blossoms high up on the grey old walls of the château itself.

"'Tis the garden of my dream," she said softly,
"the garden of roses."

"How could you dream of what you had never seen?"
asked the girl in a tone of awed curiosity.

"I cannot tell you, my daughter," replied her
mother, "but so it was. On that terrible night in the
boat when I at last became unconscious of my surroundings, I seemed to find myself of a sudden in a
garden of roses, just such a garden as this. Let us descend into it."

A flight of stone steps from one end of the balcony
gave access to the garden, and down this the two women
went.

"Yes," she continued, looking about her, "this is

44

the very place. I seemed to be walking here, looking at the roses, and enjoying their sweetness. I stooped to pluck one, when suddenly something impelled me to look up. I did so, and saw at the window yonder the figure of a man."

"That is the room where we found the book on the table," interrupted Madeline in a low voice.

"I saw his face distinctly, as he looked out of the window ; it was that of a man no longer young, with large dark eyes, an acquiline nose and a full mouth. It was a handsome face, but marked by a look of extreme melancholy and weariness. He did not appear to see me, though his eyes rested upon the very spot where I was standing. Presently he raised his eyes to heaven, his lips moving as if in prayer, then he stepped back into the room and I saw him no more."

"Had you ever seen the man of your dream in the waking world?" questioned Madeline.

"His face was strangely familiar," replied her mother musingly, "and yet I cannot tell who it was. Nay, it eludes me like a bit of flying thistle-down. But our companions are beckoning to us; perhaps they have made some further discovery."

"We have explored every room in this part of the château," said Baillot, as they approached, Madeline with her hands full of roses. "And while we have found no sign of a living being about the place, we have made a discovery which will not be unwelcome to two ladies, who have been forced to leave their effects behind them."

"And what is that, monsieur," asked Madame de Langres, glancing down, with a quiet smile at her travel-stained garments.

"A suite of apartments, less gorgeous, it is true, than those we have just seen, but seemingly replete with everything you will need after your toilsome adventures."

"Ay, a deal of woman's gear, but not a grain of 'baccy, so far," said Winters, discontentedly fingering his empty pouch. "I'm like to die for a smoke, sir."

"You'd best explore the lower regions with Cato, Winters," said Baillot, "while I show the ladies to their rooms."

"Ah, how homelike and delightful!" exclaimed Madeline, as the young man threw open a door on the left of the corridor. The sunshine lay in bright patches upon the rich carpet, and glimmered gayly upon gilded cornice and crystal chandelier, while an abundance of comfortable chairs and couches seemed to invite to repose. "Let us stay here while we are forced to remain —at least till some one comes to dispossess us," she added. "As for the rooms we have seen, I do not covet them, gorgeous though they be."

"This is very comfortable," said her mother soberly. "I suppose we have the right born of necessity to make ourselves at home here. Let us keep within easy reach of one another, for I confess to a feeling of timidity, homelike and hospitable as the place appears."

"There is something uncanny about its perfect order and its emptiness," observed Baillot with a shrug. "We should be less at a loss to explain a musty and mouldering ruin; yet these mysteries have often very prosaic explanations. We will keep together, as you suggest, madame. I will occupy the apartments which we first examined. Winters shall sleep here in the little room at your right—if I am not mistaken there is a bell-rope;

yes,' here it is, which will enable you to arouse him with ease. While Cato shall form the connecting link by curling up outside upon a couch, à la guard of the bed-chamber," he added with a smile and bow.

The two women left to themselves found, as Winters had said, an abundance of woman's gear : linen, fine as cob-web ; gowns, sober in hue, yet of rich material, but all a world too wide for the slender figures of the two homeless wanderers. Nevertheless they donned them, discarding with sighs of relief their own travel-worn garments.

"How perfectly delicious !" cried Madeline, as she stood before the dressing-table fastening up the masses of her dark hair with jeweled pins. "I am sure if the inhabitants of the island have obligingly left all these good things for us, I should like nothing better than to remain here. What say you, dearest mother?"

"It is certainly very beautiful and very homelike," replied Madame de Langres, her eyes wandering about the comfortable chamber. "But we could never feel at ease here."

Madeline glanced over her shoulder with an apprehensive shrug ; then she laughed, and threw open the door of the wardrobe. "Which of these ample robes, mother dear, will you choose to appear in ? This black satin, when I shall in some way have disposed of its superfluous fullness, will become you rarely. For myself, I choose this gown of ruby silk, and with it this lace-trimmed neckerchief. Only fancy if the door should open now, and the stately dame to whom all belongs should appear !"

Even as she spoke there came a light tap on the door of the outer room. "It's only me, lady !"

said the voice of Cato. "I'se done fixed dinner all ready !"

Both women started at sight of the figure which awaited them at the end of the corridor. Clad in a habit of green velvet, which set off his athletic figure to perfection, ruffles of costly lace half concealing his hands, a sword hanging at his side, they at first failed to recognize the young sailor.

He came forward, a dark flush rising to his cheek at sight of their astonishment.

"I do not wonder that you are surprised to see me so gayly attired," he said hastily, "but I could find nothing plainer, and the temptation to rid myself of my wretched travel-stained clothing was too great to withstand the sight of an ample wardrobe."

"You need not apologize," said Madame de Langres smiling. "We have also made free with what we found ; I trust the owners will forgive us the liberty we have taken."

The party now moved forward to the room which Cato had chosen for a dining-room, and where he had set forth an inviting meal. "Where is Mr. Winters ?" said Madame de Langres, pausing as she was about to seat herself at the table.

Cato looked slightly scandalized. "He am smoking in de courtyard off de kitchen, lady," he said with an apologetic duck of his woolly head. "He done ate a saucepanful of meat, an' a loaf of bread 'bout half an hour ago."

Madeline laughed outright. "Then we need feel no further anxiety about our good friend for the present," she said. "What are your plans for the afternoon, monsieur ?"

"There is nothing to do more important than to finish the exploration of the castle," replied the young man; "then if time serves us Winters and I intend making a hasty tour of the island."

"Will not that involve a further separation of our little company?" said Madame de Langres. "I confess to feeling timid about being left alone in this place, and I fear I am not equal to much further exertion today."

"Especially as neither of us slept last night!" said Madeline impulsively.

Baillot turned his dark eyes upon the young girl with a gravely inquiring expression, but he said nothing.

"We were in momentary expectation of your return, monsieur, and could hardly be expected to guess that so trifling a cause as a wandering breeze had detained you," she said, returning his look with a haughty lifting of her small head.

The young man smiled. "If mademoiselle had been with us in the more than Egyptian darkness of the château last night, I think she would have been ready to forgive what otherwise had been unpardonable. I was ready to plunge ahead in the darkness at whatever risk to life or limb, but Winters cried a halt, or rather in his own phraseology he insisted upon 'dropping anchor' for the night."

"And he was quite right!" declared Madame de Langres. "I am astonished, my child, that you so petulantly criticise our brave friend. But to avoid another occurrence of the kind could we not defer the exploration of the island till to-morrow? We shall then be refreshed, and can dare the perils, if perils there be, together."

4   49

"The island is very small; I learned that much with a single glance from one of the turrets, which I ascended this morning!"

"And did you see any further sign of human habitation?" questioned Madeline eagerly.

"That you shall see for yourself," replied the young man.

CHAPTER VIII

A cry of disappointment broke from the lips of Madame de Langres as the party emerged from the narrow winding stairway which led up into the turret.

"How small, how very small it is!"

Madeline advanced in silence to the battlemented verge. Directly beneath lay the garden glowing with color, flanked on either side by orchards wherein the yellow glow of oranges shining amid the masses of dark foliage could be distinctly seen. Below the orchards stretched a park-like expanse of glade and meadow, interspersed with groups of lofty trees ; and beyond all the sea, its dim blue reach unbroken by land or sail, swept about the vast rim of the horizon.

"Are not those the roofs of cottages?" said the young girl at length, pointing to a little opening among the trees at the left.

"Yes, miss," said Winters, who had joined them, "cottages they be, but as empty as this 'ere place of human beings. 'Twas there I found my 'baccy by rare good luck; an' this suit of fustian which I made free to borrow," and he glanced down at his person with evident satisfaction. "Whar the owners of all these things be, God A'mighty knows! Mayhap they all be dead of some plague."

At this grim suggestion the women turned pale.

51

"What a terrible explanation of the mystery!" exclaimed Madeline faintly.

"A most unlikely one to my mind, Winters; your find of tobacco should have brought you more cheerful imaginings!" said Baillot frowning. "There is no trace of any such tragedy, no sign of disorder, and above all, no survivor dead or alive. They could not all have buried themselves, man!"

"True, cap'n," said Winters, scratching his head reflectively. "Mayhap the last one went crazy an' jumped into the sea. I heerd of the like once when I was cruisin' in the Indies."

"The devil take you, Winters! What do you mean by such nonsense?" exclaimed Baillot wrathfully. "We must explore the island now, whether or no, or 'tis little sleep will visit our pillows to-night."

"Best board the yacht, sir, an' git away to sea," said the old sailor with a hitch at his trousers. "I've been looking her over; she's a beauty, she is, an' as sound as a nut. We're sure to strike one of the larger islands before many days. What do you say, ma'am, to a bit of a cruise, with Winters at the helm?"

"I cannot bear the thought of entrusting our lives to yonder frail vessel after our terrible experience of a few days since," said Madame de Langres in a voice which trembled slightly, "though you may be assured of our confidence in you, my friend."

"'Tis not to be thought of," declared Baillot decidedly; "we shall undoubtedly find maps and charts somewhere about the place which will render such a course less certain to end in disaster. But to start out in yonder cockle-shell not knowing whither to steer our course—*Peste!* I wonder at you, man, for proposing it!"

"Ay, ay, sir! 'Tis not for me to think, only to obey orders. I only hope the next twenty-four hours will find us all alive and hearty," said the old sailor in an aggrieved tone.

"Even should your horrible conjecture be true, sir, what advantage would there be in being aboard the yacht?" asked Madeline with a shudder. "If we must die, let it at least be on solid ground, without the accompaniment of the *mal de mer.*"

"Ay, that's what a landsman thinks!" cried the sailor. "But no bed of wormy earth for Jack Winters; twenty fathoms of blue water for me, where the honest brine will keep my old bones in pickle till the resurrection trumpets call 'em to the daylight!"

"Tut, man, have done with your fool's talk! Let's get us about our business!" said the young Huguenot. "Could not you ladies explore the library for the maps and charts which were so singularly missing on board the yacht, while we take a hasty tramp about the island?"

"We can and will," declared Madeline stoutly; "this is no time for idle fears. Let us be about it at once!"

Accordingly all descended the narrow stairway, the women with Cato remaining in the château, while the two men set forth on their tour of investigation.

"Let us finish the exploration of the castle, while they are absent," proposed Madame de Langres. "The sooner we learn all the secrets of this old pile, the better for our peace of mind."

"I'se done looked in all de cellars," said Cato, "mighty dark and cold. Nuffin dere but heaps of boxes an' barrels, an' all full ob good victuals, praise de Lawd! More'n we eat in a year. Dere's ben a heap

53

ob folks in dis yer castle not many days ago ; de Lawd knows whar dey all is.''

"Did you find anything which would lead you to think that there had been sickness in the château?" asked Madeline anxiously.

" Not a ting, lady ; all jes perfec', as dough dey jes' stepped out, 'spectin' to be right back. Der was bread bakin' in de oven, an' a roas' hangin' on de spit. An' a power ob cold victuals in de larder, all fresh an' good. Dey surely went sudden !"

The three were traversing the picture-gallery during this conversation, and Madeline's eye wandered idly over the walls as they passed. Under any ordinary circumstances she would have lingered in delight before many of the pictures, but now she only remarked one thing.

"Have you noticed, mother, that while we see here pictures of land and sea, of fruit and flowers, that there is not a single portrait?" she said. "Is not that a curious circumstance ?"

"I had not thought of it," confessed her mother, "but surely we should find in such a collection some evidence of family pride. There is at least an indication of the peaceful taste of the owner, since we see no battle-scenes. For my part I am coming to believe that this has been the scene of a very tranquil existence."

"Tranquil—yes, but how dreary, shut in by yonder impassible barrier of blue sea !"

Meanwhile the two men were tramping silently along towards that part of the island where were the cottages, whose roofs they had seen from the turret of the château, and which, as we have seen, had already been visited by Winters.

"This is the place, sir, where I found my 'baccy, an' where I helped myself to some clothes," said Winters, as they approached a small cottage built of rough-hewn stone and thatched with straw. The rustic porch was garlanded with a climbing rose, whose luxuriant branches had flung themselves in graceful festoons to the roof, whereon it had burst into a very carnival of bloom, over which looked forth the sleepy eyes of two dormer windows.

"If we must stay on this 'ere island," continued the old sailor, "this place were more to my mind for our little company. More wholesome, sir, an' not so ghostly as yonder pile of stone."

"My faith, man, I believe you're right!" said Baillot. "How about the inside?"·

"Come in an' see, sir. Honest folk have bided under this roof; it has the right look to it," replied Winters, opening the door.

Baillot entered after him and looked about the little room. There was an ample chimney-place on one side, a heap of white ashes showing where the last fire had burned itself away. By the hearth stood a high-backed chair and near it a cradle, its draperies hanging carelessly upon the floor, as if its little occupant had been hastily removed. In one corner a dresser displayed upon its spotless shelves shining mugs and platters of pewter, and upon the table near the window was a bit of sewing, the needle still sticking in its folds. Upon this quiet scene, quiet, yet many-voiced in its quaint simplicity, looked down the white face of the old clock, silent too, its hands pointing to eight o'clock.

Both men instinctively uncovered their heads in this humble interior.

"Is there anything upstairs that we need see ?" said Baillot, after a long silence. "If not we must go on."

"Nothing, sir, but the chambers; nothin' fancy about 'em, but plain and neat. I tell you, sir, not all the brine was in the sea yonder, when I first clapped my eyes onto this little place. It's been a home to somebody, an' there's been a deal of love here, I'm thinkin'. It put me in mind of the place I used to have years ago in England. Many a time when I was on the deck of a stormy night, that little place 'ud rise before my eyes as plain as day, and I could almost hear a little yellow-haired lad a callin' me daddy ! But he's quiet now for many a long year in the churchyard, an' his mother beside him, poor lass. She'd a deal of trouble, an' I fear I wasn't the least of 'em, with my wild ways. The sight of this quiet little place an' yonder empty cradle's brought it all back to me, though I left it astern a matter of twenty years ago." And the old man drew his sleeve across his eyes. "Yonder's the barn-yard," he continued. " I saw two fine cattle grazing in the field behind it. Down this way there are two other cottages, laborer's huts, empty like the rest ; I didn't go no further."

"Very well, then," said the Huguenot, "let us go in this direction ; it was among the trees on yonder slope that we caught the gleam of something white from the deck of the yacht."

They now turned their steps towards the left, and soon came in sight of a graceful little gothic building of white marble. It stood on a slight elevation and was almost concealed from view by the thick masses of foliage which surrounded it.

56

"And what may that be, do you think, sir?" said Winters.

"It may be a summer-house," replied the young man, "since it commands a fine view of the sea, or—" he did not finish the sentence, for they had now approached the entrance of the building.

"It is unmistakably—a tomb," he added in a low voice.

The dome of most graceful shape rested upon groups of clustered pillars, and beneath it the figure of an angel, with half-furled wings, stood as if. guarding the sarcophagus at its feet. The attitude of this figure at once attracted the attention; with one hand outstretched, as if in warning, the forefinger of the other resting upon its lips, it seemed to entreat eternal silence. Upon the tomb itself was neither armorial bearing nor inscription, only a single word carved in bold relief, *Eheu.*

For several moments the two men stood motionless, gazing at the beautiful downcast face of the silent guardian. The sunshine streamed cheerfully in across the marble floor, a crimson rose dropped its petals noiselessly upon the velvet grass, the low thunder of the surf upon the beach below sounding a fitting requiem for the dead.

"There be the others!" said Winters at length in a hoarse whisper, pointing outside.

"None of them are of recent date," said Baillot stooping to examine the moss-grown stones. With some difficulty he deciphered the words on one of them. Pierre Michaux, died June 16, 1630, and Désiré his wife, April 3, 1635.

"There is nothing here, Winters, to bear out your

horrible explanation of the uninhabited condition of the island," he continued. "There have been no burials of late, except perhaps—" and he pointed significantly towards the mausoleum. "But we must hurry on if we would complete the circuit of the island before sundown."

"I'm not afeared of anything we may meet," said Winters. "Suppose you go in one direction, an' I in another. "We'll meet at the castle in less than an hour."

Accordingly they parted, the young man turning to the left along the brow of the cliff. He walked rapidly, stopping now and again to look about him. The country through which he passed was comparatively open, and resembled a well-kept park on any gentleman's estate. Here were the covers for game, and there a pond white with lilies, a tiny boat fastened under the overhanging foliage on its bank. Now he startled a quiet group of sheep, or caught the tinkle of a bell from the neck of some sleek cow grazing tranquilly in the shade. Of human habitation or presence there was no further trace. He arrived at the castle gate before sundown, and was greeted by Winters who had entered just before him.

"There's not a soul on the island, sir," said the sailor, "unless you found somebody; I made thorough work of my half an' saw nothing except a few cultivated fields an' a group of barns. But when I climbed a tree yonder to take a good look in every direction I tell you what I did see," and he lowered his voice slightly, "I saw a sail!"

"A sail!" repeated Baillot, "coming this way?"

"That I couldn't say for sure, sir. That little craft

skims like a swallow; we might overhaul her after a bit, an' so escape."

"If we were perishing for food and drink, and were forced to it, man, we might try it," replied the young man slowly. "But night will soon close in on us, and I fear we should repent our rashness before morning."

"Ay, ay, sir! jes' as you say," said the old man in a disappointed tone. "But God knows when we'll git another such chance."

"If the ladies have succeeded in discovering any maps we might attempt it," remarked Baillot after a thoughtful pause. "Let us go and find them."

A very few moments sufficed to settle that question.

"There are neither maps nor chart!" declared Madeline. "And we have made thorough search in every nook and corner of the library. The left wing of the château contains a chapel," she continued, "with altar, candles, and a beautiful picture of the Ascension; there is a great hall on the ground-floor opening upon the terraces, and a wilderness of chambers and corridors, above that the turret chambers and the battlements. That is all."

"Then you may rest assured of safety to-night!" said the young man bending his dark eyes admiringly upon her glowing face, "for Winters and I can assure you that there is no living being upon the island."

The party, fatigued by the day's excitement, retired early to rest, the arrangement of the sleeping apartments being as Baillot had suggested. For a long time after the others were wrapped in slumber, the young man sat in the great chair before the empty fireplace of the mysterious bedchamber, deep in thought. His own past, his uncertain future, the mysteries of his surroundings, the haunting loveliness of Madeline, all in turn flitted through his wearied brain, till at length his head fell forward on his breast and he slept profoundly. He was aroused suddenly by the sound of some heavy object falling to the floor ; in an instant he was on his feet, dazed and half-blind with sleep, but instinctively reaching for his pistol which he had placed on the table at his side, when of a sudden he was seized from behind, blindfolded, bound and gagged with incredible strength and swiftness.

CHAPTER IX

A CRY IN THE NIGHT

DESPITE her extreme fatigue, or perhaps because of it, Madame de Langres slept but little during the early part of the night. Towards midnight she was aroused from an uneasy doze by some sound, the nature of which she was unable to determine. Raising her head from the pillow, she listened intently. The noise was not repeated, and after awhile she again fell into a light slumber. But she was shortly aroused a second time by her daughter.

"What is it, Madeline?" she asked in alarm.

"I heard some one cry out." .

"Where?"

"I do not know. I was sound asleep and dreaming; suddenly I heard a cry; 'Winters, help!' were the words; then immediately I awoke. The words were no dream, and the voice was that of M. Baillot."

"The voice was doubtless but a part of your dream, my child. . That you should be visited by disquieting visions is not to be wondered at. Come back to your pillow and rest till morning, you are over weary."

The young girl obeyed reluctantly, but she lay for a long time open-eyed in the darkness, her ears strained to catch the slightest sound. Save for the wind which sighed drearily down the wide chimney, and the drowsy chirping of insects on the lawn below, there was no sound to break the silence of the night. At length reassured by the peaceful quiet, and the soft regular breathing of the sleeper by her side, the young girl's eyelids fell and she too slept.

It was morning when she awoke, and the bright sunlight streamed cheerily in at the open window. Madame de Langres was standing by the dressing-table putting the last touches to her toilet.

"Good morning, my daughter," she said cheerfully. "You see that I was right after all. Did you not rest well after your disturbing dream?"

"I slept profoundly," replied the young girl drowsily. "As for my dream, I have forgotten it all—save the shout for help, and that was doubtless fancy like the rest."

"Come to the window, dear, and you will see that we have some other visitors which we did not see yesterday."

Madeline needed no second bidding; she was out of bed in an instant. On the lawn below several magnificent white peacocks were strutting about; one of them, evidently the master of the flock, with his tail spread to its widest extent, was displaying his gorgeous plumage to his admiring consorts.

"What beautiful birds," exclaimed Madeline. "I never saw white peacocks before!"

"They are very rare," replied her mother. "But I remember to have seen some of that color once while travelling in England.—But there is Mr. Winters, and evidently disturbed about something; perhaps an accident has befallen the yacht."

Madeline was dressing with rapid fingers. "I must play housemaid to-day, mother," she said gleefully. "Old Cato will scarcely be able to do the work of this mansion unaided. I mean to gather a quantity of those lovely roses and trim that charming drawing room which looks out upon the terrace.''

The two now emerged from their chamber into the corridor, where they shortly encountered the old sailor. He stopped short on beholding them with so distressed an expression on his broad weather-beaten countenance that Madame de Langres who was on the point of greeting him cheerfully exclaimed in alarm :

''What has happened, sir ? You look as woe-begone as if you had met with some great misfortune.''

''That I have, ma'am,'' said the old man, shaking his head with a dismal groan. '''Twill prove a misfortune for us all, unless I find him somewhars.''

''Find whom? Who is missing?'' cried Madeline anxiously.

''No other than young Baillot, miss, an' things look pretty black. I turned out early an' went to rouse Cato who was sleepin' on the bench yonder, by the cap'n's orders. I found him tied up hard an' fast an' gagged into the bargain. 'What does this mean, you black rascal,' I says, loosin' him. 'Who trussed you up in this ere fashion?' He was so stiff and frightened that he could hardly speak at first, but after a bit he limbered up his tongue an' told me as how he'd been sleepin' sound for a matter of a couple of hours, as nigh as he could tell, when on a sudden somebody made a grab at him in the dark ; he tried to yell, but they choked a monstrous gag into his mouth, then tied him up an' left him. He had a notion that if he could only call me or the cap'n that everything would be ship-shape directly, so he wiggles and twists, an' being near the edge of the bench, pretty soon off he goes on to the floor with a tremendous whack.''

63

"Did he see who his assailants were?" asked Madeline with trembling lips.

"I was just comin' to that, miss; when he succeeded in rolling off onto the floor, he lay there for a bit half-stunned, for the bench was high and his head got a stunning thwack; he hears somebody steppin' cautiously near, an' by the light of a lantern sees two men lookin' at him. 'Let him be,' whispers one. 'He's hard an' fast an' we must make haste.' There were two of the scoundrels; sailors by their dress, says Cato, sailors by the knots in the ropes as bound him, says I. Wall, I then puts for the cap'n's room, and after knocking an' gettin' no answer, I tries the door; it opens easy, and I go in to find the cap'n missin' while his window is wide open an' a handsome bit of tackle hangin' out. Yes, miss, by that ere tackle, some time in the course of the night the cap'n took leave, for he ain't no whars to be found on the island!"

"Do you mean," said Madame de Langres, "that he left us of his own accord, or that he was carried off?"

"How can you ask, mother?" exclaimed Madeline indignantly. "Do you think for a moment that he would abandon us to our fate now, when he remained behind on the wrecked vessel?"

"In course, it's plain enough," said Winters gloomily. "He was carried off; but how they done it, I don't see, for he's monstrous strong is young Baillot, an' a pluckier lad ne'er climbed a mast. Another thing I can't see for the life of me is who carried him off, an' why?"

"He was carried off because he slept in that dreadful room!" wailed Madeline, wringing her hands. "Where is Cato? I must ask him about it, and—oh, Mr.

64

Winters, did you climb the tower and look? Perhaps the ship that carried'him away is visible.''

"I ain't so sure that he was carried off in a ship, though 'twas sailors as done the job plain enough. Suppose now that this 'ere place belongs to smugglers or pirates ; they might have some hidin'-place, a cave or suthin of that sort, an' be a layin' low for the rest of us.''

"That is true !'' cried Madeline with a quick shudder. " Did you hear any noise in the night?'' she asked, dropping her voice.

"No, miss, I was dead tired, an' slept like a log. They must have been mighty quiet, though Cato says he is sure that he heard the cap'n cry out once somewhars outside.''

"Ah !'' cried Madeline, with a sobbing breath, ''I heard it also ! Why—why did I not rouse you at once, for it was for you he called? 'Winters, help !' were the words. Oh mother, why did you persuade me that I was only dreaming? We might have saved him.''

The old sailor shook his head. "They that took him was prepared for anything that might happen ; if I had tried to save him there 'ud be no Jack Winters here this morning.''

The young girl silently wrung her hands. "Where is Cato?'' she repeated.

But Cato could throw no further light on the subject beyond confirming the fact that the missing man had shouted for help in the words that Madeline had heard.

" Dey didn't hurt him, lady,'' he said consolingly. " Der ain't no sign of blood anywheres ; mebby dey bring him back, when dey fin's out who he is.''

"But we don't know who he is," said Madeline despairingly.

"He ain't never sailed afore the mast till this v'yage. An' that's been plain to me sense the day we sailed," observed Winters. "But now let's get a bit of suthin to eat, an' then see what's best to be done. I ain't in favor of spending much more time in this blarsted castle —askin' your pardon for the word, ma'am. I never thought much of stoppin' here; 'tain't suitable quarters for shipwrecked folks. Now thar's two things we can do, we can move down into that little cottage yonder— a snug and wholesome place, an' good enough for any-body, or we can take to the yacht and put to sea. If we'd done that yiste'day, we'd 'a' been many a mile away from this tarnal place."

"Yes," said Madeline sorrowfully, "and no one missing, while now—" and she turned and stared with unseeing eyes at the wide blue horizon.

"Our position is certainly a most difficult one," said Madame de Langres anxiously. "I hardly know what to advise. Would it not be well-nigh impossible to navigate the yacht with so small a force? Madeline and I hardly count as able seamen," she added with a shadowy smile, "while old Cato must needs be somewhat inexperienced in nautical affairs."

"Ay, ay, ma'am," replied Winters, rolling a quid of tobacco about in his capacious mouth with the air of a ruminating ox. "You're land-lubbers all, an' more's the pity; but I reckon ye don't want to stay here to be et up alive by a lot of pirates, do ye? We'd have to take on board a plenty of cooked victuals, an' I'd soon shake some sea sense into that black rascal, Cato."

Madame de Langres was silent for several minutes;

she was evidently thinking deeply. "I am not of the opinion," she said at length, "that this is the abode of either pirates or smugglers; nor do I think that our companion was spirited away by such, for there is no evidence of brutality on their part. For example, it would have been far easier for them to have stabbed the negro, and thus silenced him effectually. Nor is there the slightest sign of any lust for plunder, though the place is not lacking in objects of value. I agree with you, my friend, in thinking that our small company would be better housed in yonder cottage, where we would be within easy reach of one another, than in this deserted pile. But I confess to shrinking back appalled from a voyage in the yacht, without chart or map, in a region of ocean with which we are entirely unacquainted. Such also was the opinion of our unfortunate companion."

"You are right, mother," said Madeline in a low voice. "We are in a horrible strait; disaster seems to threaten us in whichever direction we turn; but anything, rather than commit ourselves into the power of the dreadful sea."

"Ay, land-lubbers all," repeated Winters with a shrug. "Heaven help us, miss, if we stay here. But you shall have your way about it!"

The party now partook of some breakfast, which Cato had made ready, and immediately thereafter prepared to occupy the little cottage, which had already been twice visited by Winters in his unavailing search for the missing man.

"'Tis a comfortable-enough place," said Madeline looking about her, "a pretty cottage and doubtless occupied by worthy folk; but to me it has even a sadder look than the empty castle. Where are the busy hands that scoured these pewter dishes to their silvery whiteness? where the little downy head that rested on the pillow of that vacant cradle?"

"God knows, miss," said the old man, shaking his head, "but we must hope for the best; they may all be as right as trivets somewhar, an' as happy as ever. I'll jes' set this 'ere cradle out of sight, and tidy up the place a bit afore we come to stay. Some of them fine sofys and chairs—ay, an' cups an' plates from the castle won't come amiss, an' Cato will want a lot of victuals."

The day passed quickly, for all were busy. By sunset the cottage presented a very snug and cosy appearance; all saddening signs of its former occupancy had been removed, and much of the humble furniture replaced by articles more suited to the use of the ladies.

Many times during the day Madeline had sought the lofty tower of the château and had swept the horizon with the glass, in vain search for some token of the man who had so mysteriously disappeared from their midst.

"He will return—he will surely return," she said to her mother—"if he is alive."

"I do not doubt it, my child," replied Madame de Langres. "For myself, I have not yet given up hope that he may still be on the island; not many hours have passed since we saw him last."

"True, but the condition of Cato; the midnight cry for help; the telltale ropes hanging from his window, and also this—" and she lowered her voice slightly. "I found it among the bushes near the landing." And she held up to view a bit of blue cloth, evidently torn from some garment.

Madame de Langres examined the fragment. "It looks to me like the material of which clothing worn by officers in the navy is made," she said at length. "I have not forgotten," she added with a deep sigh, "the days when I used to pack your dear brother's sea-chest. Would God, we knew what had befallen him."

"We must not think of the past, sweetest mother," murmured Madeline. "It only serves to dishearten and unnerve us. We will—we must—believe that God is in heaven, and that somehow all things will turn out well, for us—and for those whom we love."

"You are a living ray of sunshine in this dark earth, my child!" cried her mother passionately. "As long as I have you, I ought not to despair."

CHAPTER X

KIDNAPPED

Unable to move or cry out, yet with all his senses keenly alert, Baillot felt himself raised and borne cautiously forward, the feet of his captors making no sound on the thick carpet.

"Have a care, now, with that rope!" came a hoarse whisper in English, as he was lowered to the floor. "'Tis as much as your life is worth to hurt a hair of his head!"

He perceived that he was being invested with a sort of harness of ropes and bands, firmly secured about his body; in another moment he was again lifted and felt himself swiftly descending to some unknown depth, swaying and swinging dizzily in the cool air; but whether the coolness was that of the night or of some subterranean passage-way he was unable to determine.

Presently he was seized from below, and the bands and ropes hastily cut away from his body, his hands and feet still remaining securely tied. A moment's pause followed, then a whispered word which he did not catch, and he was again lifted and borne noiselessly but swiftly onward. A chance crackling of a stick under the foot of one of his bearers, and a sprinkle of dew on his upturned face from some overhanging spray, convinced the young man that he was in the open air. With a desperate effort he succeeded in disengaging one hand from its fastenings; in an instant he had torn the gag from his mouth, and shouted with all his strength.

"Winters! Help!"

A heavy hand was clapped over his mouth before he could follow the cry with a second.

"Faith, but he's strong!" whispered a voice. "Give me your handkerchief; another such shout, and they'll be about us like a hornet's nest. Bind up that hand there; make it secure this time!"

Convinced that resistance was useless for the present, the young man made no further effort to escape, but instead bent all his faculties to the task of discovering who his mysterious abductors were, and whither he was being taken.

"Set him there!" said the same low voice, "and slip that cushion behind his head!"

In another moment the muffled dip of oars and the liquid ripple of water informed the captive that he was in a boat, and that it was being urged swiftly forward by a trained and powerful crew.

For the space of perhaps a quarter of an hour they pursued their onward course, the regular sound of the oars in the rowlocks and the heavy breathing of the crew alone breaking the silence.

"If I could but loosen these bonds about my feet," thought Baillot, "and get my hands free from these straps, I could slip overboard and swim for it."

Cautiously he moved and twisted about, and presently to his great joy he again succeeded in wrenching one hand from its fastenings, then slowly and stealthily he reached down and began to work at the ropes that bound his feet. And now the low booming of the surf told him that they had reached the mouth of the stream, and were about to enter the sea.

"'Twas neatly done!" exclaimed a low voice.

"That black rascal though was like to have been our undoing; and when he cried out for help I thought we were lost. They don't look for midnight visitors, and no wonder!"

"Silence, sir!" said another voice sternly. "You forget yourself."

Baillot had by this time succeeded in unfastening the last knot that bound him, and was on the point of springing to his feet, preparatory to a plunge overboard, when to his dismay he perceived through the bandage that covered his eyes the gleam of a lantern.

There was the sound of a smothered oath, and he was seized by a pair of strong arms.

"Help, quick!" cried an alarmed voice close to his ear. "He is loose, and I cannot hold him alone!" The young Huguenot struggled violently with his captor, but half a dozen strong hands had clutched him by his legs, his arms, his body. He was forced into a sitting posture and held there.

"I beg, monsieur," said a low voice, in excellent French, "that you will not again attempt to escape us. You are in no danger; but, on the contrary, are in the hands of those who are most deeply interested in your welfare! You will, however, pardon us if we make your bonds secure."

Which was at once done, and this time in such a manner that the captive was convinced of the futility of any further effort to free himself. He was somewhat reassured on his own account by the words which had just been spoken, but what of the others?

By the sounds that came to his ear, he was convinced that they were approaching a large vessel. He could hear the rattle of chains, the shrill whistle of the boat-

swain, and the sonorous voice of the commanding officer. A quick order from some one in the boat, and
the oars were dropped into their places with a single
click; another, and he could feel that they were being
drawn swiftly upward. In a moment more he was lifted
gently from his place, the bonds which secured his feet
loosened, and he was marched between two of his captors across the deck of a vessel. He counted the steps;
it was a large ship.

"Now, monsieur, carefully; we are about to descend
some stairs," said a voice which he recognized as being
that of the man who had spoken to him in the boat.

His hands were released, the gag removed from
his mouth; he heard the click of a key turning in the
lock. Raising his head he tore the bandages from his
eyes and looked about him. He was entirely alone.
The bright light of a lamp which was secured to the
ceiling revealed the interior of a large cabin, comfortably and even luxuriously furnished. There were two
doors, both of which were closed. He sprang forward
and tried one of them, the thought of escape still uppermost in his mind; it was fast.

"I must get away," he groaned aloud; "they will
think that I have deserted them!"

The other door yielded to his touch and disclosed a
smaller cabin furnished for sleeping. He paused for a
moment and listened intently to the sounds above;
there was the greatest hurry and confusion which his
trained ear could not mistake. They were getting under
way.

Hopeless now of making his escape, he returned to
the outer cabin and sat down by the table, his mind a
turmoil of distracting thoughts. He was aroused after

some moments spent in unpleasant revery by the opening of the cabin door. He sprang to his feet and confronted the man who had entered.

"How is this, monsieur?" he cried sternly. "What is the meaning of this proceeding? By what right do you seize me in this way? For whom do you take me? There is some grave mistake here!"

"Monsieur will pardon me," said the officer, for as Baillot now observed, the man who addressed him was clad in the full uniform of the British navy.. "Monsieur will pardon me if I excuse myself from answering these, or any other questions which he may be pleased to ask. I am forbidden to answer questions, but am permitted to assure monsieur of his personal safety, and of every attention which he may require while aboard my vessel. Pray consider me your humble servant and use me in every way for your convenience save the one, which I have just specified. These cabins are yours and "—striking as he spoke a small gong—"this man is at your command as body-servant. He cannot speak," he added significantly, "but you will find him an excellent valet."

As he spoke there entered on noiseless foot a man with a face as silent and expressionless as a statue of bronze. He was clad gaudily in a livery of scarlet velvet, trimmed with gold lace.

"Zed, you will attend Monsieur during the voyage!" said the officer addressing him. "See to it that he lacks nothing; report to me for further orders."

The man bowed in token that he understood, but he did not speak.

"And now, monsieur," resumed the officer, turning to Baillot, "permit me to wish you a very good

74

night. If the present wind holds, our voyage will soon be at an end; in the meantime I beg that you will give yourself no uneasiness, and believe me when I assure you that all is well."

He bowed profoundly and was about to withdraw, when the Huguenot sprang forward.

"There is some terrible mistake, I assure you!" he cried. "It cannot be that you wish to carry me off in this way. Do you know who I am?"

"There is no mistake," replied the officer with an air of decision, "and I beg once more to assure monsieur that all is well! further than that I cannot go. Good-night."

"But my companions on the island! Stop—I assure you that you have made a terrible mistake!" But the officer was gone.

"This is infamous!" muttered the young man under his breath. "He shall answer me!" and with that he sprang toward the door.

The black gave a low inarticulate cry and made a gesture as if to prevent him.

"Out of my way, fellow!" said Baillot fiercely, throwing open the door. In the passage-way were two marines standing as if on guard. They presented arms with an air of profound respect.

"Where is the commander of this vessel?" demanded Baillot in French, then bethinking himself he repeated the question in English.

"Yonder, excellency," replied one of the men jerking his thumb over his shoulder, but without removing his eyes from the handsome angry face before him. At the top of the companion-way he was confronted by two more marines; these dropped their pikes, in

75

token that further progress in that direction was cut off.

"Let me pass!" he said angrily.

One from a little group of officers standing near instantly came forward. He bowed low as his eye fell upon Baillot.

"Ah! monsieur desires the air?" he said courteously. "Let him pass at once."

"I desire to see the commander of this vessel," said Baillot haughtily.

"In order that you may—"

"Demand my release, sir."

"That is impossible, monsieur," said the young officer. "Impossible, and, I may add, little to be desired by monsieur. Were you not a prisoner on yonder island? Now you shall shortly be free, and—" here he checked himself suddenly.

"But my companions who are left behind?"

"They are quite safe, and their removal only a matter of time. There will be no further reason for their presence there," said the young officer in a soothing voice. "And now let me beg of monsieur to descend to the cabin. It is quite impossible for me to explain further. Monsieur will understand me when I say that I am under oath to say no more."

"Allow me, sir, to explain to you how—"

But the officer had turned away with a low bow. Baillot stared after his retreating figure. "I am dreaming doubtless," he muttered with a short laugh; then perceiving that the marines were eyeing him with undisguised curiosity and amusement he slowly descended to the cabin he had just quitted, and there as it was still night he lay down in his berth and was shortly sound asleep.

The officer who had spoken with him was presently accosted by the commander of the vessel.

"How now, St. Clair! Did you have any trouble with our passenger?"

"He was bent upon speaking with you, my lord, in order to demand his release. But I assured him of the impossibility of the thing, and finally prevailed upon him to retire to his cabin."

"Our rude English tongues doubtless alarm him!" remarked the other with a chuckle. "But he might be in worse hands. What think you of his appearance?"

"I am bound to say, my lord, that I was surprised. He is apparently much younger than——"

"You forget, sir!" said his superior sternly.

"He is a man of tremendous physical strength," continued the young officer with some confusion; "we had great ado to hold him in the boat."

"What do you mean, sir?"

"Did not Marston tell you how he worked himself loose just before we made the ship? He would have been overboard in another moment."

"Gad, sir, but that would have been an awkward thing for us," remarked the other shrugging his shoulders. "We shall do well to keep a sharp eye on him during the rest of the voyage. Ay! and a close tongue in our mouths!" he added with a stern glance at his companion. "Did he question you at all?"

"He seemed much concerned about his companions who were left behind," replied the young man. "I made bold to assure him that they would be at once removed from the island."

"I'll warrant me that they will be removed! You

were not far out of the way there. His concern for them does him credit. If the wind holds we shall soon be quit of him,—and a good riddance ; this kidnapping business is not to my liking.''

''Nor mine.''

''Well, sir,'' said the older man after a short silence, ''I shall go below for a few hours. Remain on deck till I return, and stay—'' he added with a significant gesture, ''keep him where he is !''

CHAPTER XI

WHEN the young Huguenot awoke it was to find the sunlight streaming cheerfully through the skylight of his cabin. He looked about him for a moment at the milk-white walls and crimson curtains of his prison with that dazed wonderment which often hangs about the recent traveller in the land of dreams; then his eye fell on the black servant standing by his bedside in a deferential attitude. He bore in his hand a small silver tray containing a delicate cup of Sèvres china and a silver pot; this he offered to the young man with a low bow.

"Chocolate?" inquired Baillot; "but I am neither a woman nor a sick man, my good fellow. Take it away and fetch my clothes—for I see that they have disappeared."

The negro instantly obeyed, and Baillot stared at him in puzzled silence, as with perfunctory deftness he laid out a grand array of costly toilet articles together with a complete suit of apparel of gorgeous material and fashionable cut. He roused himself as the valet approached him with towels and a silver basin containing water which he had previously dashed with eau de Cologne.

"You may leave me now, fellow, Zed—Zip—whatever your name is! I will dress myself. But first re-

79

move that pink satin waistcoat and the velvet coat, and bring me something plainer and more ship-shape."

The negro again made obeisance, and immediately replaced the articles in question with others of black satin overlaid with silver lace.

Baillot eyed them with a scowl. "I shall have to appear like a popinjay from the court before these officers," he thought to himself; "that comes of appropriating the finery at the château." With the word came a sudden illumination. "They mistake me for the former occupant of the castle!" He sprang up with a smothered exclamation, pushing the proffered basin to one side so roughly that the perfumed water was spilled upon the floor. Then seeing the alarmed and puzzled look upon the face of the negro, he laughed outright.

"I am in the habit of waiting upon myself at my toilet, my good fellow; I shall do so now, and do you inform the commander of this vessel that I wish to speak with him as soon as convenient."

The man at once left the cabin, and Baillot, left to himself, made rapid work with his dressing.

"Ay, thou art a pretty-enough coxcomb, in thy lace ruffles and satin coat!" he exclaimed with a grim laugh, as he faced his reflection in the glass. "Erstwhile officer, convict, refugee, sailor, castaway, what for the moment are you?"

But he was none the less accurate in all the details of his toilet, leaving his cabin a few moments later a complete picture of the gentleman of the period, his keen dark face, with its slightly aquiline nose, brown eyes and well-cut lips, shaded by dark locks of hair which he wore unpowdered.

Upon entering the outer cabin he found a sumptuous breakfast awaiting him, which he proceeded at once to discuss with an excellent appetite, Zed attending him with great ceremony. When he had finished he bethought himself of his resolution to attempt another interview with the captain.

"Did you tell the commander that I wished to see him?" he inquired.

The man bowed.

"What did he say?—Confound it, you can't speak, but why, since you hear perfectly?"

The man uttered one of the strange inarticulate sounds, which Baillot had before noticed, then with an apologetic grin opened his mouth. He was tongueless.

"*Diable!* What a shame in this age of the world! —But the captain?"

By way of reply the negro produced a letter which he handed to the young man with his accustomed obeisance.

"Monsieur will pardon me if I find it impossible to accede to his request for an interview," he read. "We have just sighted a ship of the enemy, and my presence is imperatively required upon deck. Monsieur need give himself no uneasiness but had best remain below during the day.—TORRINGTON."

"*Peste!* does he think that with a fight in prospect I shall remain below stairs like a sea-sick woman? I shall go on deck at once!" But he found the marines still on guard before the outer door, evidently under orders to keep him below decks. The hot color flew to the young man's face and he was on the point of bursting into an angry protest, but he bethought himself of his perfect helplessness, and turning on his heel without a word, strode back into the cabin,

"What then shall monsieur do with himself to-day?" he exclaimed aloud with a short laugh. "Monsieur may look at his pretty new clothes and play with his fingers. May the enemy make it so hot for them that they will find themselves unable to spare four good men to guard monsieur, then we shall see!"

In his anger he had forgotten the presence of the man who could hear though he could not speak; but as he turned in his rapid stride up and down the narrow confines of the cabin his eye fell upon the negro. The man stood staring at him with such an expression of anxious alarm upon his sable countenance, that the young Huguenot stopped short.

"You think that I am a madman, fellow? Well I promise you that you shall not suffer at my hands unless—" and he scowled fiercely, "you presume upon your position and attempt to make yourself my jailor; in that case I shall make nothing of tying a double bow knot in your black neck. Now fetch me some books—or stay, fetch me a sea map and some charts."

"I will see if I can place our mysterious island," he thought to himself. But the negro presently returned with one or two volumes which, with many apologetic duckings of his woolly head, he deposited upon the table.

"How now; am I not permitted to have a chart or map?"

The negro rolled up his eyes in evident fright, but he shook his head emphatically.

"Hum! Monsieur is requested to employ his

mind with a romance; 'tis a fitting employment for a man who wears a satin coat on blue water. What is here—Corneille—Racine? I shall perhaps be able to while away an hour in your company." And flinging himself upon a chair he opened one of the volumes.

The better part of an hour had passed away, when some unusual sounds on deck attracted the reader's attention. "That sounds like action," he murmured, casting aside his book; "they are about to engage or I am very much mistaken."

A glance at the open door revealed the marines still standing motionless, with no sign of interest or excitement on their stolid red faces.

"*Sacre bleu!*—but these Englishmen," muttered the captive with a shrug, "they are made of wood!"

While the Huguenot arrayed in his costly satin and ruffles sat staring morosely at the imperturbable marines, on deck all was bustle and excitement. The enemy's ship had been sighted about six o'clock in the morning. It was at first deemed advisable to keep out of her way, and thus avoid an engagement, but it soon became evident that this would be impossible, for the English vessel, though a first-class ship heavily armed, was not equal to a chase with the fleet-winged stranger.

"Our consort should have met us hereabouts," said Torrington to St. Clair as he uneasily paced the quarter-deck. "What can have become of her? A stiff brush with the enemy might prove embarrassing with our present passenger aboard."

"I'll warrant me that the smell of gunpowder will be new to the gentleman," replied St. Clair flippantly;

"but to my mind it is more wholesome than the odor of sanctity, to which no doubt he has been accustomed heretofore."

"You are an irreligious dog, St. Clair!" growled his superior with a chuckle. "See to it that our friend does not escape his quarters; if it becomes necessary to remove the men on guard bid the negro lock him in securely. He'll stay there willingly enough when the cannonading begins."

"Perhaps," replied the young man, lifting his eyebrows.

"Make him secure in any event. And now set every man to his post; we shall be within range inside of twenty minutes. A couple of broadsides from *The Conqueror* may cool them off a bit."

The enemy, flying the French flag, had now approached within hailing distance, and presented, with her towering mass of snowy canvas, her massive hull bristling with cannon, and her yards alive with seamen, a most imposing sight.

"What ship is that?" roared Torrington through his speaking-trumpet.

"Come a little nearer," was the derisive answer, "and see for yourselves!"

"Ay, that we will, the impudent rascals!" cried Torrington throwing down his trumpet, while a dark flush of wrath rose to his cheek. "Run her athwart the enemy's bow and give her a broadside!"

Slowly *The Conqueror* swung about to her helm, but the enemy perceiving the design of the Englishman turned also, and at the moment *The Conqueror* presented her bow, poured into it a deadly blast of eighteen-pound shot.

That it had taken effect was immediately evident, and Torrington shouted angrily, "Close with the enemy! No quarter!"

The two ships had now approached so near that the faces of the crew on the French ship were distinctly visible, and their bearded grinning countenances seemed to fill the Englishmen with a kind of dull rage.

"Give them something to laugh at!" was the cry, and a sheet of flame burst forth from the dark side of *The Conqueror*.

"Ah, that was good—look at the rascals now! Give them another!"

But the enemy was not idle; from her yards skilful marksmen kept up a deadly fire, while her guns roared incessantly. A dense cloud of smoke enveloped the vessels, through which the glare of the bellowing cannon, the forms of the combatants, and the tattered canvas overhead, could be seen dimly, like the imaginings of an awful dream. The ships had drifted so close that the rigging had become entangled—a signal advantage to the English vessel, which, owing to her heavy construction was slower in answering her helm.

"Put some of our people over her sides!" roared Torrington. But the boarding-party, headed by St. Clair, was repulsed and driven back with heavy loss. Things now began to look serious for the English, their decks were piled with the dead and wounded, and a number of their best guns silenced; the ship, moreover, was leaking badly and on fire in several places.

"The day is going against us," groaned Torrington between his shut teeth. "But I'll not be taken alive!"

Just at this critical juncture he saw, to his astonishment, that a small party from his own vessel had succeeded in boarding the Frenchman, and that a deadly conflict was going on. Seizing a pike he pushed forward with an encouraging shout. Ten minutes of sharp fighting followed, a hand-to-hand struggle with cutlass and pike, at the end of which the Frenchmen were evidently worsted, for they raised a loud cry for quarter; at the same moment a triumphant shout burst from the English crew.

"They strike! They strike!"

The battle had lasted but little more than an hour, but the havoc which that hour had wrought was indescribable. The crew of *The Conqueror* now addressed themselves with vigor to the task of extinguishing the flames, which threatened to destroy both vessels. This being accomplished and the prisoners made secure, Torrington, who had by some miracle escaped without a scratch, bethought him of his passenger.

Approaching St. Clair, who was having a wound in his arm looked after by the ship's surgeon, he said in a low voice, "What of our friend below stairs, is he safe?"

"I cannot tell you, sir," replied the young man, "we were obliged to remove the marines on guard early in the engagement, so many of our gunners were killed. I gave the negro orders to lock him in. He is probably in his cabin stiff with fright. I will go below," he added, "as soon as this nasty cut in my arm is attended to. But can you tell me, my lord, who led that last boarding-party?"

Torrington stared at the young man in surprise.

"Did you not lead it yourself, sir? I was about to congratulate you for the service; it was that, and that alone which saved the day."

"'Twas not I, my lord; I was on the point of asking you whether we ought not to strike, when I heard a great shout and caught a glimpse through the smoke of a party rushing by, led by some one whose face I could not see."

"'Twas Euston then!"

"Euston was wounded when we tried to board her the first time," replied the young man quietly. "I saw him fall."

Torrington turned on his heel with a smothered exclamation; some one was pulling at his coat from behind.

"Well, you rascal, what now?"

The negro was kneeling upon the slippery deck, his hands clasped, and a most piteous expression of appealing agony on his ashen face.

"Are you hurt, fellow? No—well then, what does this mean? Where is your charge?"

"Something has happened to him, my lord," interposed St. Clair hastily. "I will look to it at once." And wrenching himself out of the hands of the surgeon, he crossed the deck and disappeared down the companion-way.

One of the younger officers now approached the commander, he saluted respectfully, then said in a somewhat hesitating way:

"A sailor who has been severely wounded has just told me an extraordinary thing. He insists upon it that the boarding-party was led by the person whom we took on board last night."

"What?" exclaimed Torrington. "The fellow is mad! But here is St. Clair."

The young man came quickly forward looking pale and anxious. "The—ah—gentleman is not in his cabin, my lord," he said.

CHAPTER XII

A HUGUENOT

"Where is he then?" demanded Torrington with
an oath. "For once in my life I wish you could
speak!" he continued, fixing his eyes gloomily on the
negro, who still sprawled at his feet. "Get up, and
help look for the Frenchman!—the devil take all
Frenchmen dead or alive!"

"But, my lord," interposed the young officer, "if
the sailor yonder spoke the truth, we owe our victory to
this same Frenchman!"

"Gad, sir, do you believe such idle ravings? Would
he fight his own countrymen, man?"

"We must at all events ascertain what has become of
him," put in St. Clair. "'Twill be an unlucky cruise
for us all should we fail to do so."

"Unlucky enough!" growled Torrington, turning
on his heel. "Get you about the quest; look carefully
among the dead and wounded."

A systematic search of both vessels was at once instituted, and before many minutes a cry from one of the
sailors called Torrington to the spot. On board the
enemy's ship, which was still lashed to the side of *The
Conqueror*, amid a heap of the slain, marking the spot
where the fiercest fight of the day had taken place, the
marines had uncovered the body of the man.

St. Clair and Torrington reached the spot at the same
instant. They looked at one another without a word.

"Bring him out here," commanded Torrington; "call the ship's surgeon."

St. Clair was already tearing aside the lace ruffles at the breast of the unconscious Baillot that he might listen for a possible heart-beat. "He still lives, my lord!" he said briefly.

At this moment the ship's surgeon, a short stout man with a bustling and authoritative manner, arrived upon the scene.

"Out of my way, gentlemen," he said with an imperative wave of the hand. "You impede my vision."

All obeyed save St. Clair, who still supported the unconscious man's head, and Torrington, who stood at his feet like a grim statue.

"What do you make, sir?" he asked gruffly, as the surgeon paused for a moment in his cautious proddings and manipulations.

"I find no serious hurt, m' lord, so far," replied that functionary cautiously. "We had best remove him below where he can be stripped; I shall then shortly be able to ascertain the full extent of his injuries."

"Give him some brandy," commanded Torrington. "I'm no leech, but damme, that'll fetch him up, if anything will!"

"I was about to administer a restorative, m' lord," replied the surgeon with dignity.

This he at once proceeded to do, and with such good effect that the young man's eyes opened, and to the great surprise of all he presently sat up and looked about him.

"Is the day ours?" he asked eagerly.

"What does he say?" inquired the surgeon, with

another meditative prod; "I do not understand the French language myself; it is not necessary to my profession."

Baillot turned upon him a look of perfect intelligence, then glanced at the anxious faces about him.

"I see that we did beat them," he said slowly, this time in English. "My faith, but it was a close brush! I caught the fellows just as they were about to board us, a hundred strong."

"Where are you hurt, sir?" questioned the surgeon, thrusting his round anxious face into the young man's range of vision. "I have not yet been able to locate the injury." And he again made as though he would continue his investigations with a cautious forefinger.

"Sheer off, man!" said Baillot, waving him off. "I escaped the onslaught of the enemy by rare good fortune, but I can bear no more of your mauling. Somebody fetched me a blow on the head with the butt of a pistol that knocked me senseless for a moment; other than that I haven't a scratch."

"Thank God!" ejaculated Torrington fervently; "'twould have been a sorry day for us, had you been as dead as you looked when we found you!"

Baillot eyes him curiously. "That is a question that I wish to discuss with you, sir. I think that I can shortly convince you that my death would make very little difference in your fortunes."

"Let me assist monsieur to his cabin," said St. Clair, coming forward. "In the meantime we all realize that we owe our freedom—perchance our lives, to his valor."

"True!" growled Torrington, as Baillot slowly rose

to his feet. "But how does it happen that you were willing to fight your own countrymen?"

A mingled expression of bitter sorrow and hatred swept like a tempest across the young man's expressive face. He glanced at the shattered vessel, the heaps of dead and wounded about him, then he turned and faced his questioner.

"Sir, I am a Huguenot!"

A low murmur of amazement ran about the little circle of listeners. Torrington was the first to recover himself. "Take him below!" he said, with a fierce scowl at the curious faces of the sailors; "the blow on his skull is more serious than we feared. Look carefully to it, doctor. Go below with him, St. Clair; your own hurt needs nursing."

Half an hour later as the English commander stood on the deck of his own vessel, which was already reduced to a state of wonderful order by the small body of uninjured marines, St. Clair approached him.

"How many have we lost, my lord?"

"Forty killed, and as many wounded."

"'Twas a bloody battle. How fared the Frenchman?"

"Seventy killed, and the rest prisoners. I have placed Fortescue in command of the French ship with enough of ours to man her, and divided the prisoners. I wanted you here," he added, observing the quick flush of annoyance which rose to the face of the man at his side; "besides you are wounded."

"My wound is nothing," said St. Clair hastily,—"a mere scratch. But what think you of our prisoner's, perhaps I should say our—"

"Call him what you like, sir!" interrupted Torrington impatiently. "What do I think of his declaration? I have had a dozen minds about it. I begin to think that we have made some atrocious blunder."

"That can hardly be, my lord," observed his companion thoughtfully. "We found everything exactly as was told us; the postern unguarded—as was previously agreed upon, the door opening to our key; the black man on guard, everything— No there can be no mistake on our part."

"If he is by some miracle a Huguenot!" exclaimed Torrington.—"But hold, we are gossiping like a couple of women. His religion concerns us not a whit. What confounds me is his fighting; why man, he fought like a soldier!"

"All the better, my lord, but a miracle of itself, for how—"

"Tut, the how of it is nothing to us. Yet we must recognize his services—if by chance he be not crazed by his hurt. Let him up on deck freely for the rest of the voyage, but look to it that he gets speech with none of the others."

Meanwhile the young Huguenot in his cabin was passing a *mauvais quartre d'heure* with the surgeon.

"I must insist, your excellency," the little man was saying, "upon making a very thorough examination. From the nature of your remarks we apprehend perhaps an injury to the corinal suture of the cranium, which might necessitate a very interesting operation—very interesting! I am sure, your highness, I should be most delighted to perform such an operation upon you, and should it chance to be successful—"

"But I tell you I am not hurt, go and look to those who are; there are enough of them, poor fellows."

93

"The cases you refer to are in the hands of my assistant, your grace," replied the little man with airy dignity. "And also I may say that I believe the surgeon of the French vessel is at work among them. You need give yourself no anxiety concerning them—though I am sure it does you great credit. But as I was saying an injury to the stephanion sometimes occasions—"

"There is no injury, I tell you! save a bruise; give me a lotion for that, if you must do something, then leave me."

"A lotion, my lord, would not be amiss, and I will presently apply it after I have satisfied myself that the ophryon is quite uninjured. Now in regard to internal injuries, in the region of the xiphoid appendage when I examine it in this manner do you feel any pain?"

"By the powers, man! Such prodding would be apt to produce a feeling of some sort! Once more I tell you that I am not hurt. Come, I shall fare very well with Zed here to attend me."

The surgeon rolled his round eyes in the direction of the negro, who was standing near.

"Ah!" he cried, "what have we here? A cranial wound of some seriousness I believe."

Baillot looked up hastily. "You are hurt!" he exclaimed, noting the ashen pallor of the man's face, and the thin dark stream of blood which trickled down his dusky cheek. "Why did you not say so? But I forget, you cannot speak. I left you tied up securely enough, as I supposed. Did you get loose and follow me?"

The negro gasped slightly once or twice, then fell heavily to the floor.

"There's a case for you, doctor. Do your best for

him, poor fellow; he has already suffered enough for one man."

"As I thought," remarked the surgeon with an air of satisfaction, after a superficial examination of the wound. "A most interesting case—most interesting. I shall be able, I trust, to demonstrate successfully my theory of—"

"Don't do it here!" interposed Baillot hastily. "Have him removed to his own quarters; let me know later if I can be of any service to him. I verily believe that the poor fool was trying to follow me into the action. Not so much of a fool after all," he added thoughtfully, "for he was trying to do his duty, while I—" and he broke off with a smothered groan.

A couple of marines now entered and removed the negro, the surgeon bustling along in their wake with his instruments and bandages. Baillot seeing that he was alone quietly opened the door of his cabin, and in another moment had reached the deck unobserved. Advancing to the rail he looked about him with a deep breath of pleasure; to be free even for a moment from the galling espionage to which he had been subjected was a wonderful relief. He presently drew back into the shadow of a drooping bit of canvas, hoping to avoid recognition, but here he was soon spied out by the keen eye of St. Clair. The young Englishman came forward with a frank smile of greeting on his handsome face.

"Then you are not seriously wounded as we at first feared," he exclaimed, genuine pleasure evident in his voice.

"Not a scratch, sir," replied Baillot. "In the encounter with your excellent surgeon below stairs I might

95

not have fared so well, had not his professional attention been fortunately diverted. I say fortunately," he
added in response to an inquiring look from the officer,
"but I fear that it will hardly prove fortunate for
yonder poor fellow ; the negro—my attendant or jailor,
whichever you like best to call him—was severely
wounded in the fight."

"I beg, monsieur," began St. Clair with evident
embarrassment, "that you will not consider yourself
other than an honored guest on board *The Conqueror.*"

"I have yet to learn that honored guests are removed
by force from their bedchambers in the dead of night,
and that they are placed in charge of servants who have
full liberty to incarcerate them," observed Baillot with
a shrug. "Besides—"

"It is impossible for me to explain to you why we
must do these things," interrupted St. Clair eagerly.
"But the fact remains, you are our honored guest,
trebly honored since you are also our preserver. Believe me that these unavoidable mysteries will soon be
at an end, and that you will fully understand our unfortunate position—unfortunate in that we have been
forced by circumstances into playing a part which seems
unworthy."

Baillot turned and faced the young officer. "You are
an Englishman, I am a Frenchman," he said slowly ;
"'tis the custom, born of the centuries, for us to hate
and distrust each other. You think us flippant, frivol-
ous and untruthful ; we think you stupid, obstinate and
cold-hearted. But for all that, we are in the sight of
God but two human beings, neither more nor less, and
putting aside all foolish mystery and intrigue I beg that
I may talk to you as man to man. Believe me when I

say that there is some terrible mistake here, and that the lives of others depend on its being put right at once. Will you listen to me?''

St. Clair was visibly moved by this appeal; what he might have said on the spur of the moment he afterward confessed that he did not know. But he was spared further embarrassment by the approach of Torrington. That worthy officer having seen the two young men in close conversation, and knowing the impetuous nature of St. Clair, deemed it wise to interfere.

''I have the honor to congratulate monsieur on his speedy recovery,'' he said stiffly, as he approached. '' I find that monsieur's body-servant had the misfortune to be wounded, and is incapacitated for further duty. The fellow deserves the rope's-end for disobeying orders,'' he added with a frown.

'' The negro was, on the contrary, faithful to his duty in the face of death itself.''

'' How so, your—that is, monsieur?''

'' The poor fellow had received instructions to keep his prisoner below at all costs,'' said Baillot; ''accordingly he locked the cabin-door, and concealed the key. This not jumping with the wishes of his prisoner—a difficult fellow to manage—he presently found himself unable to cope with the situation. In short, the prisoner bound him, forced the door, and escaped to the deck. The negro escaped his bonds and followed his charge into the action with the hope of being able to shield him from harm, and so he was wounded. Is my Lord Torrington satisfied with the explanation?''

Torrington bowed stiffly; his face was a study.

''I shall place one of the marines at your service,''

7   97

he said at length, "but I fear he will prove but an indifferent valet."

"That is of no consequence, sir. But now that I have the opportunity, let me explain—"

"Your most humble pardon, monsieur," interrupted the other, with a wave of his hand, "it is quite out of my power to enter into any explanations at present. Explanations must be postponed, till we set foot on English soil, which will be I trust at no distant hour. St. Clair, a word with you in my cabin; monsieur, the marine who will attend you!"

CHAPTER XIII

AT WARHAM CASTLE

The remainder of the voyage passed monotonously enough. The young Huguenot found that more liberty was accorded him in that he was permitted to go upon deck at will, but wherever he went, at his elbow like a shadow, was the marine who had been detailed to his service.

After one or two attempts to enter into conversation with the man, Baillot had abandoned any further effort in this direction. The fellow was apparently quite stupid, and beyond a stolid "Ay, ay, sir!" in answer to some request, obstinately refused to talk. Officers and sailors alike saluted him with profound respect whenever he appeared, but any attempt at conversation on his part was met with courteous but persistent discouragement. Neither St. Clair nor Torrington had spoken with him since the day of the battle beyond the ordinary greetings of the day.

The young man haughtily accepted the situation; he ceased to attempt any communication with those about him, passing long hours in reading, of which luckily he was fond. At other times he paced the deck, moodily thinking of those left behind on the island. At such times the lovely face of Madeline seemed to arise before him, her large dark eyes full of fear and sorrow. "Good God!" he thought, in a fury of impotent grief.

"I am helpless in the huge coils of another's fate! I must break away, I cannot endure it."

He resolved a thousand times that he would escape and make his way back at any cost. How he was to accomplish this, penniless as he was, and totally ignorant of the whereabouts of the island, he did not stop to consider. The first thing was to get away. And this he determined to do as soon as possible after landing.

He awoke one morning to find that the vessel had come to anchor in the night. Springing out of his berth, he began to dress hastily, observing to his dismay that a suit of unusual richness and splendor had been placed ready for him.

"Hardly the thing," he muttered. "Here, you, Jones, fetch me a plain cloth suit—cloth, understand, with no trimmings."

"'Aven't got it, m' lord," said the marine stolidly.

"See here, my man," said Baillot impulsively, "these people have made a big blunder in bringing me off on this vessel. I am not the man they want, and I must get away; this ring now is a valuable one, take it, and help me ashore. You'll not regret it," he added persuasively.

The man regarded him furtively, a gleam in his fishy eye. "You don't 'appen to 'ave any gold about you, do you, m' lord? I hain't no use for that 'ere ring; it 'ud get me into a 'eap of trouble."

"Confound it—no! I have no gold, they brought me away in the dead of night—but look you, I can get money, and I'll pay anything you like. Only help me now!"

The man shook his head. "I've 'eard hoften an' hoften as 'ow a bird in the 'and is worth two in the bush. I'm a goin' to get paid 'andsome for keepin' you all safe, and by parties as 'ave plenty of good Henglish gold. That's good enough for me, and a deal safer.''

And with that he went stolidly on with his preparations for breakfast, a most edifying expression of unimpeachable honesty on his broad red face.

Baillot bit his lip. He felt that he had made a serious blunder in attempting to corrupt the man, who would now be doubly on his guard.

"Where are we?'' he asked abruptly.

The man looked at him in surprise. "I thought m' lord, as 'ow you knowed by this time that I was hallowed to hanswer no questions. I make no doubt but that you'll know where we are all in good time.''

After he had breakfasted in gloomy silence, the young man caught up a book from the table, intending to go on deck for awhile, but he was confronted in the passageway by the guard. Reduced to the necessity of passing the day in his cabin, he resigned himself to his fate with outward composure, though inwardly he was boiling over with impatience.

About four o'clock in the afternoon, Torrington accompanied by St. Clair entered his cabin.

"I have the honor of informing monsieur,'' said Torrington stiffly, "that having reached anchorage he will now disembark. I regret most heartily the unpleasant circumstance of the battle, which afforded monsieur serious annoyance, but which it was impossible to avoid, and trust that in the future he will remember not unpleasantly his voyage in *The Conqueror*, together with its commander, who is, and will ever be, most devoted to his interests.''

Having delivered himself of this speech with the air of one who had committed it to memory, the officer indicated with a wave of his hand that the young man was to follow him.

Upon deck Baillot found to his surprise the entire force of marines drawn up as if for inspection. They uncovered upon his appearance with a ringing cheer. On the quarter-deck stood an imposing group of men, gold-laced and bejewelled, apparently awaiting his approach.

"I have the pleasure and honor of presenting to monsieur the governor of the castle of Warham," said Torrington solemnly.

Whereat one of the gold-laced and bejewelled individuals stepped forward and bowed profoundly. He was a small man with a yellow wizened countenance, and sharp grey eyes, which he fixed upon Baillot like a pair of gimlets. Something that he saw evidently surprised and discomfited him exceedingly, for he continued to stare, without speaking, for a full minute, his mouth half-open as though the words had suddenly frozen upon his tongue.

"Will your excellency proceed at once to disembark," said Torrington, observing his discomfiture. "My orders permit of no unnecessary delay."

The governor turned a lack-lustre eye upon the officer; he seemed about to speak, but evidently changed his mind, and backed toward the open bulwark, where an elaborate barge was in waiting. Here he paused and with another obeisance waved his hand to Baillot to descend before him; several of the marines sprang forward to assist him; the governor followed, and presently the barge swung slowly away from the ship, while a hearty three times three burst from the throats of the sailors assembled on her decks.

Baillot saw St. Clair leaning over the bulwark watching him ; he waved his hand by way of farewell ; the young officer doffed his cap, and bowed low.

"Can you tell me, sir, whither I am bound?" he asked, turning to the governor who was seated by his side.

"You are on your way to the castle of Warham," replied the little man with another penetrating look into the face of the questioner, "where I shall have the pleasure and honor of entertaining you until further advices reach me."

"Yes?" returned the young man interrogatively. "So much I had already gathered from our good friend the commander of yonder vessel. Perhaps you will be good enough to inform me whom you suppose me to be? I fancy that there is here some curious misunderstanding which a word of frank explanation would serve to do away, to the mutual relief and advantage of all concerned."

The governor cleared his throat loudly and moved uneasily about in his place, casting a half-frightened glance at several attendants who stood near ; at length he spoke in a slow and cautious way, as of one who carefully weighs each word ere he utters it.

"Your question is a most natural one under the circumstances—most natural. I do not wonder that you have given it utterance, nor that you feel the greatest anxiety to have it answered. And yet my duty compels me—I assure you that it compels me—to ask you to—await—further—developments."

Baillot was on the point of returning an impatient

answer to this speech, but on second thought he forced
back the hot words which had risen to his lips. " The
castle of Warham, I presume?" he said, turning his
eyes shoreward upon a massive pile of buildings, flanked
by long irregular lines of fortification and straggling
rows of whitewashed cottages, which shone brilliantly
in the afternoon sunshine.

"The castle and town of Warham," assented the
man at his side with a comprehensive wave of the hand.

As he spoke the barge shot into the black shadow of
the castle walls, glided easily beneath a massive archway of masonry, between the iron jaws of the water-
gate flung wide to receive it, and stopped before a flight
of broad stone steps. On either side of this entrance
was drawn up a line of men-at-arms as silent and apparently as immovable as the hoary towers above their
heads.

"Warham castle," repeated the governor rising, and
performing a stately obeisance. " I make monsieur
right welcome to the securest stronghold in merry England !"

Ascending the steps the party entered a large courtyard, on all sides of which looked down the dark walls
of the castle, pierced at intervals with narrow windows.
Baillot's eye was irresistibly drawn upward to one of
these casements in which stood a brilliant nosegay,
flaunting its bright blossoms of scarlet and yellow in
pleasing contrast to the somber grey of the ancient
stone.

A passing gust of wind served at that moment to
overthrow the slender glass vase which contained the
flowers, and it fell with a musical tinkle to the pavement below, scattering a swift shower of brightness into

the gloomy place. A little cry followed and a small golden head was thrust out of the window, to be withdrawn instantly at sight of the group below. In that instant, however, Baillot had caught a glimpse of a charming face, lighted up by a pair of dancing blue eyes. With a sudden movement he seized one of the falling blossoms and fastened it carefully in the lappet of his coat.

"Monsieur is quick of eye and hand!" observed the governor dryly. "We have now to go this way," indicating as he spoke a narrow stairway.

At the top of the stairway one of the attendants produced a huge iron key and with some difficulty unlocked a heavy oaken door, which further admitted them to a narrow corridor paved with stone. A second flight of steps, of such ancient date that the very stone of which they were composed was worn into hollows, brought them to another door heavily bound and clamped with iron; this being opened, with much puffing and straining on the part of the man who carried the keys, the party entered a lofty room, also constructed solidly of stone. A look of warmth and even luxury, however, was imparted to this grim chamber by the priceless tapestries which covered the walls, while upon the floor the foot sunk noiselessly into carpets of the texture and softness of moss. A small fire of fagots blazed upon the hearth, which was overhung by a monstrous chimney-piece of curious design. In strange contrast to the stern massiveness of the place were a number of trifling ornaments, a French clock, a buhl table containing a vase of flowers, an escritoire, and in one corner a lute, with pendant blue ribbons, leaning up against a gay little sofa.

The governor cast a hasty glance about him, then turning to Baillot said gravely, "Monsieur will, I trust, find himself quite comfortable here. He is assuredly as safe as one can well be in this uncertain world. You will observe—" he added with some pride evident in his voice, "that the castle walls are here ten feet in thickness."

"Safe from what?" demanded Baillot, planting himself directly in front of the little man.

"Safe from what?" repeated the governor, with an amazed look. "I wonder that you ask, and yet perhaps it is not, under the circumstances, to be wondered at. But I can only repeat what I have said; you are safe. I must now leave you for the present. Your bedchamber adjoins this on the left. Refreshments will be served at once."

"Stay, sir!" cried Baillot, "I must—" But the little man was gone, the great oaken door shutting after him with a loud bang; the grating of the key as it turned in its clumsy lock informed the unlucky Huguenot that he was still a prisoner. He listened intently, there was nothing to be heard save the sound of retreating footsteps which reverberated in faint echoes along the corridor without.

"So I am safe," he said aloud,—"this looks like it; and evidently left entirely to myself in a corner of this old pile." A faint cough from the other side of the door informed him that this was not the case; he bent down, and peering curiously through the great keyhole was rewarded for his pains by a glimpse of the scarlet livery and motionless halberds of two of the men-at-arms.

"No getting away there," he muttered. "Now the windows."

But these narrow apertures, guarded by iron bars as thick as a man's finger and opening directly over the water at a perilous height seemed to promise little better.

An agreeable diversion now occurred in the shape of dinner, which made its appearance borne on silver trays by two gigantic lackeys. With portentous solemnity these worthies drew forth a small table upon which they spread a repast, almost barbaric in its profusion, and for which the young man found a hearty appetite. When he had finished, they gathered together the appurtenances of the feast, still in the same noiseless and solemn manner, and after lighting a couple of silver lamps withdrew.

Left to himself, Baillot proceeded to examine the bedchamber. He soon satisfied himself that it had but the single door by which he had entered; its windows two in number looked out over the sea. He swung himself up into one of the narrow embrasures and looked out. The sun was setting amid a fiery pageant of cloud and its ruddy beams shining into the chamber, subdued to a sickly glimmer the light of the lamps. As far as the eye could reach there stretched the boundless panorama of sea and sky glowing with golden and rosy light. From the ships which lay at anchor in the bay he could catch the faint "Yo, ho!" of the sailors, and somewhere nearer at hand sounded the soft music of a lute.

Insensibly the young man yielded to the influences of the hour; he sat quite still, his head resting against the hard stones of the wall, his mind full of melancholy thoughts. Suddenly he was aroused from his revery by a soft whirring of wings, and with a gentle cooing sound a white pigeon alighted upon the ledge of the window ; presently it crept between the bars and quite unmindful of his presence began to peck at the stones as if in search of something to eat. Leaning forward to examine his little visitor more closely, he saw to his surprise that the pigeon was invested with a slender band about his body ; he loosened this, the bird submitting without fear to his touch, and drew from beneath its wing a small square packet.

CHAPTER XIV

FULL of wonder Baillot unfolded the paper, which he saw at once contained several lines of close handwriting, and spreading it open upon his knee, bent himself to the task of deciphering it by the fading light. He read as follows:

"Since your cruel father has denied you the privilege of attending church—where, sweet saint, I could at least adore you from a distance—I have languished in vain for a single smile. At midnight await the signal, and lower the cord which you will find secreted within the body of your lute. Before dawn we shall be in a position to defy the wrath of those who would fain separate us. Farewell, my own Helena, *yours until death and after.*—RODERICK."

When the young Huguenot had finished reading this precious epistle he smiled, then laughed aloud softly.

"Ha, little one," he said, addressing the pigeon, which was still pacing up and down the embrasure, "you have made a sore mistake in your homing this time. This pretty letter should have called a blush to a fairer cheek than mine. It was doubtless intended for the maid with the golden hair and the merry blue eye, whose nosegay took such a sad tumble this afternoon."

He again glanced thoughtfully at the paper which he

held in his hand—"the cord which you will find secreted within the body of your lute" were the words
which met his eye.

A sudden thought struck him, he sprang down from
his perch, and seizing the blue-ribboned lute thrust his
hand into its body. There was something within ; he
drew it forth—it was unquestionably a long cord rolled
neatly up into a little ball.

"An elopement at midnight," he murmured. "Ah,
yes, if now I can but persuade this brave gallant that
I am quite as desirable a companion as the blue-eyed
lady. But how will my unknown adorer effect an
entrance into these iron-clad windows? Stay, it is
possible that the bars are not so formidable as they
appear."

Which surmise was shortly proven correct, as he
found to his great satisfaction. Four of the bars in one
window had been cut completely through, and were
ready to yield to the slightest touch, though they presented to the casual observer the same impregnable aspect as the others.

But the young man was not to be left to himself for
the night without further attention from his noble host.
Shortly after he had examined the windows, a light tap
sounded upon the door of his chamber, and an elderly
man-servant entered, wearing the crimson livery of the
house, and bearing a small silver tray, containing pre-
sumably some slight refreshment for the honored guest
should he chance to hunger in the night. This functionary proceeded in discreet silence to lay out a great
array of ivory-backed brushes, crystal flasks, and other
toilet appurtenances, together with a silken night-robe
and an embroidered dressing-gown.

He then approached the door, and opening it made some signal to those without. Immediately there entered two footmen bearing a small truckle-bed, which they set down in one corner, after which they noiselessly withdrew. Baillot perceived that this meant the presence of the elderly man-servant for the night. He started up from the great chair where he had been lounging, idly watching the methodical movements of the lackey.

"See here, my good man!" he said, frowning. "I never permit my *valet de chambre* to sleep in my apartment; you must remove your couch to the corridor without—and at once."

The man looked startled. "Pardon, monsieur," he said humbly, "but I have my orders from the governor, and—"

"That makes not the slightest difference, sirrah. The governor will not presume to dictate to me about a matter of my personal comfort. Remove that bed instantly."

The lackey hesitated a moment longer, but an imperative gesture from Baillot evidently decided him. Muttering something about asking the governor's gracious permission, he again opened the door, and the offending couch was removed.

"You may find the corridor a draughty and rheum-provoking place, my good fellow," remarked Baillot graciously, "but for all that you must pass the night there for once. It will not be necessary again, I trust. Now, as everything is in readiness for the night, you may leave me. I will make my own toilet. Do not disturb me before ten in the morning, and, above all, do not enter the room unless I ring."

The man bowed low, his hand upon his heart, then backed slowly away.

The hours until midnight passed slowly enough. Baillot had placed himself in the window where were the loosened bars; these he cautiously removed, and with the cord in his hand awaited the signal—no doubt preconcerted between the lovers, but of which he was unfortunately ignorant. The night was intensely dark, and as the appointed hour drew near a fine rain began to fall. "All the better," he thought with a smile, as he pictured to himself the crestfallen countenance of the eager lover. Then another thought occurred to him.

"The donkey will come up to encourage mademoiselle to descend," he said to himself. "And indeed she must needs be a daring maid, and desperately in love, to essay a rope-ladder from this dizzy height. I must prepare myself for his reception."

From his bedchamber he procured a pillow, a couple of damask towels, which he ruthlessly tore into strips, and a bit of the voluminous white drapery which hung about the bed. It was now verging close upon midnight, and he resumed his post in the embrasure with a beating heart. Presently he became aware of the muffled dip of oars directly beneath his window, and then the cry of an owl echoed with startling distinctness from the rocky walls of the castle.

"Idiot!" muttered Baillot, unrolling the cord and lowering it rapidly into the darkness.

A gentle pull on the cord presently informed him that it had reached its destination; he waited a moment longer till a second jerk gave the signal to raise it, and shortly the first round of a strong and well-made rope-ladder came to hand. It was provided with a pair of stout hooks, and these he made fast without delay. A pause in the proceedings followed; those in the boat below were evidently waiting for the signal to ascend. The young man was nonplussed for an instant, then he leaned out of the window and shook the ladder three times.

Immediately the ropes became taut, and presently he could discern the head of a man below. He withdrew himself cautiously into the shelter of the window draperies, and waited, his heart beating quite as loudly as if he had been the yellow-haired maid.

The head of the man was now on a level with the window. "Sweetest Helena—adored lady!" came a passionate whisper, "Where are you?"

"Here, Roderick," whispered Baillot faintly, allowing a bit of his white drapery to appear from behind the curtain.

"My angel!" And the slender figure of a very young man scrambled quickly in through the window, and leapt lightly down. "Come to my arms!"

In response to this tender invitation Baillot sprang suddenly forward, seized the stripling about the waist, and forced him down to the floor, smothering his frightened outcry with the pillow. In another instant he had bound and gagged him securely; then he arose, turned up the light—which he had thoughtfully lowered in keeping with the tender romance of the scene which had just been enacted—and surveyed the prostrate lover. He could not forbear a smile at the expression in the eyes of the youth; rage, surprise and entreaty were mingled in the anguished look with which he regarded his captor.

"You have had a cruel surprise, my young friend," remarked Baillot gently, "a most disagreeable surprise ; but I think I shall be able to convince you that worse things might have happened. I have every sympathy for you in your undertaking, I have been in love myself, my dear fellow. In fact I am in love now, and it is for that reason that I encouraged you to go on with this little affair, which has apparently ended in such a fiasco—I say apparently, my dear Roderick, because your cause is quite uninjured by this circumstance, if you will do exactly as I say."

The young fellow writhed convulsively, with a dull groan expressive of the deepest anguish, and Baillot stooped to satisfy himself that his bonds were not uncomfortably tight.

"I should be happy to relieve you of your gag, sir," he observed politely, "it is no doubt very uncomfortable ; and as soon as I have succeeded in convincing you that it is to your interest to be quite still I will do so. In the meantime let me assure you that your lady is safe," and he proceeded to relate the circumstances of the afternoon. "You see," he continued, "that perhaps fearing your prowess, her father has caused her to be removed from her apartments to another part of the castle, and so unexpectedly that she had no time to communicate with you ; the matter is perfectly plain. Now at this moment there are, on guard outside of my door, several men-at-arms and a *valet de chambre*. I have only to open my door and call them in, and *voila !* You are removed, the stern parent is aroused from his slumber, and—ah, you follow me. I shall shortly be able to loose you. But first, attention ! I am a prisoner here ; that rope-ladder means safety ; I shall descend it, either with, or without you. I much prefer that it shall be with you, for in that case you will give orders to your people to take me to a place of safety. If you think best to refuse, my course is perfectly plain. I shall descend the ladder; I shall escape! And you? You shall remain; the valet will come in at ten; you will not be neglected. You understand me? I will loose one hand, if you are prepared to follow my very reasonable suggestions, be so good as to lift one finger. Ah, you consent!"

"Who are you?" said the young fellow, rising from the floor, and ruefully rubbing his wrists. He was a handsome stripling, with frank, honest brown eyes, which he fixed upon his conqueror with a curious stare.

"Who am I?" repeated Baillot. "I am really in doubt on that score. I should be very glad to know who I am personating at present. However, that doesn't matter in the very least to either you or me. We must get away, and speedily. But first, tell me what you were intending, had this little affair gone as you wished?"

"Intending?" exclaimed the youth, "why, to get married, sir, and as soon as possible. The devil take you!" he added in a sudden rage.

"Not yet, I hope," observed Baillot soothingly. "Don't get excited, I entreat you, my young friend; remember that there are sharp ears on the other side of that door; an explanation of your presence here at this hour might prove a little awkward. What I meant was this: where were you intending to go when the descent of the rope-ladder should have been successfully accomplished?"

"By carriage first, to a clergyman in an adjoining parish ; after that—I—"

"You mean that beyond that point you have not made definite plans, possibly a return to the stern father and a reconciliation—eh ?"

"That's none of your business, sir," said the stripling sulkily.

"You are right, boy. I beg your pardon for my seeming impertinence. Once out of this confounded place I will tell you who I am, and how I came to be a prisoner in Warham castle. Meantime I must not fail to observe a time-honored custom and leave behind me an explanatory note for the eye of the stern father."

And seizing a quill which lay together with an ink-horn on a table near at hand, he hastily scrawled a few lines.

Just as he was signing his name he heard a cautious cough outside the door. Turning to the lad, who was standing near watching his movements with a cloudy brow, he whispered, "Out of the window, sir, instantly—the valet !"

The boy needed no second bidding. Like a flash he sprang to the window and disappeared. Baillot hastily drew the heavy curtains before the tell-tale opening, not an instant too soon, for the door opened cautiously, and the elderly man-servant appeared upon the threshold, bearing in his hand a small rush-light, and winking and blinking like a man newly aroused from sleep.

CHAPTER XV

"How now," said Baillot sternly, "did you hear me ring?"

"No, your honor, humbly begging your honor's pardon, I did not hear you ring, but—"

"No buts, fellow. I ordered you to remain outside till you should hear the bell. Go, and do not again intrude yourself into my presence unbidden."

The man cringed visibly before the young man's stern eye, but he stood his ground obstinately. "The guard, your noble honor—the guard aroused me; he insisted that he heard voices within. I thought—"

"You have no business to think; that is for your betters. If it pleases me to talk with myself that concerns neither you nor the guard. Is it then forbidden to speak in Warham castle! and if so, why do you stand chattering there when I have already twice bidden you begone?"

But the man's sharp eyes had not been idle, and now instead of retreating, he cautiously closed the door behind him, and advanced into the room, evidently bent upon examining the bits of cloth with which Baillot had bound the adventurous lover.

As he stooped the young man sprang upon him, and in another moment he too lay gagged and bound upon the floor.

117

"Now, sirrah, is your curiosity satisfied? Perhaps you will conclude that it is best to obey in future." And extinguishing the lamps, Baillot crawled cautiously out of the window, and began a swift descent of the rope-ladder. When he had neared the bottom, he paused, and listened intently; there was no sound save the rippling of the waves as they lapped gently about the base of the tower. He whistled cautiously through his closed teeth; there was no response.

"The young rascal!" he thought. "He has left me. 'Tis a lucky thing he was unable to take his ladder with him. I must swim for it, there's no telling how long that villain lackey's mouth will be quiet; I gagged him too lightly I fear."

Cautiously divesting himself of his coat, he threw it into the sea, then descending a few more rounds of the ladder, he was discomfited to find that although he was still at some distance above the water his foot encountered the empty air.

"*Peste !*" he muttered, "did the idiot expect the girl to drop into a boat from this height?—ah, I perceive that my gallant young friend has cut the ropes, and as high as he could reach. Well, I must drop— Heaven send that there be a good depth of water below !"

Clinging to the last round of the ladder, and hanging motionless till it should cease its giddy swaying, the young Huguenot endeavored to pierce the thick darkness which surrounded him. A ghastly vision of a crushed and shapeless body washing helplessly against the base of the grim tower, arose before his mental vision. And for an instant he was tempted to reascend the ladder to the snug security of the chamber above, but the thought of Madeline, and the hapless party on the island, gave him fresh courage; breathing a brief prayer to heaven, he let go his hold, and fell with a sounding splash into the sea.

As he arose and struck out, he heard the drowsy call of the sentry from the top of the tower. Swimming as noiselessly as possible he made for the nearest point of land. Before many minutes his foot struck bottom, and he cautiously emerged upon the shore. He paused to shake the water from his clothing. All was quiet in the direction of the castle, which loomed up darkly on the right, illumined here and there with a twinkling point of light. Not far from the spot where he had landed a large fire blazed cheerily amid the trees; there were several persons in its vicinity, for an occasional dark figure passed and repassed betwixt him and the red blaze. By degrees he had approached near enough to hear scraps of the conversation which was going on briskly between two of the persons at the fireside—an old woman, who held between her teeth a short black pipe, and a tall swarthy young man, his head bound about with a scarlet handkerchief. Near them were half a dozen brawny fellows stretched at full length and snoring loudly, while behind the fire loomed the dim outlines of two or three covered wagons.

"You bungled the job, my lad, and so lost a handsome bit of gold. You should have done as I said a week ago."

"I was ready but he wasn't," replied the young fellow sulkily. "You can't hurry these fine folks. He was afraid, poor fool."

"Not so much fool as you!" snarled the old woman, removing the pipe from between her lips and spitting viciously into the fire. "I've a mind to lay the rope's end onto you for a doddering blockhead."

"Ay, and have you, old woman," sneered the other. "You'd best keep a civil tongue in your head, for I'll not hear your dotard ravings. I've had the rope's end from you for the last time. Nay, if I should choose to whisper something I wot of into yonder magistrate's ear, somebody else 'ud get the rope's end with a loop in it—hey, my lady queen?"

"Ay, the rope's end with a loop in it!" retorted the crone with a shrill, quavering cackle of laughter. "You will make a pretty gallow's bird one day, lad. How you flop about, and gasp and struggle—I see it now as plainly as I see the fire here. You are strong and young, and die hard—hard! As for me—an old woman, as you say—I've had my day, and I no more fear death than I fear you!"

"You lie!" growled the man; "you fear death and you fear me." And seizing her by the throat he flashed a bright knife over her head.

"Coward!" cried Baillot, springing forward. "Would you murder a woman?"

The fellow dropped his knife and turned slowly about. "And who may you be, my fine gentleman, that you meddle in what concerns you not? I have a mind to try my blade in another quarter!"

"Put up your knife, Bill," commanded the old woman, who was still smoking her pipe, apparently quite unmoved by all that had passed. "You have been in the water, sir," she continued, fixing her ferret-like gaze on the young man's dripping garments.

"That is true, mother," replied Baillot; "will you give me some dry clothes and a seat at your fire?"

The hag ran her curious eyes over his clothing. "Ay, velvet and lace and satin—yet he asks for clothes from poor wandering gipsies!" she muttered. "Now where might the bonny coat be that belongs with that gay suit, my lord?"

"Never you mind that, mother; but give me a suit of fustian like the one this young man is wearing, and these shall be yours."

"Ay, give him some clothes, Bill. A fair exchange is no robbery." She added a few words in the gipsy dialect to the young fellow, who had sulkily arisen to do her bidding.

A few minutes served to transform a very sorry gallant into a sufficiently common-place laboring man. And in this guise Baillot presently returned to the fire, closely followed by the young gipsy. "I have travelled far, and am weary," he said, as he threw himself down at the fireside. The old woman had shaken the ashes out of her pipe and was sitting motionless staring at the darting flames. "I shall sleep till day-break," he added, hoping that the gipsies would follow his example and thus afford him an opportunity of slipping away unobserved.

The old woman paid no heed, but went on muttering and mumbling to herself. Suddenly, however, she broke out in a high quavering voice: "I see gold in the fire—much gold, and it has to do with this bonny gentleman; ay, lad, it was a happy hour for us when he strayed into the light of our fire like a wandering night moth. I see a great ship with the fine gentleman on its deck. I see many great folk standing about him. I see him—but now it grows dark, and out of the darkness he comes to us with the salt brine dripping from his fine clothes." Then she burst into a fit of her cackling laughter, and prodded the young gipsy in the side with a skinny fore-finger.

"You are merry, mother," said Baillot as the eldritch laughter died away.

"Merry—merry? Yes, my fine gentleman, and well I may be. They are mistaken, though—a pretty jest! I could have told them better!"

Baillot made no further remark; he was inwardly cursing himself for his folly in interfering. "The old hag," he reflected unhappily, "would have been well out of the way—even had this young worthy carried out his threat—and I should have been many miles away."

"You could not have gotten far," quoth the gipsy, wagging her head; "but Bill would never have hurt me; 'tis just his little playful way. Ay, my fine gentleman," she continued, sucking away at her pipe, "you wonder because I can read your thoughts—your thoughts and the thoughts of many others as well. A hundred years have not passed over this head for naught. I live in both worlds, and the flesh is but a clumsy cover for sharp eyes like mine." With that she fell to puffing vigorously, blowing out great clouds of smoke, amid whose misty wreaths she appeared as some grotesque and ugly idol seen through its votive incense.

Baillot watched her for some time in silence, then observing that the young gipsy had followed the example of the others and had fallen fast asleep, he also lay down, pillowing his head upon his arm. About an hour passed in this manner, the woman smoking, the men snoring loudly, and the crackle of the fire dying away to a low purring sound. At length the old gipsy arose, and taking a knife from her belt stealthily approached the young Huguenot. He was on the point of springing to his feet, but on second thought he remained motionless, breathing gently and regularly. The hag leant over him, approaching her knife within a hair's breadth of his naked throat. "Ay, he sleeps," she muttered softly, "sleeps like the dead; so much the better."

She turned and crept away in the direction of the wagons. Baillot watched her till she was well out of sight, then he crawled noiselessly into the black shadow of a thicket behind him. For some minutes he stole along hardly daring to breathe, then hearing the sound of barking dogs, and the high quavering tones of the old gipsy he broke into a run, which to his great relief soon brought him to a high-road, stretching dusty and dim between the dark hedgerows on either side.

"I've made a pretty mess of the night's adventure so far," he muttered. "What if I drop anchor till daybreak, when I can look about." And spying presently the irregular outlines of a group of farmbuildings somewhat back from the road, he slipped through the hedge and was soon snugly ensconced in the shelter of a great rick.

"Not so much of a mess after all," he reflected, as he leaned back comfortably in the warm straw. "I am free; I have a capital disguise. I shall have no trouble in getting aboard a ship to-morrow, and *then*—" And then—he plunged into the bottomless abysses of sleep, giving his uncertain future not a single thought till he was aroused some hours later by a rough hand at his rustic pillow.

CHAPTER XVI

THE PINES

LIFE on the island had settled down into a peaceful monotony. Nothing further occurred to alarm the occupants of the little cottage, whose days passed quietly in the performance of the varied duties which existence imposes on all human beings, in a degree varying with the amount of their so-called civilization. With our islanders there was the usual routine of housework, cooking, cleaning, washing and ironing, gardening and the care of the various domestic animals and fowls that soon gathered about them. To the share of Winters fell the garden and the cows, while Madeline was delighted to feed the pigeons and poultry, which in their turn contributed largely to the comfort of the table. Cato was "the chief cook and bottle-washer," and early and late was to be found devising delectable dishes for the ladies. On the shoulders of Madame de Langres had fallen quite naturally the mantle of general director of all affairs both within and without, and so discreetly did she manage her little kingdom that a most delectable peace reigned therein.

As the days passed the inhabitants of the island gradually lost all fear of their surroundings. They almost ceased to speculate on the strangeness of the place, and settled down to a comfortable enjoyment and appreciation of its advantages. Though the castle had been abandoned as a place of residence, scarcely a day passed that some member of the family did not visit it. Now it was Madame de Langres and Madeline who must needs make the rounds of the gardens and libraries, to return laden with books and flowers; now Cato and Winters, who explored the vast cellars and storehouses in search of fresh dainties for the table.

The old sailor moreover had occupations of his own, which he talked little about, but which evidently cost him much time and thought. Madeline came upon him one evening as he sat in the little garden of the cottage, surveying with pride the neat rows of vegetables and smoking a short black pipe.

"Who would think," she said glancing about her at the peaceful homely scene, "that we were many thousands of miles from home, and indeed from any human habitation. One might suppose that behind that group of trees nestled other cottages as pretty and homelike as this, that up the path yonder might come at any moment a group of laughing children. How very delightful it would be to live always in this peaceful spot, far from wars and persecutions, if only—"

"Then you are lonesome, miss," interrupted Winters, removing the pipe from his mouth, and ramming down its glowing contents with a horny fore-finger. "You are lonesome, and would like to get away from our island. Wall, thar's the ship." And he fell to smoking with renewed vigor.

"I did not see the yacht this afternoon when we were at the castle," observed Madeline; "both mother and I noticed and remarked its absence from its moorings; where is it?"

"Whar is it?" chuckled the old man,—"whar is it? Who supposed you'd care? Jes' walk a bit an' see if we can find her; mebbe she's slipped her cables agin an' run away; she's a ticklish beauty.''

Full of curiosity at the old sailor's mysterious air, the young girl accompanied him towards the shore of the lagoon. Near the pier was moored the small row-boat, used by Winters in his fishing and exploring expeditions, upon which he was often accompanied by Madeline; but the yacht was nowhere to be seen.

"Where can it be?" she asked in a tone of consternation. "Do you not know?" turning to Winters.

"Look sharp, miss," said the old man with a triumphant chuckle, "she ain't far from here. Your eyes are as good as most, if you can't see her, I guess she's safe enough."

The young girl looked wonderingly about. "I can see nothing," she said at length, "and yet you say she is near."

"Wall, I reckon I'll have to tell ye then," said Winters, a gratified grin overspreading his mahogany features. "You see, 'twas this way, miss, I got to figurin' as how some rascals cut her hawser once: an' she slipped off to sea—that's the time we found her, you'll remember, jest as we was on the p'int of founderin' in that blowed cockle-shell of a boat. All right it was that time and mighty convenient for us. I reckon the A'mighty put the idee into the head of the scoundrel as done it—though it allers struck me as mighty cur'us how willin' we be to lay things to the A'mighty when they turn out to suit us—and contrariwise. Wall, as I say, I was figurin' the thing out to myself, and I says to myself, folks hev visited this 'ere island twice within —say two months, once to carry off the folks as was here afore us, and once to carry off poor Baillot.''

The young girl visibly winced at this, and Winters noticing the change in her expression, continued craftily, "I say *poor* Baillot, but Lord love ye, miss, I 'xpect it'll prove a mighty lucky thing for the 'hull of us—his takin' off. He's nobody's fool, is young Baillot, and if he don't get clear of whoever nabbed him, I'm mighty mistaken. I'm expectin' him back most any day now. He's jest as true as steel, and I'll bet has spent more hours thinkin' about us than you could rightly figure, miss, however smart you be."

"Do you really think so?" cried Madeline, a delicious blush rising to her cheek.

"Think so!" cried the old sailor gallantly. "Nobody as ever clapped their eyes onto *you* is going to forgit you in a hurry—and the rest of us 'll come in for a share on it, as long as we're in the same spot of earth."

"But you were telling me about the yacht," said the young girl demurely.

"Ay, so I was; as I say, I thought to myself that mebbe we'd have some more visitors of the same sort, as 'ud think best to carry off or burn up our little beauty—an' we may have a use for her yet. So I made up my mind to put her out of harm's way. One day I was pokin' round in the boat, and I come acrost a little creek, as runs into the lagoon just beyond that bunch of trees thar; it didn't take me long to find that thar was water enough to hold the yacht. So I fastens back the trees on either side—being mighty careful not to break 'em, and after a deal of tuggin', I pokes my lady into her new quarters—jest got her in and that's all; back flies the trees, and she's completely hid, all but her tops. That puzzled me for a spell; but arter a

while I figured that out too; I found a pot of green
paint in one of the huts below us, up I goes and paints
the tops of her masts a good green color, then I cuts
some evergreen branches and fastens 'em on, and what
do we see now, the masts of a ship? Naw, by thunder,
nothin' but a lot of trees. What do you think of that?"

"I think it's wonderful," exclaimed Madeline;
"even now I cannot guess where she lies."

"Right over in thar. Thar's a light tree, then some
evergreens, do ye see? The evergreens is the tops of
our ship."

"But the branches will wither," objected Madeline.

"Pines don't wither, miss. They'll drop off mebbe,
then the evergreen 'll be dead—nothin' strange or
startlin' 'bout a dead evergreen, hey? I've got another
scheme too, 't I'm figurin' on. I'm goin' to work on
it to-morrow. We're a needin' a lookout. An' I'm
goin' to make one, as 'll be a lookout."

Not many rods from the cottage stood a group of
giant pine trees, and here it was that Winters proposed
constructing the lookout, or crow's nest, as he called it.
Pressing Cato into the service, he conveyed to the foot
of the trees a quantity of boards and light timbers, as
well as a liberal supply of rope for the necessary tackle,
and here for several days he labored incessantly, scarcely
taking time to eat.

"This 'ere contrivance is goin' to be the finest crow's
nest as was ever constructed by man or fowl," he remarked one evening to Madame de Langres after a hard
day's work in the tree tops. "I'm goin' to have a
rope-ladder from the ground to whar the branches begin
—a good strong one, fastened taut at top and bottom;
you women-folks must learn to go up it."

"I fear that would not be an easy matter for us to accomplish," remarked the lady with an indulgent smile. "For my part I am quite willing to entrust all such matters to you; my poor eyes would be of little use in spying out ships."

Winters scratched his head meditatively. "You'll hev to turn your petticoats up," he said, a quizzical twinkle in his eye. "I suppose it ain't for me to say, but I ain't never been able to see why any creatur' of God's make with two good legs should be trussed up in such all-fired onhandy riggin'. Come a shipwreck or a fire, it's as much as you can do to save the women-folks—and why? Their petticoats is in the way. Ye can't run, ye can't climb, ye can't scarcely walk, and all on account of your consarned petticoats!"

Madame de Langres looked slightly scandalized at this speech; but Madeline laughed heartily.

"I'll engage to clamber into your crow's nest," she said, "in spite of my petticoats. But tell us, why do you wish us to go up there?"

"Wall," said the old man cautiously, "in the first place I want ye to see what I've been doin' up thar. I reckon you'll be surprised; I've got the neatest little place you'd want to see. Then ag'in it might come in handy to have a place of that kind if we was to have company of the wrong sort some day. When we git up to whar the stairway begins, we jest draw the rope-ladder up out of sight, and thar we be as snug as the ship yonder."

"But I can see the timber shining through the branches," objected Madeline.

"You won't see it when I git it painted and fixed; I'm goin' to rig her out same way I did the ship."

Two days later he announced triumphantly that the job was finished, and invited the family out to inspect the airy retreat.

"I fear that I shall never be able to go up that ladder," said Madame de Langres, eyeing the frail-looking structure of rope with manifest disfavor.

"I hope you'll try, ma'am. It ain't so resky as it looks. Will you go up, miss?"

Madeline was already tucking up her gown.

"Indeed, yes," she said stoutly, "I am going up; the view from the top must be superb."

"I'll go ahead," said Winters, running up the swaying ladder with cat-like ease and agility.

"It wriggles so!" cried Madeline, pausing on the third round and looking down at her mother with a nervous laugh.

"That won't hurt ye!" bawled Winters from above. "Ye can't fall ef you only hang on! Don't stop to think about it!"

Thus encouraged the young girl kept bravely on till at length she had reached the spot where Winters awaited her, and where the wooden ladder, which he dignified with the name of stairway, began. This was furnished with a pair of side rails, and certainly presented fewer difficulties to the novice than the more primitive mode of ascent below. By means of this stairway the two mounted in a narrow spiral to a curious-looking structure in the branches.

"Are you sure it is safe?" asked Madeline in a voice which trembled slightly, as they emerged upon a tolerably broad platform surrounded on all sides by a stout railing.

"Safe?" echoed the sailor. "It's as safe as a ship!

—a ship in her docks, I s'pose I must say for you, miss.
But I've anchored them timbers so they'll stay as long
as the tree holds together—mebbe longer. Take the
glass, miss, you can see miles an' miles in every direction. Here's cupboards whar we can stow victuals
enough to last a week. Here's curtains of canvas
painted green to let down in foul weather. Yonder
we'll sling a couple of hammocks. Thar's room enough
for the 'hull of us; and I'd like to see the man as'ud
find hide or hair of us once safely stowed up here!''

Madeline admired everything to his heart's content,
and indeed it was an achievement to be proud of, and
would certainly form a well-nigh perfect retreat in case
of danger.

"The only thing to look out for 'ud be noise," remarked the old man thoughtfully. "We'd have to be
as quiet as a ship in a calm if there was mischief abroad,
for a couple of stout axes at work below would tumble
our nest to the ground faster than we'd care to come as
was in it."

Madeline shuddered at the thought. "What about
wind?" she asked rather faintly.

"Wind?" said the old sailor, thoughtfully expecto-
rating over the railing and giving his trousers an extra
hitch. "Wall, miss, I don't reckon as anything short
of a hurricane 'ud do us much damage. We've got to
take our chances, same as in anything. These 'ere
trees have stood here for quite a spell, I reckon."

"How perfectly we can see the château," said Madeline, "and the cottage—such a speck of a thing, and
the whole island like a tiny fragment torn off the skirts
of a continent and set afloat on the ocean. This is like
being a bird."

"All but the wings, miss," said the old man. "I'd give a good year off my life for the wings of an albatross for jest one day; I'd soon know whar we was. But if I'm not mightily mistaken thar's a sail yonder!"

"A sail? I see nothing—ah, suppose you were right, and that this should prove to be our brave friend in search of us!"

CHAPTER XVII

WINTERS was silent for a moment. Then he slapped his leg violently.

"Thar's no doubt of it," he exclaimed. "That's a sail! Now we must be movin' lively, for thar's a deal to do afore we're ready for company." And with that he began a rapid descent. "Best come down to your ma!" he shouted back to Madeline, who was still trying to discover the sail on the dazzling rim of the horizon.

The young girl accomplished the descent without difficulty, and found her mother anxiously awaiting her at the foot of the tree.

"I am relieved, my child, to see you once more on *terra firma* without an accident," she said. "I should try and be satisfied with this one experiment, since it is surely a most hazardous one."

"It is not so difficult as you imagine, mother," replied the girl. "And if we are to carry out the plans of our good Winters, you may shortly be forced to make the experiment yourself; he declares there is a sail in sight."

"A sail? How very fortunate! Why should we conceal ourselves from our rescuers, pray? On the contrary, why not attempt to attract the attention of the vessel with a signal or beacon?"

Winters emerging from the cottage red-faced and

133

panting, loaded down with baskets and bundles, chanced
to hear this question. He threw down his armful of
stuff upon the ground and exclaimed somewhat roughly :

"Thar's no time to argufy the question, ma'am ; but
it's as plain as a marlinspike, that if yonder ship's crew
are good harmless folk we can soon find it out by their
actions. But thar's a deal too many pirates and bloody
men of the like on the seas to resk givin' ourselves
away. We'll lay low—or ruther high, till we're sure.
You women-folks git together what traps you're likely to
want for a couple of days or so an' fetch 'em out here
lively. Cato, douse your fire, an' hide anything that
looks too new about your diggin's. They'll suspect
thar's folks here by lots of signs, best we can do, but
if they can't lay their hands on us we shan't care."

"It seems to me, sir," said Madame de Langres with
dignity, "that this is a very curious idea of yours ;
most shipwrecked people welcome with joy any passing
vessel. I do not like the idea of concealing ourselves
in the way you suggest."

"Don't git me mad, ma'am !" said the old sailor
solemnly, "I'm a howlin' terror when I'm mad. I'm
willin' to slave for you women-folks till my fingers is
wore through to the bone, and you can hev your own
way about most everything ; but I tell ye, that you
must git up into this 'ere crow's nest, an' wait till I
give the sign that all's right and ship-shape !"

"Do not cross him," whispered Madeline, pressing
her mother's hand ; "it cannot harm us to do as he
suggests, and perhaps we shall be very glad if we do."

"But the ladder, daughter. I can never—"

"Ay, that's what's the matter !" chuckled Winters,
who had just returned with another load. "I'll tell ye

what, ma'am, I'm goin' to rig up a tackle to haul up these 'ere things, and if you say so I can take you up as neat as a pin!"

"Oh, dear no," exclaimed Madame de Langres nervously. "I could never think of such a thing. When will it be necessary for us to ascend,—in case," she added somewhat severely, "you persist in your strange idea?"

"I shall persist like a trade-wind, ma'am," replied the old man, working busily at his tackle. "There ain't no great hurry 'bout your goin' up, but get your fixin's together; a few books might come handy to pass away the time, a lot of shawls, an' some pillows, mebbe."

"Why surely you do not apprehend the necessity of passing the night in the tree-tops?"

"Wall now, I can't say rightly what's a goin' to happen; I was a goin' to store these 'ere things up there in any case, so as to have everything handy; I can't be sure yet as yonder sail 'll come our way. She may be out of sight by the time I git up thar agin, but thar's no harm in bein' ready."

Somewhat reassured, Madame de Langres returned to the cottage, and began to collect a few articles in leisurely fashion.

"Of course," she remarked in an indulgent tone to her daughter, who was similarly employed, "there is no harm whatever in humoring this strange caprice of our good old friend; this crow's nest, as he calls it, is his latest darling and he quite naturally wishes to bring it into play, but I am sure it is all very absurd."

"I trust that it may prove so, dearest mother," said Madeline gravely. "We have almost forgotten what a strange place this island is, so accustomed have we become to it, but as Mr. Winters very justly remarked, strange folks on strange errands have been here of late, and a little caution is not amiss.''

"Perhaps so, my child, and if it were not for that ladder, I should not be opposed to a few hours in yonder airy retreat. But although I am thoroughly ashamed of my cowardice, I confess that even the shipwreck did not possess such terrors for me as does that bit of swaying rope.''

"It isn't so bad if you only look up, and do not stop to think,'' said Madeline consolingly. "Perhaps we shall not have to go after all.''

"And at the next alarm our useful Winters may have mounted another hobby,'' added Madame de Langres comfortably.

But this hope was not to be realized ; the words were scarcely out of her mouth before the old sailor thrust his head in at the door and announced that the sail was clearly visible, and seemed to be rapidly approaching.

"All hands must git aloft before they git near enough to try their squinters on us,'' he bawled as he hurried away. "If they do that our game's up.''

Madame de Langres was a woman of determination and courage. No sooner did she perceive that she must mount the dreaded rope-ladder than she tucked up her petticoats snugly and advanced toward it in the same calm manner in which she had faced the terrors of the shipwreck.

"I will go first, mother,'' volunteered Madeline. "I am not afraid this time.''

"No, child, I will go first and you shall see how nimble I am,'' said Madame de Langres with a faint smile.

136

"Bravo, ma'am," cried Winters, as she mounted steadily and firmly. "Thar's sailor blood in your veins, I'll bet; anybody with half an eye could see it. Now, miss, look lively! I'll run up this 'ere stuff, then I must let the cows out of the barnyard, lock the cottage door, and a few other odd jobs, then I'll follow ye."

Madame de Langres was as much surprised as Madeline had been at the extensive structure in the pine trees. Cato was arranging the stores in the cupboards, a dozen inviting books reposed on the table and a couple of comfortable-looking hammocks, woven by the sailor at leisure moments, swung near.

"Isn't this delightful!" cried Madeline. "A cottage in the tree-tops. And yonder snowy cloud on the horizon is the ship!" She caught up the glass and studied the distant vessel attentively.

"The hull has not yet emerged from below the horizon," she remarked, handing the glass to her mother.

"When it does they'll be for studyin' us," remarked Winters who had just approached; "but they'll not find us if they look for a week. I've drawed up the ladder and made everything as snug as— Hold! Blow my buttons, but I've forgot one thing! I'll jest slip down and look to it—no need of a rope-ladder for me." And the old man hastily disappeared.

"I wonder what it was that he has forgotten," said Madeline anxiously, as she watched his distant figure dart away in the direction of the château.

"Mabby de boat," remarked Cato. "I hope dat he gits back afore dey comes."

"We cannot be sure that any one will deign to notice our little island," said Madeline with a nervous laugh. "One moment," she contined, turning to her mother, who was seemingly absorbed in the prospect without, "I am wishing so earnestly that the ship would come, bringing us relief and a means of escape from this sea-girt dot of earth; the next, I find myself wishing not less earnestly that it would go away and leave us undisturbed in this peaceful spot."

Madame de Langres sighed. "I can well understand your feelings, my child," she said soberly. "The future unfolds its pages all too slowly for our eager eyes at times, and again we would fain push away from us the inexorable hand that bids us read."

"We's boun' to have a picnic supper wiv de birds to-night anyhow!" cried Cato gleefully, preparing to spread the table with a snowy cloth.

"I don't know about that white cloth, Cato," said Madeline, looking at it doubtfully.

"Law, miss, der ain't nobody within seein' distance yet; dat 'ere table ain't fit for yer lady moder." And he went on with his preparations. Delicious bread, roast fowl, and an abundance of fruit and milk, composed the repast.

"Have we plenty of water?" asked Madame de Langres anxiously.

"Plenty of eberyt'ing," replied the negro. "We might stay a week, fur's dat's concerned. You tink dat ol' sailor done stockin' a ship for sea. He's been a gettin' ready for a week; when he wasn't hammerin' up here, he was tinkerin' away at boxes and baskets of victuals. 'Bake a plenty ob bread, Cato,' says he, 'an' bake it hard, so it'll keep.' He's got salt fish, an' salt meat, an' biscuits, an' de Lawd knows what all. It kep him mighty contented dough, and it may come in handy."

138

"The ship is certainly coming this way," said Madeline in a low tone. "I wonder why Mr. Winters does not return?"

The wonder deepened into positive alarm when several hours had passed and the old sailor was still absent. Meanwhile the ship had approached quite near; with the glass they could see her rigging swarming with seamen, and the glint of brasswork here and there about her white decks. Though evidently not a man-of-war, the vessel was heavily armed, and as she glided slowly under the lee of the island the watchers in the tree-top could distinctly hear the "Yo! yo! yo" of the sailors, as they furled and clewed down the canvas. Then came the rattle and splash of the anchors, and later a boat loaded with men shot off from the vessel's side. They were evidently not strangers to the spot, for without hesitation the steersman made for the hidden inlet, and before many minutes the watchers caught the sound of their voices from the direction of the lagoon.

A rocket fired from the terrace of the castle evidently conveyed instructions to those on board the vessel, for another boat-load shortly followed the first. It was now growing dusk, and myriads of twinkling lights in the windows of the château, and the sounds of loud laughter and boisterous shouts, showed that a revel of some sort was in progress there.

"It is quite evident that we must spend the night here," said Madeline to her mother. "Are you not thankful that we have this secure retreat? We shall sleep as peacefully as the birds—if only Mr. Winters returns."

"It may be that the owners of the castle have arrived," said Madame de Langres hesitatingly, "though

I see no women among them. It is, of course, possible
that the castle is being prepared for their reception, and
that they will disembark to-morrow."

"That does not sound like it!" exclaimed Madeline, as an outburst of bacchanalian shouts reached their
ears. "But, hark! I think I hear some one approaching."

"It am Winters!" cried Cato joyfully. "De Lawd
be praised!"

"Consarn ye, suppose it had not been Winters!"
growled the old sailor wrathfully as he clambered into
view. "Make another noise like that and I'll throw
ye overboard. You've got to clew down yer jaw, I tell
ye; those fellows yonder 'ud like nothing better than
the rare sport of a bird's nest like this!"

"Where have you been?"

"Who are these people?" exclaimed the two women
in a breath.

"I went down to the boat to hide my fishing-tackle,
and make everything look kind of lonesome and for-
saken along shore; I heerd 'em comin' afore I finished,
so I jest lies low to take a squint at 'em—I ain't rightly
figured what they be," he continued cautiously.
"They're agoin' it in some kind of a furrin tongue;
French mebbe, a kind of gab I don't keer much about
as a rule. Thar now!" he added in a tone of deep
contrition, "I'd clean forgot that you ladies was
French. Not 'at anybody'd ever guess it by your
looks, or by the way the good English rolls offen your
tongues."

"We don't mind being French," remarked Madeline demurely, "which is probably fortunate since we
cannot help it; but it is very handsome of you, Mr.

Winters, to assure us that we had made you lose sight of the damaging fact. But tell us, did you succeed in ascertaining what the errand of the ship is? Are her people the rightful owners of the place, and likely to remain? If so, we shall be obliged to discover ourselves sooner or later.''

"I didn't get wind of much," replied the old man. "By the looks of 'em, I should say they wa'n't the folks for that castle, though there was two or three of 'em in some sort of uniform. We'll see what we see— to-morrow. I ain't over and above sorry myself that we're whar we be; don't know how you feel about Jack Winters' currus idee by this time, ma'am.''

"I am beginning to think it was a most fortunate one," confessed Madame de Langres, to whom this last remark was addressed. "They seem a lawless company, whatever their nationality," she added, as a sound of breaking glass, followed by angry shouting, was heard from the château.

"We had best get what rest we can," said Madeline, "and let the morrow take care of the things of itself. Mother, let me make you comfortable in one of these swinging couches; here are pillows and blankets— thanks to Mr. Winters' thoughtfulness.''

"The other hammock is yourn, miss," said Winters. "Cato and I will roll up in a blanket, and nap on the soft side of one of these 'ere planks. Tell ye, I got this place ready jest in the nick o' time!" With which congratulatory reflection the old man composed himself to rest.

Madeline lay for a time looking up through the branches of the old pines at the stars which winked sleepily at her here and there from out the soft darkness of the heavens. The air was laden with balsamic fragrance, occasionally swept aside by a nimble breeze from off the ocean, only to roll back in languorous waves of sweetness. The hammock swayed softly, and soon, despite the noisy revelry in the château and the novelty of her airy couch, she fell sound asleep.

CHAPTER XVIII

A SUNBEAM which darted its golden arrow directly into her sleeping eyes caused the young girl to open them without delay the following morning. She lay for a moment staring, as she had done the night before into the twinkling branches of the old pine; directly above her head a red squirrel sat scolding and chattering in the branches.

"What are you doing here?" he seemed to say, with an indignant flirt of his bushy tail. "Is it not enough for you impertinent giants to possess the earth, without intruding your unwieldy bulks into our private haunts?"

Madeline shook her finger at him laughingly, and he turned and fled to a higner limb, where he again paused to deliver his philippic with renewed energy.

"Be you awake, miss?" came a cautious whisper from below. She raised her head and looked over the side of the hammock. "The rascals is abroad early this morning; I'll be blowed if I can make out what they're up to. A couple of 'em passed here not five minutes ago; thar they be agin!"

Madeline crept cautiously to the floor. "Where?" she whispered.

In reply the old sailor pointed out the figures of two men who were strolling along in leisurely fashion almost directly beneath. They were dressed, as the girl could see, in the uniform of the French navy, and for a

143

moment she could scarcely repress a cry of joy at sight of the familiar and well-loved trappings. A chance word, however, caused her to draw back, though she still listened eagerly.

"We'll scarce be able to finish the job properly under four days," remarked one of them,—"and work hard at that. I say, de Loignac, this isn't a bad place for a morning smoke." And the speaker flung himself upon the ground directly beneath the trees wherein our party of adventurers was hidden.

"We'll take a look at yonder cottage when you've finished," continued the speaker, whose words, unintelligible to the old seaman, were distinctly audible to Madeline's quick ear. "It hardly seems possible that the place has been empty so long."

"Not a bad place," said his companion, who was puffing busily away at his long pipe. "By Jove, I shouldn't mind spending my summers here with the right company. What do you make of this business, anyhow? What's the need of making ducks and drakes of the place?"

"I fancy that's of very little moment to us, my dear fellow; a close mouth and blind eyes are the thing. You know what our orders were—to leave no living thing on the island, and—" The speaker leaned forward and whispered something into his companion's ear.

"*Mon dieu!*" exclaimed the listener. "I don't wonder that you hesitated to profane the desert air with such an atrocity. What in the name of all that is hideous, is the reason for that?"

"They are all condemned convicts," replied the other coolly, "and a part of them slavering, whining

Huguenots into the bargain. I tell you that you may
not be disagreeably surprised later.''

The other smoked in silence for a few moments, then
he broke out with a savage oath. "This is not to my
liking, de Morney! Who knows but that the Bastile
will forever close our own mouths when we return?''

"Who indeed!'' echoed his companion with a light
mocking laugh. "Perhaps 'twere better not to return;
suppose we settle down here for the balance of our
lives, far from the dear delights of Paris and Versailles.
'Twould be quite as safe as the Bastile, and infinitely
more agreeable.''

"Ah! You can afford to jest, you have friends at
court, and powerful ones. As for me— How do I
know that I am not included in the precious arrangement you just mentioned?''

"You are not—upon my soul, you are not! I jest
because I do not fear anything untoward for either of
us, if we but accomplish the thing properly. But
come, let us be on foot. We can finish inspecting the
place, then take a look at our workmen.''

"I shouldn't mind owning some of those tapestries
and paintings, to say nothing of the plate. Why man,
some of the books alone are priceless!''

"Not for your life!'' exclaimed the man whom his
companion had addressed as de Morney. "You might
well fear the Bastile should you attempt to so disobey
orders.''

The listeners, as may well be supposed, were breathlessly silent during this conversation, but as the voices
and steps of the two officers died away, Winters ventured to inquire of Madeline what had passed.

She informed him briefly.

"Donno as I'm any wiser than I was afore," he commented, "except for one thing; it's middlin' sartain
from what they said, that it wouldn't be over an' above
healthy for any of us to show ourselves. Guess we'll
have to stay here for a spell till they git through their
little job, whatever it is."

The party in the tree-tops saw no more of the new-
comers for several hours, and the time passed heavily
enough. Winters especially chafed in the narrow confines of the place.

"This is a mighty slow business," he declared;
"now if I only understood their tarnal lingo, I'd sneak
down and take a squint at 'em."

About the middle of the afternoon, despite the entreaties of the two women, and at the imminent risk of
being observed from the deck of the vessel, he cautiously descended the tree and stole away in the direction of the château.

Under cover of the shrubbery, he advanced to a point
where he could observe the landward façade of the
castle with comparative security. Peering out from his
leafy screen with the greatest curiosity, he at first saw
nothing to indicate any human presence, and was on
the point of attempting a bold run across a little open
space to a clump of bushes somewhat nearer the building,
when a gang of workmen armed with picks and shovels
came into view; they were followed closely by a squad
of armed men, under whose surveillance they presently
set to work with a will near the foundation of the château.

After a deep hole had been excavated, a second party
carrying a number of small casks appeared; these busied
themselves for some moments in the place just made
vacant by the men with the picks and shovels.

"What in thunder!" muttered Winters to himself, as he observed these proceedings. "Looks mighty like blowing the place up to me. Them there casks now—gunpowder, as I'm a livin' sinner!"

That the old sailor was correct in his surmise presently appeared. One of the men who had been actively engaged in bawling out orders to those at work, now waved his arms violently and shouted something in a loud voice, which Winters could not understand, but which he rightly took to be an order to get out of the way of the impending explosion.

He was now in a position of extreme peril, and for a moment heartily regretted his boldness. The workmen still closely shadowed by their guard were almost upon him; while the man who had given the order was manifestly preparing to light the fuse, which would start the buried gunpowder.

To retreat was impossible, to advance was equally so. Hastily scooping out with both hands a hollow place in the soft mold, the sailor flung himself down upon his face among the bushes, worried most of all lest some one should perceive his blue shirt through the green leaves, and drag him from his hiding-place. But workmen and soldiers had already retreated to a safe distance, and now he could hear the rapid footfalls of the man who had remained behind to light the fuse; he almost stepped on the prostrate body of the sailor as he pressed through the bushes in his haste. A moment of silence and suspense followed, during which Winters dug a little deeper into the soft earth, burrowing into it with closed eyes like a mole. Then followed a deafening report. A shower of broken fragments spattered with stinging force upon the body of the old man, but fortunately inflicted no serious injuries. Congratulating himself on his escape, he was about to rise from the ground, when a second explosion followed; he was conscious of a terrible blow on the back of his head; then he knew no more, but lay like one dead, the white petals of the shattered roses half concealing his motionless body.

"At this rate it will take us six months to blow up the place," grumbled the man who had fired the fuse, cautiously advancing. "A pest on the place! I shall set it on fire now, the heat will cause the stone to be more friendly to the gunpowder."

"Twere a pity, my Gaston, not to remove a *soupçon* of the valuables first," said one of the others who had followed him.

"But the orders?"

"The devil fly away with the orders! Who will be the wiser? You and I must needs look through the place a little, in order that we may select the best place for setting the fire. *Tiens!* Our pockets will not be searched."

His comrade replied with a sly wink, "I am not so sure of that, Pierre; but we shall see. Call back those dogs with the picks, and set them to work again under the tower yonder. *Bon dieu!* what is this? The body of a man, and dead as a stone; which now of the fools remained behind when I gave the order to retreat!"

"But this man is not one of the workmen; I never saw his face before."

"*Ciel!* You are mad; there has been no one here for two months. He has a nasty cut in the head."

"He is not dead, man, only stunned by a bit of the flying stone. What shall we do with him?"

148

Gaston removed his cap and wiped the perspiration from his forehead. " Do with him ?" he echoed. " Why let him be till he comes to ; then set him to work with the others."

" But I tell you he is not of the number we brought with us."

" What matters it ; they will all go the same road when they have finished. If this fellow has been cast away on the island, or if he sneaked away two months since, 'tis all the same ; there can be but one way out of the thing for him. Let him earn his passage into the next world."

Winters now opened his eyes, and one of the men who were still staring at him greeted his returning consciousness with a careless kick. " Get up, dog."

" Something has hit me !" faltered the old man, putting his hand up to his head with a dazed expression. " Oh, but wasn't I a tarnal fool to poke my neck into this noose ?"

" What kind of talk is this ? Do you understand his gibberish ?" growled Gaston turning to his companion.

" He is speaking English ; I know a little.—Who air you ?"

" Who air I ? Wall, sir, I *air* Jack Winters—a dumfounded idiot with a crack in his blamed old skull ; that's who I air."

" You shall wark ; get up, *vite !* You hear ? *Diable,* I hate English !" he added testily.

Gaston laughed. " I can move him," he said with an oath. " Up and out of this, you crack-brained English cur ! You shall live just three days longer ; then you shall have the distinguished privilege of dying with some who are your betters." He accompanied his words—not one of which was understood by the old sailor—with a vicious prick of his rapier, and a gesture in the direction of the gang of workmen who were busy at their labor of excavating.

Winters understood the prick and the gesture well enough; and inwardly cursing himself for his folly, he got slowly on to his feet and hobbled off under the watchful guardianship of the Frenchmen, who lost no time in providing him with a pick and shovel. As he bent to his unwelcome task, he cast a hasty glance at his fellow-workmen. Most of them had the sullen brutalized faces of those well-versed in crime and inured to hardship; but there were several, whose pale haggard countenances and painfully blistered hands moved him to pity. The guard of armed marines stood at some distance from the pit where they were working, and seemed to pay but scant attention to anything save their own half-whispered conversation. Perceiving this, Winters, under cover of stooping to remove a loosened stone, ventured to speak to the man who was digging next him.

"Can you talk?" he whispered cautiously. The man to whom he had spoken shook the matted hair from out his eyes, and turned with a start of surprise.

"Who are you?" he asked in excellent English.

"Jack Winters," replied the old man succinctly. "Whar do they stow you at night?"

"We slept in the cellars last night."

"Under guard?"

"Under guard—yes; but the guard was drunk."

"Why didn't you git then?"

"Escape? We are counted night and morning; were one missing that one would be hunted down and shot like a rat. But you are not of us. I do not remember your face. How is it that you are here?"

"Hist, man! they've got their blinkers on us!" whispered Winters.

A moment later, he again ventured to address his companion. "What are you doin' here—you seem a decent sort, an' you can talk English?"

"I am a Huguenot," replied the man bitterly; "'tis my crime to worship God in a different way from our holy and righteous king and his new mistress."

Winters surveyed the speaker more narrowly. He was a young man of medium height and slender build. In singular contrast to his dark skin and black hair shone a pair of vivid blue eyes. These eyes had burned with a baleful glitter as he spoke of the king and his mistress, but they grew dim with anguish or fatigue as he again bent to his labor.

"What's arter this 'ere job?"

"Death, for all I know—or care," replied the Huguenot dully.

"Be there any more of you?" whispered Winters after a moment's silence.

"Yes, there are six of us. The two old men yonder, and three who are working on the other side."

Winters said no more; the wound in his head throbbed painfully, but to that he gave little thought. He was revolving a plan in his mind whereby he might save the lives of the six Huguenots as well as his own.

"Onrighteous villains," he muttered under his breath, "they have the audacity to put an honest able-bodied seaman to work with a gang of convicts! Mebbe they'll wish they hadn't, afore they git through with Jack Winters. The low-lived lubbers!"

CHAPTER XIX

"A BEASTLY morning for shooting, Rod; we may as well turn back for breakfast. There's so much water in the air that the very dogs have lost the scent; look at old Balfour's drooping tail."

The speaker was one of two young Englishmen, who were tramping along, guns in hand, their dogs at their heels. They had been overtaken by a dense mist, which rolled in wet billowy masses all about them.

"Suppose we stop at the farm for breakfast," continued the first speaker. "You evidently need feeding, sir; you are as glum and unsocial as the fog itself. What's the matter with you?"

"If I told you I might get myself into more trouble than I am in now, and that's unnecessary, heaven knows!"

"Then you are in trouble, youngster? I guessed it the moment I put eyes onto you; you're not the same lad I left behind me when I started on my last cruise. Come now, tell your big brother all about it, and I'll engage to set the matter right, whether it's a lame pony, or a row with the keeper."

"You evidently think I am still an infant, Edward," replied the other with a toss of his handsome blonde head. "What do I care for a lame pony! As for the keepers, let one of them dare dictate to me, I'll lay him flat, and teach him to obey his betters."

"Good-morning, good-morning to you, sirs! You are out fine and early; but a bad day for shooting, sirs."

"You are right, Reynolds. It bade fair to be clear when we started out. If your good wife can give us some breakfast, I think we'll stop at the farm for a bit."

"Ay, sir, you'r 'eartily welcome! My mistress is wearyin' for a sight of you, my lord. As for Master St. Clair—'e's always welcome, God bless 'im! They've a 'ot time at the castle, sir, this morning, I 'ear," continued the speaker, a burly, red-faced farmer.

"What has happened at the castle?"

"Why, sir, a fine lord from furrin parts—as was wanted for somethink himportant, the Lord knows what —was a stoppin' at War'am; he were lodged in the tower chamber, I'm told, and somebody carried 'im hoff hunbeknownst in the night, sir—along of a rope-ladder. The villains tied up the serving-man 'ard and fast, and left 'im on the floor."

"What is this you are saying?" exclaimed the elder of the two young men, who was no other than our friend St. Clair. "He has escaped then?"

"Hescaped, sir? No, sir, not accordin' to what the guard and serving-man say. 'Ow could the poor gentleman get 'old of a rope-ladder?"

"This is a pretty business, Roderick!" exclaimed St. Clair. "I must go at once to the castle and inquire into it. Will you come with me?"

"I—I—no, Edward, that is—" replied the youngster turning white and red by turns. "I think perhaps I had best take the guns and dogs home. Don't you say so, old man?" with a desperate attempt to appear easy and unconcerned, which however did not impose in the least on his keen-eyed brother.

"Reynolds here will take care of the tackle," he said sternly ; "you boy, come along with me !"

"I—I don't think I care to go up to the castle this morning, Ned," blurted out the young fellow in an injured tone. "You seem to forget that I'm not a midshipman under your orders, sir."

"Well, my boy, perhaps it would be quite as well if you were. I think I'll speak to the governor about the matter. You've been into some mischief or other, I know ; come, out with it at once !"

"Upon my word, I'd like to tell you, Ned, if you wouldn't make sport of me."

"Never a bit of it, lad. Don't you know me well enough for that ? Fire ahead, youngster !"

"I wish you'd quit calling me *youngster* and *boy*. Confound it, man, I'll be twenty in a fortnight."

"Twenty ? Humph ! Well then, my reverend sir, proceed !"

"You're making game of me," said the boy sulkily.

"Come ! You're as difficult as a woman, or a baby a year old ; speak up like a man ! They're spoiling you, lad. You must get to sea, and this folly 'll drop off you like last year's leaves from yonder oak. But again I say, get at your yarn, and spin lively, for we must needs get up to the castle at once."

"It would never have happened if old money-bags up yonder had carried a decent tongue in his head," said the lad defiantly.

"Whom do you mean by old money-bags ?"

"Why, you know ; haven't you grown stupid lately. You've called him that yourself many a time ! I mean

Sir John Rich, the worshipful governor of Warham castle, at your service, Lieutenant St. Clair. Does that suit you better?"

"That suits me better. Go on," said St. Clair with a grave inclination of the head.

"There's Helen, you know," murmured the lad hanging his head.

"What, little Helen, with head as yellow as a dandelion, and cheeks the color of a ripe apple?"

"She's lovely—she's beautiful! You've no idea, Ned, how beautiful she is!"

"No, I dare say," said his brother, carefully suppressing a smile. "And so you fell in love with the fair Helen; and what followed?"

"I didn't say so; how did you know?"

"How did I know, you Zany? Why I know because I am so peculiarly clever and learned. Didn't Sir John smile on your youthful affections?"

"He's a beast!" declared the youth succinctly. "A regular old brute. Why he shut up that girl for a week because he saw me kiss her hand. Told me to go home to my—to my—pap! Wasn't that nasty of him? But I was too smart for the old fox."

"You've a positive talent for invective, Rod," interrupted St. Clair, with an air of relish. "What did you do to circumvent the old—er—animal?"

"Why, I had a couple of carrier-pigeons—bought 'em of Browrig; regular little beauties," continued the lad enthusiastically, "and with a few gold pieces handed on the sly to Janet, Helen's maid, we got those little creatures so they went back and forth as regular as the clock. But we got tired of that after awhile, so I made a big plan to carry off my darling—"

"What's that, sir! What were you going to do with her after you carried her off?"

"Why marry her, of course. What do you suppose? Have done laughing or I won't go on."

"You'll be the death of us all yet, Rod," gasped St. Clair, wiping his eyes. "What a Benedict you would make! Go on, I'm done now. You made a plan—"

"—To carry her off, as I said," said the boy scowling fiercely. "I had the ring, the priest, and all—sent my message by the pigeon as usual. By Jove, I'd like to wring that villain's neck!"

"What villain?"

"Why a great hulking beast of a Frenchman that I found in her rooms. In her rooms, sir! What do you think of that? The old miser had moved her out just at the wrong moment, and lodged the fellow in her place."

"Ah, I begin to see; you found the Frenchman in the place of your lady. And how, may I ask, did you make your way into Warham castle, my young Lothario?"

"By a rope-ladder."

"Then *you* liberated him?"

"Not I; the fellow had me at a disadvantage. You see he was on the lookout for some means of escape. He got my message by the pigeon—which, of course, homed as usual, and when I came up the ladder—"

"—He gave you a warm reception; just so, I can depict the scene. He is a clever gentleman," put in St. Clair quietly.

"Do you know him? Who is he?"

"Not so fast, boy. So you were the means of his

escape. Hum ! You've been the undoing of as pretty
a plan as—well, it may be that we can mend the matter
still. How did he persuade you to elope with him?
It must have been a sore disappointment to find such a
stalwart pair of arms awaiting you in place of the dainty
maiden, Helen.''

The boy's face grew dark at the remembrance of the
scene. ''He bound me and gagged me,'' he said bitterly. ''Ay, and laughed at me, as I lay helpless at
his feet. He was for forcing me to take him away by
boat and carriage, but just as he was penning a note
to the governor, somebody came sneaking around the
door and he bade me begone. I took him at his word,
and got me away with my people as quickly as possible.''

''Leaving the rope-ladder?''

''Of course; how else? But I cut it, up as far as
I could reach; I did not care to help him off; the impudent—''

''Hold, boy!—You would have done the prettiest
stroke of business for yourself possible, had you hailed
the guard at once, and prevented his escape.''

''Hailed the guard! How could I have explained
the matter? He himself threatened me with the
guard!''

''A clever—clever gentleman,'' repeated St. Clair
thoughtfully, ''and a brave— Well, youngster, here
we are at Warham. Best let me do the talking. Your
tale is sweetly interesting, but it may be well to keep it
to ourselves for the nonce.''

''For your life, don't mention my name; Old Rich
hates me like poison already !''

''Tut, boy, there is nothing against the alliance,

157

when you are of the proper age. He would jump at me for a son-in-law."

' "Yes, you. Very likely!" replied the boy, in an aggrieved voice. "You are the heir, and 'tis a very different matter. But surely, Ned, you—you—"

"I am not your rival, boy! My hand on it," said his brother. "You shall have your Helen all in good time. But no more of this rope-ladder nonsense. You must remember that you are no play-actor, but an honest English gentleman, and fit mate for any lady in the land."

"'Thank you, Ned, thank you!"

The two shook hands in the hearty fashion of men who love each other, looking steadily and squarely into one another's eyes, as befitted Englishmen and brothers; then without another word, they strode up to the great entrance of the castle.

They were admitted without delay into the presence of the governor himself. The little man was striding up and down his hall, his face drawn and wrinkled into a thousand rueful puckers.

"Good morning, my lord," he cried. "You have heard—I see that you have heard! Now what am I to do?"

"Good morning, Sir John," returned St. Clair, bowing ceremoniously. "Allow me to present my brother, Roderick."

"I already have the honor of the young man's acquaintance," returned the lord of Warham with a frown, at which the lad blushed a furious crimson.

"Ay? And you do not mislike him then; an honester lad never drew breath, nor a braver. He joins me, sir, on my ship ere long."

"That were well; Satan has ever a task for the un-employed!" growled Sir John, an ominous glitter in his small deep-set eyes.

"What do you mean, sir? Your speech is not over-friendly in its sound."

"Look you, the boy here has been making love to my daughter, and that I will not have; she's only a child, and shall be mine for awhile yet. This slaving and worrying over a woman-child does not profit, sir!" —working himself up into a fury—"for no sooner is she come to an age when she ceases puling and whin-ing, than along comes some miserable whiffet of a boy, and is for carrying her off. Dawdling and palavering and kissing of hands! I'll have none of it, I swear I'll have none of it!"

"Of course not at present; the thing is not to be thought of," said St. Clair soothingly. "But in time, sir, you must acknowledge that one of the family of Arundel is not disqualified for an alliance with your daughter."

"Humph! perhaps not.—But a truce to this talk! We are not a pair of match-makers. What think you of the escape of our prisoner?"

"A most serious mischance. I should like, if it be agreeable to you, Sir John, to see the chief witness in the affair. I mean the *valet de chambre*, who has such a wondrous story to tell of the escape. It may have chanced that the fellow has suppressed some important detail."

"True—true! By all means, St. Clair. You are a clever fellow, and it may be will squeeze some further information out of the rascal. The fellow is a French-man, Bolieu, by name, and I mistrust me a deep knave with a lying tongue in his head, like the rest of his confounded race.—Ay, the fellow may be at the root of the whole matter. Tell them to fetch him at once."

Bolieu presently entered. He was a fat man, with lank black hair, and a pale smooth-shaven face. He shuffled uneasily as he walked, and looked about him in a furtive way as does an animal, unexpectedly brought into the presence of a dreaded foe.

"Stand there, villain!" roared the governor in a dreadful voice, whereat the prisoner visibly cringed. "The right honorable Viscount St. Clair, lieutenant in his majesty's ship *Conqueror*, will now examine you in my presence. And do you speak the truth, sirrah, or we shall presently draw it from you to the tune of your own shrieks on the rack. You hear me!"

CHAPTER XX

THE little governor having thus introduced the luckless witness, strode majestically to his great chair, wherein he seated himself with due ceremony and deliberation.

"Now, sir," he remarked with an air of condescension, "the fellow is in your hands; ask what questions you will." He then leaned back in his chair, placed his finger-tips together judicially and assumed an attitude of attention slightly tempered with *ennui*, as of a man who has already gone over the ground with the utmost thoroughness, and therefore expects nothing of the slightest interest.

"Will you tell me, my good fellow, what you can of this unfortunate affair?" began St. Clair easily. "You were sleeping in the ante-room of his bedchamber, were you not?"

"I was, your honor," replied the man, shifting uneasily from one foot to the other, "but not on my bed; the honorable gentleman objected to my having my bed in the room. It was therefore removed to the corridor. The guard will tell you as much."

"Very good. Did you remain in the room during the evening?"

"No sir—that is—your honor, the honorable lord sent me to the corridor to wait—a most rheumy and disagreeable spot, I contracted—"

"Confound your rheum, blockhead!" interposed the

11   161

governor, with a stamp of his foot. "Your health, sirrah, has not become a matter of interest yet. It may later—to yourself," he added darkly.

"Certainly, your excellency, and your honor. I humbly crave your most noble pardons! I was only—"

"Then you were not in the room during the evening," said St. Clair impatiently. "At what hour did you enter the chamber to remain?"

"At about twelve of the clock, your honor," replied the man more briskly. "At that hour the noble lord rang the bell, I entered and performed my usual duties. I then turned down the lights, and lay down in one corner upon the rug. I must have fallen asleep, for I was very weary, but I was shortly awakened by a slight sound—I am a very light sleeper—I arose quickly, and was on the point of calling the guard, when I was seized from behind, bound and gagged."

"How many men were there who thus overpowered you?" questioned St. Clair with a slight smile.

"Three, your honor," whined the witness, "and monstrous strong men they were, with black velvet masks over their faces. One was dressed in crimson velvet, slashed with silver; the others I did not see so clearly."

"You have a nimble fancy, fellow," observed St. Clair meditatively. "Were you bound when the alarm was raised?"

The flunkey turned a shade paler, and swallowed with a visible effort. "I was loose, sir—I mean, your noble honor. I am a strong man, and I worked till morning to loose myself that I might call assistance."

"Did you call the guard at once? I mean as soon as you had gotten rid of your gag."

The man was silent a moment before replying; at length he said, "I loosened my gag, your noble honor, then I called the guard; but my voice is weak, and as I said before, my gullet was husky by reason of a rheum caught in the corridor; I was therefore unable to make them hear, so—"

"—So you must needs loose yourself," interrupted St. Clair. "Now did you—attend me carefully—did you find any writing, or paper containing a writing anywhere about the apartment?"

"Any writing, my lord! How could that be? Your honor may be sure that I thought of but one thing and—"

"Hold! I am inclined to think that you thought of two things or three. There was a writing; you have it. Give it here this instant!"

"Upon my sacred honor, my lord," cried the wretched flunkey, falling upon his knees, "I do not know what you mean. I swear that it was all just as I have said, the three men with masks, the—"

"You are lying, you rascal! Every second word that you have uttered is a lie. There was a paper; I saw it!"

Every eye was turned upon Roderick, who unable to hold his peace longer, and regardless of his own part in the story, had darted forward.

"*You* saw it!" exclaimed the little governor, springing to his feet. "*You* saw it! And what, pray, were *you* doing in my house at midnight, sir?"

The young man turned white, but he faced the governor with an air of haughty courage.

"I came to your house to carry off your daughter, sir. I meant to marry her, sir, and I mean to still.

I love her and she loves me. You may lock her up as hard and fast as you please. I shall find her. I shall marry her."

Sir John Rich stood in his place as if turned to stone. His face was a study. St. Clair had involuntarily drawn his sword, but at the first words which the little man uttered he dropped it back into its scabbard with a sigh of relief.

"And so you were going to carry off my girl—willy-nilly, hey?"

Then the governor of Warham astonished everybody present by bursting into an immoderate fit of laughter.

"Ha, you young rascal!" he cried, when he had somewhat recovered himself. "I ought by rights to clap you into my deepest dungeon, there to cool off your hot young blood at your leisure! But by the sword of Charlemagne, I like your spirit! I did that very thing myself; I did,—the very same thing; only I succeeded, young man, and carried off my lady, while you were not so lucky.—Ah, now this puts a different look on our matter altogether—eh, St. Clair? This scoundrel here has made us a fine tale to cover some rascality or disobedience of his own; that's evident enough. Now then to the rack with him!" and he made a fierce dive at the wretched Bolieu, who was wallowing in the extremity of his anguish on the floor at their feet.

"Oh, my lord! oh, my good—my excellent—my worshipful lord!" howled the prostrate flunkey. "It is true that I disobeyed orders; but the man would not have me in the room, and how could I help it! Mercy, I beg of you noble sirs—kind masters, I will tell you everything! 'Twas the strange lord who bound me—

he himself; and there *was* a writing! I have it all safe—it is here!"

The man had crawled quite up to the great chair now, and was frantically endeavoring to kiss the governor's hand.

"Get out, you whining, slavering dog! Give me the paper, but keep your distance! Ah, what have we here! 'To the governor of Warham Castle, Sir: I beg that you will pardon me for taking such an unceremonious leave of your hospitable roof. My private affairs, however, are at such a pass that I can remain no longer. I therefore take advantage of the kindness of a friend, and shall be many leagues from Warham castle before daylight. That you are the dupe of a monstrous blunder on the part of some well-meaning person, I do not for a moment doubt. There is certainly no reason why a Huguenot refugee should meet with such distinguished consideration at your hands. I have the honor, sir, to subscribe myself, with many thanks for your hospitality, HENRI BAILLOT, Comte de Lantenac, Late officer in the Royal Navy of France.'

"A monstrous blunder—do you hear that, St. Clair! I begin to think so. In short, I thought so in the very beginning. There are many things to confirm that view of the case. '—a Huguenot refugee,' "—referring again to the letter, which he had carefully flattened out in his hand.—"Now that could hardly be, you know! Well, perhaps we had best defer any further discussion of the matter; but first, who is the friend to whom he refers?"

"He must have honored me with the name, sir," said Roderick, "though I hardly reciprocated his feelings."

"No, I'll warrant me that you did not, my boy!
165

Did you assist the—ahem—the gentleman to escape by
means of your rope-ladder and afterwards ?"

"Marry, that I did not! Of course, sir, I could not
take the ladder away, for I must needs go down it myself, but I took myself off as speedily as possible when
I got the opportunity."

"And how happened it that you were so quiet; why
did you not call the guard?"

Roderick turned red and white by turns. "Why, at
first, sir, he had me at a disadvantage. I did not expect to find—"

"No, that you did not, you young villain!" interrupted the peppery little governor, his temper rising at
the thought. "Confound you, and he got the better
of you. Glad of it,—wish he had choked you! But
you were loose when you went down the ladder; why
did you not call the guard?"

Roderick was silent for a moment, then he blurted
out. "Why did I not call the guard, sir? Ask yourself; would you have called the guard had you been in
my place?"

"Would I, had I been in your place? Gad, young
fellow, but I like your impudence! No, sir, I would
not! I should have skipped down the ladder,—that's
what you did. Now then, our prisoner evidently followed you at his leisure, after trussing up our friend
here,"—indicating the unfortunate Bolieu with a con-
temptuous gesture. "He is manifestly then at large,
without a sixpence in his pocket, in a strange country
and on foot. We shall presently be able to lay hands
upon him."

"Have you taken any steps in that direction, excellency?" said St. Clair.

"Any steps? Well, just a few, sir. I have had two dozen stout fellows scouring the country for miles since daybreak. 'Tis full time we heard from some of them.—Ah, 'speaking of the devil,' as the old saying hath it, here is Browrig now. Have you any news, Browrig?"

"Sorry news, your lordship! Two of our fellows, who were out in a boat examining some of the fishing smacks that lie at anchor in the bay, found this coat floating on the water, not many rods from the castle walls. Perchance the poor gentleman has been foully dealt with."

Sir John Rich examined the dripping garment with attention. "Is this the coat worn by the gentleman?" he asked, turning to St. Clair, "—of a truth I was so taken up with his face, and with a thousand perplexing thoughts that I gave but scant attention to his attire."

St. Clair looked puzzled. "You have me at a loss, sir," he said at length. "I never had the eye that takes note of trappings. 'Tis a woman's province that."

The governor was silent for a moment, then he brought down his hand with a prodigious thwack on the broad of his leg. "I have it!" he exclaimed. "My daughter Helen will know it. She saw the man from the window. Call her to my presence, Spence. She will be with her maids in the tapestry chamber."

The man disappeared. In a few moments he returned, followed at a discreet distance by a severe and sour-faced dame of uncertain years. Immediately behind this good lady, with downcast eye and half-frightened air, stepped the lady Helen, as dainty a maid as ever breathed English air, her simple robe of green silk setting off the snowy whiteness of her neck and arms as rarely as does the leaf of a lily its blossom.

"Upon my word, Rod, I can excuse your folly!" murmured St. Clair, as his eye noted the flower-like beauty of the girl's face, and the slender grace of her maiden figure. "The little Helen bids fair to rival her famous namesake of Troy."

He stepped forward to pay his respects to the lady, but Roderick hung back somewhat fearfully, though with a world of devotion shining in his honest brown eyes. The governor perceived this and chuckled beneath his breath. "How now, sir," he cried loudly, "have you no greeting for your old playmate? This coldness ill befits a youth so fiery that he must needs beard the old fox himself in his den."

At this disconcerting remark, Roderick blushed a furious crimson; but he quickly recovered himself, and stepping boldly forward exclaimed, with a low bow: "Most gladly do I avail myself, your excellency, of your permission to pay my addresses to the lady of my heart. Since the ardent desire of both of us is for her happiness alone, we shall surely cease, from this hour, to play at cross purposes."

Having delivered himself of this somewhat theatrical speech, the young man sprang to the side of the maiden, and possessing himself of one of her snowy hands began to whisper some not unwelcome words into her ear, despite the bristling indignation of the duenna.

"Upon my word, sir, you are not lacking in boldness!" quoth the governor, regaling himself with a delicate pinch of snuff. "I did not send for you, child, in order to provide you with a husband this morning—that is a matter which must be concluded with no unseemly haste, but— Pah, this snuff would draw tears from a stone image! Tell me, daughter, did our guest, of whom you caught a glimpse from the window yestereen, wear this coat?"

"Yes, father," replied the maiden, without a moment's hesitation. "And 'twas here he fastened the rose from my nosegay; here is a fragment of the stem still sticking fast by its thorn!"

"Now is that not wonderful! What an eye hath a maiden, while we men are so dull and stupid!—What argues it, St. Clair, the finding of the coat in the water? Do you think the poor fellow is dead?"

"Dead?" murmured the maiden. "Nay, that were a pity! he was a gallant gentleman; how deftly he caught at that falling rose."

"I do not think the man is dead," began St. Clair. "Perhaps—"

He was interrupted by the trampling of many feet in the corridor without and the confused sound of voices.

"They have found him!" cried the governor joyfully, springing to his feet.

CHAPTER XXI

A FRIEND IN NEED

"YES, my lord, we have found him!" said one of the men who was grasping the luckless Huguenot by the arm. "He was sleeping in a rick of straw near a farm-house on the Arundel estate—disguised, as you see, as a gipsy. Yet were my eyes too sharp—"

"Let me speak for myself, fellow," said Baillot, wrenching himself loose from his captors with a violent effort.

"Loose him, varlets!" roared the governor. "Have you no sense of what is becoming?—Your pardon, sir, for the unmannerly rudeness of my retainers. Our anxiety for your safety must be our excuse. I fear you have suffered much in your misadventure."

"Have you read the letter I left for you?" questioned the captive moodily, his eye wandering about the room, and resting at last in the greatest astonishment on the group formed by St. Clair, Roderick, and the lady Helen. "How is this?" he exclaimed; "'tis an ill-wind then, that blows no good!"

"You thought I played you a scurvy trick, sir, in cutting the ladder, and getting away without you," quoth the lad; "yet I scarce felt beholden to you after all that had passed."

"Ay, you served me right, boy,—but the letter," turning impatiently to the governor.

"We have read the letter, monsieur," said that worthy solemnly. "If you will do me the honor to accompany me to your apartments, you shall refresh yourself. I shall then be pleased to talk with you of the matter. Pray rid yourself of the thought that you are in any sense a prisoner, but your presence here is indispensable to the clearing up of a great mystery." And the little man majestically led the way from the hall. Baillot followed with a very bad grace, still attended by the men-at-arms to whom he owed his capture.

"Blockhead that I was!" he muttered, as the door of his apartment—not the tower-room of his adventure, but a loftier and more magnificent suite on the ground floor—closed on the retreating figure of his host. "I have played the part of a witless boy; I should have been leagues away by daybreak, instead of yielding to my fatigue like a woman."

Yet his disappointment was not untempered with hope; his letter had been received, his declaration made, and from the manner of his host he inferred, not unreasonably, that an impression of some kind had been made. He observed furthermore that no guard had been posted before his door, and that the windows of his drawing-room opened directly upon the terrace. "I am a prisoner no longer," he thought with a thrill of joy; curiously enough with the knowledge he lost his desire to escape. "I will remain," he decided, "till we unravel this mystery, of which I for one am heartily weary."

He made haste to rid himself of the gipsy's clothes, which presented but a sorry appearance in the broad light of day. "When they have satisfied themselves that I am indeed but a homeless refugee," quoth he with a smile, "I fancy that this fine wardrobe will be at my disposal no longer.—Yet however fine the trappings, if the pockets be not plentifully lined, one may fare but poorly in this greedy world, as I have already found to my sorrow."

A good breakfast which was presently brought in, served still further to put the young man into good humor with his surroundings. He had no sooner finished it than St. Clair was announced.

"I was surprised to see you here, lieutenant," he said, rising to greet his visitor; "you are then on leave?"

"Surprised, and not overjoyed, I fancy," returned St. Clair. "I am sure that you reckon me among the chief of your persecutors."

"I believe I owe a somewhat strange and unpleasant adventure partly to you. Are you as averse as ever to any explanations on my part?"

"On the contrary I am here for that purpose," said St. Clair eagerly. "Tell me at once how you came to be on the island?"

"A shipwrecked party, consisting of two women and three men, found their way thither after the loss of their vessel. Destitute of clothing and of every necessity of life, they gladly availed themselves of the goods the gods provided."

"Then you found the château deserted?"

"Entirely so. There was not a soul on the island when we arrived. May I ask whom you expected to find there?"

St. Clair apparently did not hear this question. He was staring hard at the carpet as if lost in thought. After a little he aroused himself to say:

"Your pardon, monsieur, for leaving your question

unanswered; this you will grant me all the more readily when I tell you that you are free. May I ask if you would accept a commission in the British navy? There are a number of vacancies, and the gallant officer to whom we owe our latest victory would prove a valuable acquisition."

"I thank you heartily for your kind interest in my fortunes," said Baillot. "But there is that which I must do before I think of my own future. I must return and find out what has become of the helpless companions whom I was forced to leave behind."

"And for that you will need funds—which luckily you will not lack," said St. Clair in a matter-of-fact tone. "I have here your share of the prize money paid to the crew of *The Conqueror* for the captured vessel."

"But I am entitled to nothing," said Baillot, a dark flush rising to his cheek as St. Clair placed a small bag upon the table. "I took part in the action only by evading the orders under which I was placed. But may you never know how it feels to be shut up below decks when fighting is going on!"

"I can only say that it was fortunate for us that you escaped to the scene of action," cried St. Clair heartily. "And if you are not entitled to a share of the money, no one is. The enemy would be picking the bones of the poor old *Conqueror* now, with all of us hard and fast as prisoners of war!"

"A penniless refugee has little choice," said Baillot, a shade of bitterness clouding his face. "So I will accept the gold most thankfully. My estates in France are confiscate under the present laws, as you are of course aware. I have some property in America, and it

was there I was bound when our vessel was shipwrecked."
He paused as if lost in painful reminiscence. "There
is one thing I must crave of your kindness yet," he
continued after a little, "and that is the location of
the island; without that information I can scarcely
hope to rescue those who are doubtless still there—unless some mischance has befallen them."

St. Clair hesitated, and Baillot, who was observing
him narrowly, exclaimed angrily, "What monstrous
nonsense is there about that spot of earth! Am I to
understand then that the rest of my party are to be
marooned simply because they have had the ill fortune
to—"

"Hold, you misunderstand me; it will be impossible
for me to obtain what you require under three days.
Your demand is reasonable and just, you shall have the
information if it be in my power to give it. Meanwhile will you not be my guest at Arundel for the
present? It was that for which I came to you this
morning."

"I thank you for the invitation," said Baillot, somewhat stiffly; "but it will doubtless be best for me to
go up to London at once; I have some preparations to
make."

"I must ask you to remain here for a few hours at
least. I shall wish to communicate your story to our
host, and—"

"Certainly, and however great my impatience you
may rely upon me not to take French leave," said Baillot with a forced smile at his own poor wit. The air
of mystery about the affair affected him most disagreeably, the more so since he felt sure that he was mis-
trusted.

"*Diable!*" he broke out with a frown. "This affair has assumed a most unpleasant aspect. I see plainly that you are fearful lest I prate of the matter, and thus compromise you in some way. Not being altogether stupid I can understand that perhaps higher interests are involved. Now in France what would happen in such a case? The inconvenient person disappears; where? It matters not; the Bastile has nooks and corners within its walls most safe. In England you have the Tower. Perhaps if—"

"Upon my honor, sir, you are wrong! Do you suppose that I would descend to such vulgar trickery?" demanded St. Clair fiercely. "And yet—" he added after a pause, "I do not wonder at your thought after all that has passed. Now listen, you need fear nothing from me; but I confess that I do not know what to expect from another quarter. My advice is this, get you out of England without delay, for although your life is in no present peril, you might be subjected to a delay which would prove maddening under the circumstances. As for the information you require, go to the island of Terciora, of the Central Azores group, and inquire for one José de Miguel. He can give you what you require. But you should have an order to show him, and this it will be exceedingly difficult for me to obtain. I will do my best, and will send or bring it to you within the three days. Should I fail to obtain it, try gold on de Miguel. I do not see why—But where shall we make our tryst?"

"Nay, you know best; I must trust myself entirely to you in the matter," said Baillot. "London?—I shall be only an atom there, and easily enough hidden. I know the place as thoroughly as you do."

"You had best do as I suggested, come to Arundel for a day or two. It need not be known when you leave—nor whither. But I fancy I hear our host—the excellent Sir John Rich. Not a word of this to him, I pray you."

And indeed at this moment the sound of bustling footsteps in the corridor without was heard, and a brisk tap at the door announced a second visitor.

"Ah, St. Clair, my dear fellow, glad to find you still here! I have just had important advices—most important. We were not wrong in our conjectures. A very neat little affair—very neat indeed, but the laugh is not on our side this time! Yet we have all done our duty, and that after all is the main thing. I hope, my dear de Lantenac—for so I must call you, with your permission—that your enforced visit to England will not incommode you, but rather be to your advantage—your very considerable advantage, sir!"

All of this the little governor delivered with an air of the greatest relish, rubbing his hands briskly, and skipping about with suppressed excitement. "There is no discredit attached to any of us in the matter," he continued, "least of all to the distinguished officer, whom I have the honor to see under my roof. I have heard of your gallantry from my Lord Torrington, sir, and I congratulate you! You will remain my guest for some days longer, I trust."

"M. de Lantenac has done me the honor to accept an invitation to Arundel, your excellency," said St. Clair. "Though of course I shall not force his inclinations in the matter."

"No, no, of course not," said the governor frowning, "—not at all! He will remain my guest for the present; I must make amends for the affair of last night, you understand. There is a little festivity in prospect—ha, ha! That brother of yours, St. Clair! —really I would rather it were you now; but I cannot have such a thing repeated. Why bless my soul, sir; think of my little Helen clambering down a rope-ladder at midnight! And she would have done it!—ay, marry, she is a maid of a proper spirit! And you heard the young knave tell me to my face that he would carry her off? I should never have an easy moment,— not one, sir! So I must needs make the best of a bad matter. I have sent for the honorable Earl, your father, and the scriveners; and unless there be some obstacle, which I see not at present, we shall shortly celebrate the betrothal of the young couple.''

"Roderick is a lucky dog!" observed St. Clair smiling. "By my faith I am inclined to challenge him to a duel in behalf of the maiden, in the good old fashion.''

"Nay, my lord, he shall have her," quoth the governor with a great laugh; "you are too late. The only thing left for you is to get carried off in some action and leave the earldom to your energetic younger brother. 'To him that hath shall be given,' you know, as the Holy Book hath it.''

"Heaven forefend!" ejaculated St. Clair, with a shrug. "I am no Esau. The Fates may have as fair a mate in store for me.—But I must congratulate the youngster; 'tis not every ill-wind that blows so much good.''

"Let us adjourn to the great hall, gentlemen," cried the governor with a wave of his hand; "'tis there the lovers are holding court. Marry, 'tis a fine sight to witness the airs of dame Ursula, the governess! She has my orders not to interfere, but it is most irksome to her acidulated maiden modesty to be compelled to leave a pair of lovers unmolested in her very presence. You, Count de Lantenac, have played a famous part in this little Comedy of Errors, and the young people, curiously enough, are inclined to thank you for its happy ending. The ungrateful young rascals! as though I could not easily enough have banished my would-be son-in-law from Warham, and shut up the foolish maid in a nunnery!"

CHAPTER XXII

THE day following promised to be a notable one for the inhabitants of Warham castle. The weather was clear and fair, as befitted the betrothal day of the fairest maid in all England. The Earl of Arundel had arrived betimes, and had given his paternal blessing on the union ; and what was more important for the ultimate happiness of the young pair, the fathers had put their heads together to consult concerning their temporal welfare. The great oaken table in the library of the castle was littered with parchments and papers, and the lawyers and scriveners, inflated with the importance of the occasion, were busy with deeds and writings, apparently matters of the supremest indifference to the young couple themselves, who sat in one corner, content to leave all such unimportant matters as moneys and estates to others, while they basked in the radiance of love's young dream.

These matters having been happily concluded, a general air of festivity and joyousness took possession of every one. Even Baillot, though he was harassed with anxiety concerning his own affairs, could not help joining in the amusements which were going on.

" Leave us now, sir?" exclaimed the governor, when the young man had hinted to him his desire to take leave. "'Tis not to be thought of! You must at all events wait until after the ball."

And the lady Helen had added her entreaties so prettily to those of her father, that sorely against his will the young Huguenot had yielded. He had an uneasy feeling that he was being watched, and that the cordial insistance of his host had its root in something beyond a desire for his company. Once he had surprised St. Clair in close conversation with Sir John Rich, and the embarrassed air with which they at once ceased talking upon his approach had increased his discomfort.

On the morning of the proposed ball, amid the general confusion and bustle which prevailed, he stood somewhat apart from the merry groups which were occupied in trimming the great hall with garlands of greenery. His thoughts were far away. He seemed once more to stand in the corridor of the mysterious château; the delicate flushed face of Madeline with her large, sweet eyes full of reproachful questionings, arose distinctly before him. He gave an involuntary sigh. "I must get away from this place, and at once!" he muttered to himself.

"You are not happy, monsieur," said the voice of St. Clair in his ear, "and I can well guess the cause; you are anxious to leave this scene of domestic felicity which somehow grates upon your feelings. I must tell you, however, that the matter of which I spoke to you has not been neglected; I am expecting every hour to hear whether or no I have been successful. You shall know at once, whatever the intelligence. Meanwhile you are quite as safe here as anywhere, and perhaps as happy, since the delay must be endured."

"I thought you had forgotten—" began Baillot in an agitated voice; he was checked in any further utterance by the approach of Sir John Rich.

The little man had been in a state of most joyous activity all the morning. From the cellars to the turrets he had inspected everything about the castle with his own eye. He had even penetrated to the kitchen in the excess of his zeal, from whence, however, he had been routed by the housekeeper, a notable and privileged person, possessed of almost unlimited powers in her own domain.

"Indeed, your gracious honor, 'tis impossible that we should be put about by a visit from you just now," the worthy lady had declared, smoothing down her silk apron. "The maids and scullions are that in terror of your worshipful honor that they are like dumb images in your presence. Their spoons in mid air, and their mouths wide open, how can you expect the plum cakes, the jellies and the flummeries to be properly made? You must even leave it all to me."

"Very well, dame," the governor had replied majestically. "But remember that there is no mistress in the castle; and that to-night no fewer than a hundred of the first ladies and gentlemen of the country will sup here in honor of my daughter's betrothal."

"No mistress indeed!" thought the dame to herself, but she only said, "You may trust me, my lord. All shall be as proper and right as at the king's palace, though I must needs look to it myself. And who knows but that the next feast may be in honor of your own wedding; for 'twould be hard to find a more personable gentleman."

"This is a great day!" the little governor exclaimed,

approaching the two young men. "All goes well; the weather is propitious; the preparations are going forward right merrily! and best of all, I have news that the duke will be with us to-night!"

"Is it so?" exclaimed St. Clair, with an involuntary glance at Baillot. "The happy pair are indeed honored; though the king himself might well dance a measure in honor of so fair a maid."

"And should he do so, 'twould not be the first time the lords of Warham have been so honored," quoth Sir John proudly. "Why, man, in King James's time—"

"Ah, here is our happy bridegroom!" said St. Clair hastily, interrupting what was likely to prove a tedious tale, and one which he already knew by heart. "I see he has a word for my private ear; I pray you to excuse me for a moment."

"A brave officer that," observed Sir John, looking after him with a genial smile, "and the younger brother is not less to my liking,—indeed he has the more personable figure of the two. A prettier pair than that youth and my daughter Helen it would be hard to find!"

"Indeed you are right," said Baillot; "I wonder that you were so hard of heart in the beginning of their loves."

"Marry! That was only to test the youngster's metal. Had he been easily rebuffed, he would never have done to perpetuate the house of Warham. I have no son, sir, the lady Helen is my heir, and one of her sons will bear the titles and inherit the estates of Warham, by a special grant."

"A most desirable and equitable arrangement,"

murmured Baillot perfunctorily. He was weary at heart of Warham castle, and was rapidly coming to the conclusion that if he heard nothing further from St. Clair before nightfall, he would take advantage of the confusion incident to the festivities, and quietly slip away. "Do you expect many guests?" he asked turning to his host, who was watching with delight the operations of two young men who were looping with a fringy garland of green the carven gallery at one end of the hall.

"More than a hundred, Count," replied Sir John. "You shall dance with some of the fairest maidens you could hope to see anywhere on this green earth.—See now, they will finish the garlands with bunches of roses; is not that a pretty device? The musicians will sit yonder in the gallery, and I'll warrant me that there is not a better floor for a dancing foot in England than this. 'Tis as smooth as a maiden's cheek, and as slippery as a Frenchman!—Bless my soul, what have I said? Your pardon, Count!"

"You have but exercised the diplomatic courtesy for which your nation is famous," replied Baillot with a slight curl of the lip. "And I fear me that similes quite as unflattering to English characteristics are common enough in the mouths of my countrymen."

"I'll warrant me!" said Sir John with a chuckle. "Such as 'stupid as an Englishman,' as—but why be disagreeable to each other? I began it, and I sincerely beg your forgiveness for my unruly tongue. 'Tis an unseemly and churlish trick to be forever girding at those of other nations. Nay, I sometimes wonder if our so-called patriotism is not after all a kind of selfishness, which breeds disaffection and warfare."

To all of which the young man returned no answer save a grave inclination of the head. Presently the governor took himself off to oversee the decoration of the banqueting hall, and Baillot retired to his own quarters. Here he began to make some preparations for the journey which he had in mind, preparations necessarily of the most meagre description, since he was destitute of arms of any kind, and dependent still on the wardrobe furnished him by his captors. However he secured the gold, which St. Clair had given him, about his person, and attired himself in one of the plainest of the rich habits which had been placed at his disposal.

As evening drew on he grew more and more anxious, but none the less determined to get away. He could hear the sounds of opening and shutting doors, the rolling of coaches, and bursts of song and laughter from various parts of the castle. No one had inquired for him for several hours, and he began to flatter himself that he had been overlooked amid the general excitement, when a light tap sounded upon his door. In response to his summons St. Clair entered.

Closing the door behind him cautiously, like one who fears that he is watched, the young officer exclaimed in answer to Baillot's invitation to be seated:

"No, no, I must not stop! I came to inform you that it is as I feared. It is utterly out of my power to obtain for you the order of which I spoke. There remains but one thing for you to do in order to rescue your hapless companions, and that is to seek out de Miguel. I fancy from what I know of the man, that you will not find it impossible to purchase the information which you require."

"Then I shall leave at once," said Baillot rising. "I thank you most heartily for the efforts you have made in my behalf, and for the information without which I should have been utterly at a loss."

"'Twill be impossible for you to leave at once," interrupted St. Clair,—"impossible! I must tell you frankly that your actions are watched, and that every effort will be made to detain you in England."

"But—"

"Stay! hear me out; to-night when the revel is at its height, slip away to the postern gate on the east side of the castle—you reach this by traversing the terrace directly outside the great hall where the dancing is to take place. At the postern you will find a horse; in the holsters there will be arms. Ride along the highway for one mile towards the west till you reach cross roads, then north to the sea; there you will find a skiff awaiting you which will bear you to a schooner in the roads. I have represented to her captain that you are my agent in a certain matter in Holland. Once there you are safe and free to follow your own devices. I need not ask your secrecy in my behalf, should it become known that I have aided you in—"

"That goes without saying!" interrupted Baillot. "My lips are sealed not only in regard to the adventures of to-night, but to all that has transpired of late, for it is not difficult to guess the reason of my detention in England. For your own services to me, a thousand thanks are too few."

"Say no more, I must leave you. May you succeed in your venture!" and with a courteous gesture of farewell the young officer left the apartment.

A lackey now appeared to announce that the hour for

the banquet had arrived, and Baillot presently found himself ushered into the great drawing-room of state wherein was assembled a brilliant company. He could see the small figure of his host at one end of the room and standing near him, the prospective bride attended by her lover.

He advanced to pay his respects, and was shortly presented to a buxom English damsel, whose ruddy charms were set off by a gown of white muslin, at this time just beginning to be worn in England, and which with its favorite accompaniment of blue ribbons, has remained the recognized garb of youthful prettiness ever since.

The young girl looked shyly at him as if not wholly displeased with her cavalier, but she evinced no inclination to enter into conversation, and Baillot presently roused himself to say, as they were following the stream of guests to the great banqueting-hall, from which sounded the soft strains of harp and violin,

"This is a gay scene, is it not, Miss—ah—Rington?"

"Yes, Rington, that is my name," assented the young girl, blushing rosily as she glanced up into the dark eyes of her questioner. "My papa is Sir George Rington of Rington Grange. You will see him yonder with that stout lady, who has the tall feather in her hair. —A gay scene? Indeed yes, but after supper will be the dancing which must be far pleasanter than eating. I never came to a ball before."

"You are perhaps just from your convent," remarked Baillot rather abstractedly, observing a stout red-faced man who was just seating himself at the right of the host at the table of honor.

"That is the duke," said the girl, following his gaze,

"only fancy! I should like to go to court, but papa won't hear of it. He says he likes country-bred girls who know nothing of the ways of courtiers. Is not that tiresome?"

Baillot glanced down with some interest at the ingenuous face of the young girl, which somehow reminded him of a gay wild rose in its wayside tangle of greenery. "Surely this scene is gay enough to please you, is it not?" he said smiling.

"Yes, if mamma only allows me to dance all I wish. Here is mamma now, we are to sit next to her. Mamma, this is the Count de Lantenac."

Mamma, a rather severe and purple-faced matron, adorned with lofty and nodding plumes and a plenitude of old-fashioned jewelry, acknowledged the introduction with great stiffness, and immediately took the conversation into her own hands. Baillot listened with outward deference to a long account of the exact degree of relationship which existed between the families of Warham and Arundel, and of the different intermarriages which had taken place between these and other exalted personages in the county during the past hundred years. As for Miss Rington she relapsed into silence, which was evidently what her maternal ancestor designed, since she possessed in common with most British females, a profound distrust of everything French.

The attention of the worthy lady being at length diverted by the good things which were now being pressed upon the company, the flow of her conversation was necessarily checked, much to the relief of Baillot, who was thus left to his own reflections. He ate of the viands which were offered him with but little comprehension of their savor, though it was evident from the profusion of meats, cold and hot, of venison, fish, wild fowl and pastry, of cunning spiced dishes, creams, confections and fruits that the country had been laid under contribution far and wide. At length the ladies withdrew, leaving the men, as was the custom, to indulge still further in potations, which judging from the flushed faces and heavy eyes of some of the company had already been more than sufficient.

The mirth now grew fast and furious; toast after toast was given and drunk, amid clashing glasses and the merry quips and jests of the revellers, until the host in response to an urgent whisper from the youthful bridegroom, arose to lead the way to the ball-room.

As the guests passed out from the banqueting-hall in a confused crowd, St. Clair lingered for an instant at the side of Baillot to whisper—

"Now!   You will find all as I told you."

Seizing the moment when the company emerged into the dimly-lighted corridor, the young man halted in the black shadow of a suit of ancient armor, and in another moment, perceiving the coast to be clear, he darted out upon the terrace, discovered the postern gate, opened it without difficulty, and leaping upon the back of a horse, which he found tied under the shelter of a tree, galloped away into the darkness.

CHAPTER XXIII

"*Diable!* The wine in these cellars is as heavy as the waters of Lethe! My head feels like one of those unwieldy puncheons yonder."

"No doubt 'tis as empty of wit, my excellent Pierre. But we must rouse the dogs yonder and set them to work, else these same heads of ours will be knocked together by the fine gentlemen who lodge above." The speaker rose to his feet with many a stretch and yawn, and strode away to the cellars where the gang of workmen, under guard of the marines, was lodged.

"Ho, there! you lazy rascals!" he exclaimed, "are you sleeping yet?—Bah! the air here is so heavy with wine that it is enough to sicken an honest man; did I not forbid you to drink when you were on guard?"

"You swallow the fumes of your own drunkenness!" grumbled one of the marines, sitting up and rubbing his eyes sulkily. "We did but quench our thirst; would you have us anger our guts with clammy cold water in sight of an ocean of good wine?"

"Keep a civil tongue in your good-for-naught head, varlet!" roared the sergeant, with a hearty kick at the half-drunken fellow, who had presumed thus to answer him. "Fetch out the convicts till I count them. Be quick about it, or I promise you a charge of shot in your clumsy calves!"

189

The marine rose unsteadily to his feet and looked about him with a lack-lustre eye; then he proceeded with no gentle hand to arouse his sleeping companions. With many a muttered oath they unbarred the heavy door of the inner cellar in which the convicts had been shut up for the night. A rush of foul air and a smothered groan issued from this noisome den.

"Out of there, dogs!" shouted the sergeant.—"Stir them up with the bayonet; we are late, I tell you!"

"One, two, three," he muttered, and so on till he had reached forty, as the wretches filed out. Then he paused, and the scared face of one of the marines appeared in the doorway.

"There are no more of them, sergeant."

"No more of them? You are drunk! There are six more, the Huguenot dogs—nay, seven, for there is the Englishman I found yesterday under the bush."

"I tell you there are no more," repeated the marine sullenly; "look for yourself!"

With an impatient oath the sergeant dashed the man aside, and entering the cellar, began to plunge his bayonet savagely into the trusses of dirty straw which served the convicts as beds. "I'll soon have you out," he shouted, "my fine gentlemen, who must needs refresh yourselves with a morning nap!—Here you, fetch me a light!"

After a moment's delay, which the angry sergeant filled with oaths and execrations, a lantern was brought, and he proceeded to make thorough search in the nooks and corners of the place.

"A thousand devils!" he exclaimed at length. "The cursed hounds are gone. Was this door left unlocked, numskull?"

"Unlocked? No, sir, I swear it was not. I locked it top and bottom myself. Did you not see me draw the bolts just now?"

"*Comment diable!*—but there is some way of getting out inside the place. Feed the dogs, then set them digging where they were yesterday!" And the sergeant sprang out of the cellar and disappeared.

Having briefly acquainted his comrade with his unpleasant discovery, the two worthies sought their superior officers, who were luxuriously lodged in one of the wings of the château which had thus far been spared for their accommodation.

These gentlemen, whose potations had perhaps been not less deep than those of their subordinates, were still sleeping soundly, and for some moments made no response to the thunderous knockings with which the two marines assailed the panels of their chamber door.

"Wake up within there, lieutenant! Wake up!" shouted Gaston, pounding lustily with the stock of his musket.—"What if the Huguenots have murdered them in their beds!" he exclaimed, turning to his companion.

"They're either dead or dead drunk—which is not far from being the same thing as far as a man's wits are concerned," quoth his companion sagely. "What say you to breaking down the door? This tower must come down within the day, and our noble lords find their quarters elsewhere."

"Easier said than done, comrade; but we must get their ear at all events, if it be the ear of living men. Now then!" But the united efforts of the two men made no impression on the heavy door.

"*Peste!* we are losing time," remarked one of

them, pausing to wipe the great drops from his heated face. "Suppose we hunt the rascals for ourselves, without waiting further orders. They cannot be far away, nor can they escape us."

"As you say, they cannot escape us, and I choose to know at once whether the men within be dead or alive. —Awake! Awake! Fire! Murder! Thieves!"

"Ha, I hear them! That last tattoo of yours, Gaston, would serve Gabriel himself in lieu of a trumpet!"

"What do you want?" came a sleepy voice from within; "cannot you leave your betters undisturbed till daybreak?"

"'Tis long past sunrise, sir. And we have just discovered that a part of the convicts have escaped!" roared Gaston through the keyhole.

Some sort of a smothered ejaculation followed this announcement, then the sound of a heavy body leaping onto the floor.

"Hold on there, I'll be out in a second," said the voice of de Loignac from within.

The men outside looked at one another ruefully. "Hum! I relish not the task of telling the story," said one. "Our worthy lieutenant was doubtless occupied last night with the cobwebby bottles which he bade us bring him from below, but he will wreak vengeance upon our unlucky heads, for this matter."

"We'll take it out of the marines then!" growled his companion, sticking his little fingers into his armholes, and beating a tattoo on the polished floor with his boot-heels.

"And the marines will take it out of the convicts."

"And the convicts—?"

"The devil will shortly take the convicts!"

"How now, sergeant!" said de Loignac sternly, as he opened the door. "What is this you were saying?"

"We find six of the prisoners missing this morning, sir," replied Gaston with a respectful salute. "And with them a man whom I found yesterday, stunned by a blow in the back of his head from a piece of falling rock."

"What's that? You made no report of any such matter to me."

"You were at the ship, sir, at the time," muttered the man sulkily. "I set the rascal at work with the other convicts. He was locked up with them last night securely enough."

"Securely enough!" roared the officer. "What do you mean, stupid, by that, when in the same breath you tell me that you have lost six prisoners?"

"I mean, sir, that they were put into the inner cellar last night as usual. And that this morning the six Huguenots together with the Englishman are missing. But 'tis impossible that they—"

"*Diable!* You discovered an Englishman on the island and kept the matter to yourself. You infernal blockhead! I have a mind to blow your stupid brains out this minute! What sort of a looking man was this Englishman?"

"A dull-looking, oldish man, dressed in fustian like a laborer.—But as I was going to say, sir, 'tis not possible for them to escape. We can lay hands on them easily enough within the hour. What I particularly wish to know is how many men shall I detail for the search? and shall I give them orders to shoot down the fugitives when they are discovered?"

"You hear this precious rascal!" remarked de Loig-

13   193

nac over his shoulder to his brother officer, who now appeared in the corridor.

"Yes, I hear him; no thanks to him that we were not murdered in our beds last night. The beasts were doubtless all drunk." The speaker carefully surveyed his finger-nails, and proceeded to trim them precisely with a small knife which he took from his pocket.

"I believe you would think of your toilet if the heavens fell!" cried de Loignac impatiently. "What do you say to this business?"

"Since the lives of these gentlemen are of no especial value to the world at large, I should suppose the simplest method were to send out a party to pick them off. —Seven, I believe you said, a pretty morning's sport."

"Devilish pretty!" growled de Loignac impatiently. "Well, we may as well breakfast; I never hunt on an empty stomach."

"Then you propose leading the expedition in person? Truly quite a diversion. But let us by all means take the Englishman alive. There may be others of his party concealed upon the island. You remember the condition of the cottage?"

"By Jove, you are right!" cried de Loignac. "There's somebody about. It makes my blood run cold to think how easily we might have run our necks into a precious noose! But who can be here, think you?"

"I don't like the look of the thing myself," said de Morney, surveying his delicate finger-tips with an air of pleased attention. "One Englishman would hardly be here without another—the rascals flock like blackbirds. There's some deep-laid scheme of the enemy on foot, mark my words!"

"You have the croak of a sick raven, de Morney. Now if your claws are in sufficiently good order, suppose we break our fast and get about the business at once," growled de Loignac, with vast contempt evident in the tones of his voice.

"You forget yourself in your irritation, my friend," replied the other sneering. "If I overlook your offensive words and manner, it is only because I take into consideration your origin."

"No one shall taunt me in that manner without giving an account of it in blood!" cried de Loignac in a fury. "Defend yourself!" And he drew his rapier and made a vicious lunge at his companion.

"*Mon dieu!* gentlemen, remember where you are! This is no time for a duel!" exclaimed Gaston, throwing himself between the combatants. "Put up your swords, I beg of you!"

"You are right, fellow," said de Loignac sullenly, sheathing his weapon. "We will settle this matter later on French soil."

"As you will, my friend," replied the other with an amiable smile, as he flecked an imaginary bit of dust from the sleeve of his jacket, "a duel is always a pleasant diversion."

"But the prisoners?" interposed Gaston anxiously.

"Detail half a dozen of the marines to make search," said de Loignac shortly. "Go with them yourself. Pierre can take charge of the mining. Shoot the Huguenots, but take the Englishman alive. I shall put him to the torture," he added, grinding his teeth savagely. "We shall see whether the raven's croak be a true prophecy!"

An hour later the sergeant returned. He found the

two officers pacing up and down the half-ruined terrace smoking in moody silence.

"Your report, sergeant!"

"I have not succeeded in finding any trace of the missing men, sir."

"No trace of them?" exclaimed de Loignac. "They must be lurking in the castle," he added after a moment's pause. "Set the place on fire at once.— Stay, put heavy charges of gunpowder in the cellars before doing so ; we will have a disturbance here which will unearth the rats if they are hidden in this pile. If they do not come to light then—"

"If they do not come to light then?" repeated the sergeant interrogatively.

"They *will* come to light," replied the officer, with a stamp of his foot. "We shall see them either hurrying out before the smoke like half-smothered rats, or piecemeal after the explosion. Either way will do," he added indifferently. "What say you, de Morney?" turning to his companion.

"*Bon!*" replied that gentleman tersely. "Anything to hurry up this confounded business."

"As for our quarters," continued de Loignac. "Suppose we take possession of yonder cottage. 'Tis a capital little place, and well furnished. I took another look at it yesterday afternoon."

"Very well," said de Morney languidly. "Get about your business without delay, Gaston.—And by the by, do you search out and fetch to the cottage five or six dozen bottles of that same yellow seal before you set the place afire. But not a drop for yourself, rascal, remember! 'Twas your drunken carelessness which caused this last mischance."

The man touched his forehead in respectful silence as the two officers walked away; but no sooner were they out of sight than he turned to Pierre, who had approached as de Morney was speaking, and with an excellent imitation of that gentleman's haughty manner said:

"Fetch me five or six dozen of that same yellow seal, but not a drop for yourself, rascal, remember!"

Pierre replied by thrusting his tongue into his right cheek and winking rapidly with his left eye; then both men burst into a roar of laughter.

"Ah, you drunken villain, had you let the bottles alone, and attended to your duty as carefully as do your superior officers, this last mischance would never have come about," said Pierre, when he had somewhat recovered himself.

"Drunkenness is truly a great crime in those of low degree," quoth the other piously. "I shall have no doubt a heavy penance to perform when next I make up my accounts with a holy father. As for you, my friend, nothing short of a pilgrimage barefoot will serve to lighten your conscience."

CHAPTER XXIV

HOW IT HAPPENED

WHEN Winters heard the heavy bolts slide into their sockets after the gang of convicts had received their scanty rations of bread and water, he found himself completely at a loss. . The place was pitch dark, and in the confusion of the moment he had lost sight of his companions. He felt about in his pockets, and found to his joy a parcel of candles, which he had made up along with the rest of the stores for the crow's nest.

Unhesitatingly he struck a light, knowing that its feeble glimmer would not be noticed by the marines outside, who had already begun their night's carouse. A low growl of approval and surprise arose from the convicts.

Looking sharply about him the old sailor spied the pale face of the young Huguenot in the corner.

"Are you all here?" he whispered, stooping over him.

"All,—but what use; they have remembered to lock the door to-night?"

"Never mind that; I know this 'ere place. The others'll soon be asleep, an' then I'll show ye a trick worth two of theirs!"

"But there is no place to hide,—even if we make our escape from this place," said the Huguenot gloomily.

"Ain't thar!" ejaculated Winters with a chuckle.

198

"—Ain't thar! Wall now, jes' you leave that to one as knows a thing or two about this 'ere island. Lay low for a spell," he added in a whisper, "till all's quiet here, then we'll git."

The candle which the sailor had thrust into a broken-necked bottle shed a flickering and uncertain light upon the black walls steaming with noisome vapors, upon the uncouth figures of the exhausted convicts, who lay sprawled out at full length or curled up into wretched heaps among the trusses of filthy straw, upon the pallid despairing faces and sunken eyes of the Huguenots.

"A rum go!" he muttered, staring about him reflectively, "but I'll fetch it or bust!"

For more than an hour longer the sailor sat motionless watching and listening. There gradually arose about him a loud monotonous humming sound, like that from a hive of gigantic bees. "The convicts are dead asleep!" he said to himself, rising stealthily to his feet. He laid his ear to the great iron-bound door and listened. "And the marines are dead drunk!" he added with a grim smile. He bent over the Huguenot.

"Comrade, are you awake? 'Tis time we were moving." The young man rose slowly to his feet.

"Moving?" he repeated dully, "but where?"

By way of answer the old sailor stooped and pushing aside the litter of straw and filth which lay along the northern wall, disclosed an iron ring fast in one of the stones of the floor.

"Thar!" he said briefly, stooping over to lay hold of the ring. With a mighty pull he raised the stone from its place and pointed to a narrow stairway which plunged down abruptly into a hole of pitchy blackness. "Thar!" he repeated. "Come on!"

"You will escape, will you?—Ah, you will go, but not without me. I go first."

Winters turned with an involuntary cry; a huge half-naked convict towered over him threateningly, armed with a broken bottle.

"Give me the candle."

Winters did not understand the words, but the look and gesture were plain enough.

"In course, my hearty, by all means," he remarked coolly; "git right down thar and see for yourself; it's all ship-shape below decks," he added with an encouraging wink at his horror-stricken companions. "He'll find something mayhap as'll warm the cockles of his heart."

The convict remained below for several minutes; they could hear him grumbling to himself as he stumbled about. When he returned he was heavily-laden with wicker-covered flasks, with which he retired to his own corner, growling out something unintelligible as he passed the Huguenots.

Winters pulled another candle from his pocket and lighted it. "I'll go below for a little of the same sort," he remarked with another of his extraordinary winks. "We can't get off now till he's sound."

"Why not take him along?" asked the Huguenot.

Winters looked warily at the convict; he was a heavy powerful fellow with a thick neck, a small bullet-shaped head and a villainous eye which he turned suspiciously from time to time upon the group in the corner.

"It ain't in the pictur!" he responded enigmatically as he disappeared down the stairway.

He returned presently his hands full of the wicker-covered flasks. "Take a sup of this 'ere stuff," he said hospitably, proffering one to the Huguenot, "it'll hearten ye up a bit."

The young man waved it away impatiently. "I have no stomach for the devil's brew to-night," he said.

"Call you it that, mate," said Winters, drawing the sleeve of his jacket across his mouth after a prolonged draught. "Wall, mebby you're right. Grog has been well-nigh the ruin of me and of many a better man as well; but for all that its mighty comfortin' of a cold night."

"Warming on a cold night, and cooling on a warm night," commented the other with a short laugh.

"You've hit it, man! I shall take no more to-night though, for we shall want all our wits about us." He was interrupted by the convict who had again stumbled to his feet. "Why do you not drink?" he growled savagely, fixing his red eyes upon the sailor.

"He does not understand," interposed the Huguenot hastily; "he is an Englishman."

"He neither drinks nor sleeps, and you neither drink nor sleep!" cried the convict with a terrible oath. "Look you, I shall drink but I shall not sleep!—Ah, you white-faced whining hypocrite, I have taken a hand in your little game! Tell the English dog."

The young man translated what the convict had said. Winters replied by passing his candle to the man who hung over him threateningly. "Ay! look till your black in the face," he growled. "Ef you find the door your more'n welcome. I'm tarnal sleepy," he said as the man disappeared down the stairway, "an' look you; we're all dead sleepy when he comes back. Consarn his buttons!" he added with a scowl.

When the convict reappeared it was evident that his

greed had mastered his suspicions for he was loaded down with the flasks.

For a long time Winters lay motionless, taking an occasional sly look at the convict, who apparently quite unaffected by the quantity of wine which he had already swallowed, sat stolidly knocking the heads off bottle after bottle, muttering and grumbling to himself as he poured their contents down his capacious throat.

After a time he arose unsteadily to his feet, and moved slowly toward the stairway, chancing however to stumble over the prostrate bodies of some of his sleeping comrades he fell heavily at full length ; struggling for an instant with the stupor which was mastering him, he rolled over like a log and lay quite still.

Winters sprang up and seizing the lighted candle where it had fallen from the nerveless grasp of the drunken wretch, hastily stamped out the tiny crawling flames which were greedily feeding upon the straw. Then he seized the young Huguenot by the shoulder.

"Come, mate, 'tis long past midnight ; we must be snugly housed before daybreak, or we are lost. Rouse the others and go ahead ; I must git this 'ere stone so I can handle it somehow, I don't want to leave our tracks uncovered—not that it matters much," he added, hauling the stone partly over the opening.

He then crawled into the stairway and with a prodigious effort succeeded in lifting the stone into its place.

" But how are we to get out ?" questioned one of the men, who stood huddled together at the foot of the ladder, their faces showing pallid and anxious in the feeble flare of the candle.

" Why jes' this way, mate," replied Winters, pulling

away a pile of empty cases, and disclosing a door sunken deeply into the stone wall. "We open this so, an'—" His jaw fell, and an ashen pallor overspread his countenance. "By the powers! if that dumb fool Cato hasn't locked this door!"

"Can we not break it down—there are seven of us?" asked the young Huguenot anxiously.

"Break it down," growled Winters, wiping the cold sweat from his face. "Wall, I reckon we'll hev to try. If we don't fetch it, we're gone coons."

The old sailor together with three of the Huguenots laid their shoulders to the door in a vain attempt to force it.

"Consarn it all!" cried Winters at length. "This 'ere dummed door's clamped an' barred with iron on t'other side, and bolted top an' bottom into the bargain. The devil fly away with that black numskull Cato! we're like to pay for his miserly folly with our lives!"

"Do not yield to profanity, friend, whatever the provocation," said the deep voice of an old man who had not hitherto spoken. "'Tis ill speaking of the evil one in a plight like this; 'twere better to fall upon our knees and entreat the Source of all Wisdom for guidance in our perplexity. God ofttimes brings his children into straits in order that they may be forced to fly to him for succor."

"Aw! Mayhap you're a parson, sir?" said Winters, a queer mixture of reverence and contempt in his tone.

The Huguenot bowed his head. "Yes," he said simply. "I was a pastor,—alas! that I must say *was*. And yet it becomes me not to question the will of God, who is able to cause all things to work together for good to them that love him.''

"If that be the case, sir," said Winters, meditatively scratching his head, "suppose you clap on all sail, and try a tack on prayin', while the rest of us look about us a bit; happen there's yet another way out than what I knows of."

"Silence!" cried the old minister with an authoritative gesture. "Let us pray!" and sinking to his knees he put up a short but fervent petition for succor and guidance in their sore perplexity.

All had involuntarily fallen to their knees while the aged pastor was praying, and as they arose the faces of the Huguenots shone with a peaceful joy which did not escape the sharp eyes of the old sailor.

"You reckon we're all ship-shape arter that!" he said slowly, "I kin see ye do; an' I'm blamed if I don't think so too. If I could speak to the A'mighty in that convincin' sort of way, blow my buttons, if I wouldn't be at it half the time! But He wouldn't listen to the likes of me; I'm a turrible wicked old seadog, an' not fit to mention the A'mighty—'xcept when I swar."

"Though your sins be as scarlet, they shall be white as snow," quoted the Huguenot solemnly. "God will listen to you as willingly as to me, friend. Try it and see.—But what is that archway yonder? It is filled with masonry to be sure, yet if it communicate with another cellar we might perchance find an exit." Seizing the candle from the hand of Winters the speaker approached the light nearer the surface of the wall in question. "See," he continued, "we might easily loosen a few of these stones!"

"There's no harm tryin', parson," said Winters. "Happen you're right; I'm 'xpectin' to be got out somehow. But what'll we dig with?"

No one answered this question, which was certainly a serious one. The Huguenot however continued to search about, flaring the light into every nook and corner of the place; suddenly he uttered a cry of joy and held up to view a rusty pickaxe, which he had found lying on the earthen floor, half-hidden by a pile of broken casks. "Here is the instrument of our deliverance," he said in a trembling voice, "providentially left for this our extremity by some hand which knew not its mission!"

"And here's the man for the pickaxe," cried the irrepressible sailor, "proverdentially provided with a pair of good stout arms! Hand it over, parson, we'll soon see whether you're right or wrong!" And seizing the tool, he began a lusty assault upon the masonry of the archway.

It soon became evident that the wall was a thick one, and that to pierce it would prove no easy task. When the sailor became exhausted and paused to recover breath one of the Huguenots took his turn. In the course of half an hour they had succeeded in removing but a single stone; but the breach once made it became only a matter of time to widen it, and after several hours of hard labor the toilers had the satisfaction of hearing some stones fall from the other side. They had penetrated the wall.

"I'll take a look on t'other side!" said Winters. And seizing the lighted candle, he crawled cautiously through the jagged opening into the darkness beyond.

CHAPTER XXV

"What is there?" anxiously inquired the Huguenot pastor, thrusting his white head into the opening.

"It's safe enough," was the cautious answer. "But I'm blessed if I can make out what sort of a place it is! Best come through at once, all of ye."

The anxious listeners needed no second bidding. Winters held aloft the guttering candle, and all looked about them curiously. The feeble light revealed a low, narrow gallery arched and paved with stone, which appeared to stretch away indefinitely into the darkness.

"Let us go forward!" said the old minister after a pause. "That this place will afford us the refuge for which we entreated the Almighty, I do not for a moment doubt, else why was my gaze directed toward the arch? Why did my dim eyes find the pickaxe?"

"Hark, what is that?"

"They are at work agin," said Winters, "and not far away; 'tis the noise of the picks overhead."

"Heaven grant that they do not penetrate this gallery in their excavations!" exclaimed the Huguenot pastor. "Let us hasten!"

"Ay, ay, sir!" cried the sailor, "this 'ere's the last of the candles!"

The party hurried forward, stumbling now and then over a loosened stone, the damp mouldy air of the place, its low walls green and shining with moisture, oppressing them one and all with a sense of suffocation. They had not proceeded far when the ground shook beneath their feet, and a muffled roar and detonation echoed and re-echoed throughout the dismal place. A few fragments of broken stone fell from the roof of the gallery, then all was silent once more.

"Thank God!" murmured the old minister reverently, "we have escaped that peril."

"They're sarchin' for us with gunpowder," quoth Winters. "I'll bet my head the rascals was all-fired mad not to see legs and arms a flyin' into air with that explosion!"

One of the party, a bold-looking but taciturn man of middle age, who had been hurrying along slightly in advance of the others, now paused with a gesture expressive of great surprise.

"What is it?—What have you found?" cried the others, hastening their steps.

The gallery, which at this point diverged slightly towards the left, suddenly expanded into a large and lofty chamber. It was at the entrance of this chamber that the man, who was called Croissart, had paused with uplifted hand.

The place was, like the gallery, paved and ceiled with stone, but the great height of the roof and the curious formations which depended from it, revealed the fact that it was not the work of man, but rather a natural formation. It was manifestly one of those caverns or grottoes, in which the slow finger of time delights to work out in silence and in darkness all sorts of weird images of the living and sentient world above ground.

This cavern, however, was not dark, but illumined

with a pale greenish light, which darkened and gleamed at intervals like the light of a glowworm. This uncertain light, the adventurers presently discovered, came from the side of the cave through a number of narrow slits which pierced the solid rock at intervals. In a word it was daylight, but daylight filtered through a thick curtain of green leaves, which swaying and fluttering in the breeze from time to time caused the peculiar effect of light and shade which they had observed.

It was none of these things, however, which caused the little group to stand silent and motionless at the entrance to this strange place. In the centre of the chamber—for so we may call it—was a table roughly and massively built, and before it in a great oaken chair, his back to the entrance, sat a man. He was leaning forward, engaged perhaps in writing, for pens and inkhorn lay near at hand, while a number of papers were scattered about on the table before him. For the rest, he was dressed in a rich but somewhat old-fashioned habit of darkish velvet adorned with a profusion of lace. The long curls of a wig which fell forward on either shoulder entirely concealed his face from view. This personage was apparently not aware of their approach, for he sat quite still, his hair stirring lightly in the fresh breeze which blew in from outside.

"And who may this fine gentleman be," whispered Winters in the ear of the clergyman. "He must be as deaf as an adder or he would have heard our voices. What do you say, sir, shall I hail him?"

The Huguenot looked about him anxiously and uncertainly as if to seek advice from the others, at the same time laying a restraining hand on the arm of the sailor. No one spoke; all were gazing in fascinated silence at the figure in the great chair.

"I think I saw him move," whispered one after a little,—"or was it but the shadow of yonder leaves?"

"'Tis some bedevilment or other; the place is full of it!" muttered Winters, his teeth chattering with terror. "Let us go back and leave him."

But at this the aged clergyman with a sudden energetic straightening of his thin figure, strode boldly forward toward the silent figure.

"Friend!" he said, in a voice which sounded hollow and unnatural. The lofty roof caught up the word and flung it back in a thousand uncanny whispers. "'Tis but the echo," he said after a startled pause, glancing toward the shrinking group in the doorway.

"'*Tis but the echo—but the echo—the echo—echo—e-cho!*" repeated the airy voices.

"Good Lord! I'd ruther be blowed up and done with it!" cried Winters, darting forward.

"What be you doin' here, sir?" laying as he spoke a trembling hand upon the shoulder of the man who sat in the chair, still apparently quite unmoved by all that had been going on about him. "He's—he's dead!" he gasped, turning an ashen face toward the others.

And the ghostly echo whispered "*Dead—dead—dead!*"

How long this strange figure clad in the habiliments of life had sat in that great chair it was impossible to guess. The awestruck gazers shrank back before the terrible face, its lips drawn back from its yellow teeth in ghastly semblance of a smile, its withered eyeballs fixed in an unwinking stare. One skeleton hand grasped a pen. From beneath it where it rested upon the paper had spread a dark yellowish stain.

The aged clergyman was the first to break the silence. "This poor relic of humanity can do us no harm," he said, and advancing to the table, he looked down at the paper upon which the man had been writing when death had so suddenly overtaken him. After a moment's pause he continued, " I can read a part of what is written here ; it is this: ' Gracious Sire, Have I not atoned for my folly? another year of this solitude will drive me mad ! Better a cell in the Bastile with the restless heart of Paris beating near at hand than this horrible exile ! Besides I must see you ; I fear lest—' I can read no more," —glancing up at the circle of grave attentive faces ; "what follows is completely obliterated."

"This 'ere must be the man what owned the place above !" said Winters at length. " But who is he?"

"Nay, that we cannot say," replied the Huguenot. "These other papers seem to contain figures and estimates of some sort; there is nothing further.—My friend, did you bring the pickaxe ?"

"I have it," said Croissart.

" Then as we must perforce remain hidden during the day—if indeed it be the will of God to deliver us from this place, we will lay this poor shell away to rest a space from the fever of living," said the old minister solemnly.

Accordingly after removing some of the paving-stones, a grave was dug and the body of the unknown was buried. The Huguenot pastor breathed a brief prayer, the stones were replaced and all was over.

" This ain't such a bad sort of a place now that the gentleman is underground—whar he's b'longed for the

Lord knows how long," remarked Winters, wiping the perspiration from his face. "Now I'll jes' take a squint out of one of these 'ere.windows." And dragging the great chair wherein the dead man had sat close to the wall, he clambered to its back and peered out of one of the narrow slits.

"What do you see?" questioned one of the Huguenots. But the sailor only replied by a warning gesture. Presently he jumped down and approaching the others half-whispered, "Two of the rascals is jes' outside; they're sarchin' for us. But blame it, we're safe enough here if we don't perish of hunger an' thirst."

" Is there no other way out save the one by which we entered?" said the young Huguenot, whom the clergyman had once or twice addressed as St. André. "What is here?" approaching as he spoke a dark recess in one corner.

"There seems to be a continuation of the gallery, or another chamber of some sort," exclaimed Croissart, cautiously advancing a few feet. "'Tis a pity we have no light."

"I do see a glimmer of some sort in the distance!" cried St. André. "Stay, I will advance alone, if there be any obstacle or pitfall, 'twere best for one to discover it," and he pushed boldly past Croissart and disappeared in the darkness.

Presently he reappeared to the great relief of those who remained behind. "'Tis all smooth and straight underfoot," he said almost cheerfully. "I was not mistaken about seeing light. I found at the end of a gallery, similar to the one by which we entered, a door clamped and bolted to the solid rock. All we shall have to do, I take it, to emerge into the daylight will be to walk out. The door is completely overgrown with vines and shrubs on the outside and has evidently not been opened for some time."

"It won't be healthy for us to open it for some time longer!" quoth Winters. "If we had a bit of fodder now, an' a mouthful of drink,—Blow my buttons, but I'd be blamed glad of even water!"

"Even water!" echod St. André. "What liquid ever devised by the wit of man equals a draught from one of God's own fountains. Water you can have, friends, if you will but follow me."

Near the grated door of which he had spoken, there gushed from the solid rock a spring of crystal coolness and clearness, its tiny stream falling into a basin which had been hollowed out in the stone beneath, from thence overflowing into a channel which evidently had some subterranean outlet.

"Ah!" exclaimed Winters, rising to his feet after a long refreshing draught, "that will be better than the water in the crow's nest. Faith! if I had known of this snug retreat I should never have troubled myself to build that; though it sarved its turn—it sarved its turn!"

"To what do you refer?" questioned St. André.

Thus interrogated the sailor made haste to tell the whole story of the shipwrecked party, including the disappearance of the young sailor and the present whereabouts of the women and Cato.

"The only thing that worries me," said the old man in conclusion, "is that fool, Cato. He'll be dead sartain to do something to draw the eyes of those miscreants into the tree-tops. Like enough he's got a white table-cloth up there, an' 'll take it into his woolly head to shake the crumbs off onto the very heads of the varmints.''

''Could you not bring them hither—together with some of the provisions, under cover of the darkness?'' asked the Huguenot pastor, who had been a thoughtful listener to the sailor's story. ''These ladies, from what you say of them, must be of our number,—driven like so many others from the shelter of their homes.''

''The very thing!'' cried Winters, slapping his leg violently, as was his wont when an idea appealed strongly to his imagination. ''The very thing! One of you shall go with me; two of us can make shift to carry enough victuals to last several days. When those are e't up we shall have to trust to our wits to get more.''

''Rather trust God, who has guided us thus far!'' exclaimed the pastor piously.

''Who gave us our wits, man? An' what did He giv 'em to us for?'' cried the incorrigible old sailor. ''The Lord made yonder spring, but if you was thirsty would you stand up an' bawl: 'Oh, God, I'm dry!' an' expect the Lord to pour the water down your gullet? You'd dry up in your tracks afore you'd git it, I reckon; and sarve you right!''

''In your rough way you have put a very important truth,'' quoth the minister in an argumentative tone. ''And since by the goodness of the Almighty and our own wits, our thirst is quenched, I propose that we return to the chamber which we have just quitted, and there spend some time in prayer and meditation.—'Twill be a profitable employment,'' he added, ''and will help pass away the time until evening, when we shall attempt to carry out the plan of our bold rescuer here.''

THE Huguenots received this suggestion with manifest joy. As for Winters, he followed the others, but
with the air of a man who felt himself to be out of
place.

"What I can't for the life of me see," he burst out
at length, "is what all the trouble between your worshipful king and you is about. He ain't a heathen, is
he? No. An' he prays to the same God, an'.expects
to git to the same heaven, don't he? An' yet he's for
makin' you come to his church, an' you say you can't
do it, an' would ruther be killed than do it. Now what
I want to know is this. What be you goin' to do when
you all git up yonder? Wouldn't it be a heap more
sensible to quit jawin' and quarrellin' with each other
and put your heads together for the savin' of such sin-
ners as I be, say? Course I don't know nothin' 'bout
it, but 'taint good sea sense to go cruisin' 'round promiscuous like when you've got a special port in view,
and a cargo to take there."

The old pastor sighed. "I suppose," he said, "that
if the love of God could once take possession of the
church militant all dissension would cease. Sometimes," he added with a shadowy smile at the little
group of earnest faces, "I think that word militant as
applied to the church on earth is used advisedly, only,
alas! most of the fighting is within, and the foes with-

out wax mighty and laugh at the sight of an army whose whole energies must perforce be directed to quelling the quarrelsome and mutinous soldiers which compose it. Ah well, I trust that in the new world there will be a church militant which shall also be a church triumphant !"

At this one of the Huguenots forgetting his surroundings burst forth with a strain from the Psalms,

"Sing unto God, praise ye his name !
The righteous rejoice and triumph before God,
But the wicked—"

"Hist, man," cried the sailor springing forward, "you're clean out of your mind to raise such a noise. You don't want to have so much religion aboard without a good lot of common sense to keep it well up to the wind ! Blow my buttons, but it reminds me of a sloop with a whoppin' spread of canvas and no ballast !" And the old man clambered up to one of the openings in the wall once more, and peered anxiously out. "Wall, as luck will have it," he remarked after a moment's survey, "there don't seem to be any of the varmints about; but you want to batten down your hatches for the rest of the day, or you'll git to heaven quicker'n you want to !"

"You are right, friend, rough and almost profane as is your way of expressing it," said the pastor. "And as this must of necessity be a day of fasting, let it also be a day of prayer and special sanctification, each for himself and in silence, till the time shall come to act." So saying the holy man withdrew himself into a dark corner of the cavern and sat down upon the stone pavement. The others followed his example, and so the hours wore heavily away.

As night drew on, Winters, who had spent the day wandering back and forth between the door of the outer corridor and the windows, solacing himself meantime with a liberal mouthful of tobacco, approached St. André.

"The blamed rascals have kep' away from this part of the island all day," he remarked; "I ain't seen hair nor hide of one of 'em. Mebbe your prayin's kep' 'em off, same as smoke'll drive away musquitoes. Wall, all I'm hopin' is that they ain't got wind of what's up in them pine trees. I'd sooner part with my right hand than have anything happen to them two women—not that I keer much for women-folks in general, knockin' round the world as I do, a man don't fall in with the right sort very often; but a finer, smarter lady than the one I've been tellin' you about, or a sweeter, handsomer lass than Miss Mad'line, you don't often see."

"What is the name?" interrupted St. André, leaning forward and fixing his blue eyes intently upon the old sailor.

"The name of the gal is Mad'line—that is her first name," replied the old sailor. "She's French—though as I've often said, nobody 'ud ever guess it. 'I don't mind bein' French,' says she. I had to laugh, she said it so kind of cute like. I tell you she's as smart a lass as ever growed, an'—"

"But her last name!" urged St. André eagerly.

"Wall, it's something like *d'Longer*, I ain't no tongue fur— But what in thunder ails ye, man?"

The young Huguenot had sprung to his feet and was excitedly pacing the floor.

"Is the young lady very slender?" he asked in a tremulous voice, "and has she a clear pale skin, beautiful brown hair, and dark eyes?"

"The very pictur'!" cried Winters. "Her hair curls like a grape-vine if it gits loose. She's mostly pale, but I've seed her cheeks's red's a rose when our cap'n was a talkin' to her. Her mother looks a lot like her, only she's always pale, and her hair has a sprinkle of white in it here and there like the sea of a stormy day. Do you know 'em?"

"I believe that they are my mother and sister," replied the young man in a husky whisper. "*Mon dieu*— to think of their being in the midst of such peril!" he added with a groan.

"Ain't I here?" exclaimed Winters in an aggrieved way. "An' ain't I looked arter 'em for a matter of two months? They're as safe as we be—if they've only done as I said, kep' quiet, an' had the luck to keep that fool Cato quiet too, which is another thing, the blamed—"

"Why did you leave them?" interrupted the young man harshly.

"Why did I leave 'em?" repeated the old sailor, rolling up his eyes. "Why Lord, here you folks have been a goin' on 'bout God's leadin's, speshul providence and that sort of thing. S'pose I hadn't of left 'em; where'd you be now—hey? Mebbe the Lord's got more idees than you give him credit for! Looks to me like a neat little plan to bring you folks together agin—a curus way, I admit, but I don't know's under the circumstances I could ha' done better myself. Seems to me if I was a sailin' under a cap'n as I knew had good sea-sense an' a reliabul chart, I'd take my orders

without inquirin' too much into the reasons for 'em.—
An' I know one thing mighty well, I'd git the rope's
end and desarve it too, if I didn't."

"Yes—yes, of course!" replied St. André impatiently. "But when can we start?"

"Wall, not for quite a spell yet; the sun ain't been
down more'n an hour. Like's not they'll be on the
lookout for us to-night. They've blowed the castle up
pretty much by this time," and the speaker meditatively
shifted his quid of tobacco. "I hope to the Lord they
don't take up their quarters in the cottage yonder; it's
only a stone's throw from the crow's nest."

"Are you making your plans for the night's work?"
queried the old clergyman approaching. "St. André
de Langres, you have the air of a man in deep distress
of mind; what is it, my son?"

"Yes, that's the name!" quoth Winters jubilantly.
"By gum, thar'll be a big time when my ladies clap
their eyes onto you, sir. Hope I'll be thar to see it!"

"What do you mean?" again inquired the Huguenot pastor, glancing from Winters' broad smiling face
to the downcast countenance of the young man.

"He means that the two women of whom he has
been telling us, are in all human probability my mother
and sister, from whom I was parted by those devils in
Languedoc six months ago. God only knows what they
have suffered since! And now I hear of them once
more, only to learn that they are reduced to a forlorn
refuge, from which they may already have been torn by
the brutal hands of yonder villains."

"You didn't worry about 'em a mite till you found
they might be some relation of yourn," remarked the
old sailor coolly. "Beats all how resigned we be 'bout

other folks' troubles! We'll soon find out whether they're thar yet. And now you, parson, what's your name, if you don't mind telling me—I allers like to know how to hail ship or man?''

"My name is Dinant—Constantin Dinant," said the Huguenot with a courteous inclination of his white head. "Will you tell me what you intend to do? It seems to me that we must have a preconcerted plan of action, so that in case of any mischance we should not be altogether at a loss.''

"Jes' so!" quoth Winters, smiting his closed fist into the palm of his other hand. "S'pose now we should find we couldn't git at the crow's nest, by reason of the infernal French villains bein' in the way. Then we should come back—with victuals if we can lay our hands on any. Thar's another case, suppose we should git up in the tree, then should be surprised and be forced to stay. You'd have to make the best of it and lay low where you be till the rascals leave the island, which won't be long.''

"We will keep a guard at the door so as to admit you instantly in case you return, which God grant!" said pastor Dinant.

And now as it had grown sufficiently late in the opinion of Winters to make the venture, all groped their way through the passage to the end of the corridor where the grated door showed dimly in the thick darkness. This was cautiously opened, not without great difficulty on account of the rust of years, then Winters and the young Huguenot, de Langres, slipped silently out, with a whispered "God speed" from the old pastor.

Pushing their way through the thick branches they

gained the summit of the little hill, under whose over-hanging brow was the concealed entrance which they had just quitted. Winters paused for a moment to look about him. The night was dark and yet there was sufficient light from the stars and the slender new moon, which now and then plunged dagger-like into the midst of the rapidly drifting masses of cloud, to show the adventurers their whereabouts. On their right hand glowed a dull red mass, manifestly the smouldering remains of the castle, while at a little distance they could see through the trees the brilliant light of a large fire.

"Dash my buttons!" muttered Winters, "'tis as I feared, the castle is in ruins, and the blamed rascals have quartered themselves in and about our cottage."

"Let us get nearer and see if it be possible to approach the pine trees," said de Langres in an eager whisper.

"Sartain, that's what I was meanin' to do. This way!" The two crept cautiously along, skulking fearfully in the thick shadows of trees and shrubs; now and then crawling on their hands and knees through the more open spaces. In this way they gradually approached the neighborhood of the giant pines. They soon discovered to their dismay that the camp-fire which they had seen, was between the cottage and the trees, so near that one in the crow's nest could easily have tossed a pebble into its glowing depths. Around the fire lay a number of dark forms.

Winters stopped short. "Now if they be all asleep!" he whispered to his companion, "we'll make a break for the trees. Dash it!—no; the blamed rascals have posted sentries." And he dodged back behind some bushes, dragging his companion with him.

The two men lay silent, hardly daring to breathe, as one of the marines passed so near their hiding-place that they could see his face distinctly in the wavering firelight.

"What do you say to overhauling him when he gits back next time?" whispered Winters, as the sentry again disappeared behind the cottage. "We could batten down his hatches and leave him here; or I could silence his guns altogether with this 'ere knife."

"It is not to be thought of," hastily replied his companion. "There is scarcely a chance in a thousand but that he would yell before we succeeded in overpowering him; we should be seized and—*voila!* Better let him pass again, then while he is beyond we will get up the tree as noiselessly as possible. I must know whether they are safe!"

"Thar'll be no chance of gittin' the women-folks down and into the cave yonder," said Winters.— "Here he comes agin!"

The sentry emerged from behind the cottage yawning portentously, and grumbling to himself about the uselessness of his job as he passed the listeners.

"Now!" whispered the Huguenot as the marine turned his back; the two crept silently toward the nearest tree in the group. In another instant they had commenced their perilous ascent, clinging with fingers and toes to the rough bark of the great trunk. The Huguenot, being the younger and more agile of the two, had already gained the lower limbs of the tree, but Winters had still a good piece to climb when the marine reappeared from behind the cottage and came directly towards them.

It was impossible to retain his hold without continuing

to ascend, as the old sailor well knew. Trusting therefore to the great trunk to conceal him, he kept on desperately, and had almost reached the spot where the Huguenot was awaiting him in an agony of impatience, when unfortunately his foot slipped; at the same instant a piece of bark to which he was clinging gave way, and he fell heavily to the ground, a distance of some twenty feet, striking amid a clump of bushes which clustered about the foot of the tree.

CHAPTER XXVII

AT SEA

BAILLOT found his spirits rising with every foot which the good horse under him put between him and Warham castle. He felt in the holsters, and found therein a brace of pistols, which he transferred to his belt. The night was slightly overcast, yet not so dark but that he could discern the road winding dimly before him, bordered with hedge-rows and groups of trees on either side. Behind him rose the castle, every window ablaze with festive lights.

Having proceeded about a mile or thereabouts as nearly as he could judge, he drew rein and began to look carefully for the cross-road which St. Clair had mentioned. He had not proceeded far in his quest when the sound of voices warned him that some one was coming. He looked about him once more, and seeing that there was nothing for it save to advance, he spurred on his horse, intending to pass the approaching horsemen at a gallop.

"Hold, friend!" cried a loud authoritative voice. The speaker wheeled as he spoke directly in front of Baillot. "Your name and business, sir."

"By what right do you stop a traveller on the highway?" said Baillot, answering the question by another.

"We are not here to bandy words," said the man sternly; "your name and errand at once."

Baillot perceived by a struggling moonbeam that his

questioner was heavily armed. " I am a messenger from Warham castle charged with a weighty commission," he said boldly. " Hold me at your peril !"

The man who had accosted him seemed somewhat staggered by this declaration, for he fell back and conferred with one of his companions in a whisper.

"You shall go back to Warham with us," he announced presently with an air of decision ; "if what you say is true, you shall go your ways at once."

"But the time," urged Baillot, "—I am not permitted to waste an instant. You are doing something both stupid and unwarrantable in detaining me. I pray you let me pass, gentlemen."

The man stared at him without speaking, and Baillot rightly judging him to be a country sheriff, and his companions but armed plowmen, plunged suddenly through their midst, and pounded away down the highway. He heard voices calling upon him to stop, and lay forward upon his horse's neck, momentarily expecting to hear the whiz of a pistol-ball above his head. But to his surprise his pursuers did not fire, and after half an hour of hard riding the sounds of their shouts and the clatter of their horses' hoofs began to grow fainter. "I am gaining on them !" he thought with satisfaction. Ten minutes more and he drew rein and listened. He could hear nothing. " I have passed the cross-road long ago," he thought. " I must go back ; it will never do for the sun to find me on English soil."

Springing to the ground he gave his horse a slash with the bridle which sent him flying down the highway ; then slipping through the hedge be began to run in the opposite direction as fast as his feet could carry him over the plowed ground. He had not gone far when he heard his pursuers in full gallop; they passed him where he crouched motionless behind the hedge.

"Now for it!" he muttered under his breath as the sound died away in the distance, and emerging upon the highway he laid his heels smartly to the ground, keeping out a sharp eye meanwhile for the cross-road. A sudden turn in the highway brought him face to face with another group of horsemen, who hailed him loudly:

"Hold, there! tell us where you are bound in such haste?"

"I must not stop, neighbor," cried Baillot, slackening his pace a bit. "The constable is ahead riding in hot pursuit of a man whom he believes to be the very one we are looking for. Get you quickly after him!"

"Ha!" exclaimed the man. "Well met, comrade, but what is your errand this way?"

Baillot stopped short. "Nay, that I am bidden to reveal to no man. I am on my way toward the castle, do you not see, blockhead?"

"How, then—" began the man doubtfully.

But Baillot was already out of ear-shot, running at full speed as before. His questioners after staring stupidly after him for a full minute went their way.

By the glimmer of a finger-post on his right, Baillot perceived that he had at last reached the cross-road, which he had passed without notice in the excitement of the pursuit.

Plunging down it as rapidly as he was able for the sand, into which he sank ankle-deep at each step, he soon heard the sound of water running gently upon the beach.

At his approach a man sprang up from beneath the shelter of some bushes. "You are late!" he whispered. "I began to fear lest you were nabbed. Look lively now, or we shall not be able to get away with the tide!"

"I was pursued," replied Baillot, also in a whisper, stepping as he spoke into a skiff which the man had pushed out into the water.

"The devil!" exclaimed the other briefly, jumping in after him and sending the boat well out with a strong push. The little craft fairly flew over the water under the mighty strokes of the oarsman, her bow pointing toward a dim light, which Baillot rightly judged to be the light of the vessel for which they were bound. They were already several furlongs from the shore when a dark figure ran out from behind some trees, and began to gesticulate wildly. Baillot perceived this, but he said nothing to the man with the oars. In another moment they had reached the side of the vessel; both men climbed quickly onto her deck, the skiff was hauled up, and the sails set with great swiftness, but in perfect silence, at which Baillot inwardly marvelled.

During the process of getting under way Baillot had stood silent at the rail; no one had spoken to him, and he was on the point of asking one of the sailors to point out the captain that he might inquire what sort of accommodation the vessel was likely to afford for the night, when a heavy hand fell upon his shoulder, and a harsh voice exclaimed in his ear:

"Getting your wind, cap'n? *Morbleu!* but you're in luck to get off! Come below, I'll give you a sup of something I brought aboard with me—a present from you know who." And the speaker laughed with a sound as discordant and unmirthful as a human laugh could well be.

Much surprised at the peculiar way in which the man had accosted him, the young Huguenot followed across the deck and down the companion-way. The dim flare of a lantern which was secured to the wall of the stairway shone directly upon the gigantic figure of his guide; Baillot noticed with astonishment the long grizzled locks which fell about his shoulders and the scarlet sash twisted about his middle. "A strange-looking sailor for a vessel of this class," he thought, as his eye took in these details.

"Did you get what you went for, cap'n?" said the man entering the cabin and reaching to turn up the wick of a smoky oil lamp. He turned as he spoke and fixed his eyes upon Baillot. His jaw dropped, he opened his mouth as if to speak, but only gulped spasmodically once or twice. Then he took a step forward as if to leave the cabin.

Baillot, whose wits had not been idle, perceived this movement; he sprang forward, raising his hand imperatively. He had resolved on a bold part.

"Stop, sir!" he said sternly. "Another step without my permission and you are a dead man!"

"Who the devil are you?" sneered the man, whipping out a poniard and continuing his progress toward the door.

Without a word Baillot sprang upon him, wrenched the poniard from his grasp, hurled it across the cabin, then twisting one leg quickly behind his gigantic adversary hurled him violently to the floor. All this was done in a twinkling, and before the fellow had time to recover from the surprise of this totally unexpected assault, Baillot had clapped the muzzle of a pistol to his head.

"Be silent, until I have spoken !"

"You've got me," muttered the man, a savage light shining in his small deep-set eyes. "Say on !"

"You expected to find in me your captain. Look at me well ; I am your captain from this hour. Hold !" as the man again attempted to speak. "You wish to know what has become of the other. That does not concern you. I am here in his stead. You will obey me." He then withdrew a few steps still holding the pistol in his hand. "Get up."

The man obeyed sullenly. "Who are you, and how did you come here ?"

"You brought me to the ship. Obey me, well ; disobey, die !"

"But," exclaimed the sailor with a look of involuntary admiration at the sinewy frame and stern dark face before him, "suppose I kill you first? What is to hinder ?"

"You will not kill me first."

"You are at least mortal," sneered the other, "—and you are not wanted here." He was edging his way as he spoke in the direction of his poniard, which was sticking in the wall of the cabin.

Baillot perceived that he had no ordinary man to deal with ; therefore, at the risk of calling down a swarm of the crew from above, he fired his pistol at the arm of the sailor just as he raised it to grasp the handle of the weapon. Dropping his hand with a howl of mingled rage and pain the fellow rushed forward like an enraged bull.

Stepping quietly to one side, the young Huguenot

again caught his adversary about the middle, and again succeeded in hurling him violently to the floor.

"Is it enough? Will you obey? Or must I break every bone of your body as I have broken your arm?"

"I will obey," he said sullenly, scowling with pain.

"Very well then, get up. But I give you fair warning that my patience with you is well-nigh exhausted; one more rebellious word, and there will be another first mate on this vessel."

"What do you want me to do?" growled the man, rising rather unsteadily to his feet.

"First hand me that poniard," said Baillot, coolly proceeding to reload the pistol which he had just fired. The man obeyed. "Good! Now go before me to the deck and call the crew together, I wish to speak with them."

"I may as well have it out with them," he thought to himself, "or they will poniard me before morning."

Arrived on deck, the mate, as Baillot had rightly judged him to be, commanded the crew to assemble in the waist of the ship. Baillot stood at the rail watching them as they sauntered up by twos and threes. The clouds had dispersed by this time, and the moon riding high in the heavens shone boldly on the villanous faces, glittering knives and scarlet caps of the thirty ruffians which made up the crew.

"Men!" began Baillot in a loud clear voice, "I have called you together to tell you that from this time forward I am your captain." A low growl interrupted him at this point, and several voices shouted "Overboard with him!" but no one stirred to make good the threat, for the mate with a threatening gesture shouted "Hear him out!"

CHAPTER XXVIII

MASTER AND MAN

"Do you say that, mate? What do you know about this 'ere swab? How did he come here?" broke in an undersized man, whose broad black brows marking an unbroken line directly across his face, gave him a peculiarly savage and brutal look.

"Hear him out, I say!" repeated the mate with a furtive glance at Baillot.

"What you want, men, is plunder," went on Baillot, and a deep chorus of "Ay, ays," greeted this assertion. "Your captain has always taken the lion's share—"

"Ay, that he has!"

"He was a greedy, cruel cut-throat—"

"A fine gentleman!" bawled the undersized man. "A spy!"

"A spy!" cried Baillot. "Would I come into your midst were I a spy? No, men, I am not a spy. Hark you! Two months since I was shipwrecked in a region of the ocean not many leagues from the Azores, and with four of my mates was cast onto a certain island. On this island we found a great castle, empty of inhabitants, yet crammed with all sorts of valuables : we will go there; the booty shall be yours."

The pirates looked at one another. This was a strange tale ; but there was also something strangely convincing in the face and manner of the man who had told it. They were half inclined to believe it.

"How came you here? Where are the others?"

Baillot expected this question. He realized that he had not put his case very skilfully. "But, *ma foi*," he said to himself, "I am not a lawyer nor yet a professional liar—which is perhaps the same thing. I have been forced into a cruel dilemma; God grant me wisdom to deal with these cut-throats."

"Ay, ay!" bellowed the crew, closing in around him as he hesitated. "How did you come here?"

"I have already broken your mate's arm for presuming to question me," said Baillot firmly. "I say now, once and for all, the island is a prize worth trying for. It shall be yours. Crowd on all sail and make for the Azores!"

There was nothing especially convincing in these words, as the pirate crew dimly realized; but the voice, and above all the eye of the man before them carried that well-nigh irresistible magnetism which is so compelling a power in a personality born to command. All eyes were turned inquiringly upon the mate; he had thrust his injured arm into his bosom.

"Ay, ay!" he growled impatiently, "shake out the canvas lively! We may as well do as he says. Fisher is nabbed and he will blab on the rest of us."

"Come down to the cabin," said Baillot, addressing the mate in French. "I will set your arm; it must be painful."

"*Bon dieu*, you are then my compatriot!" exclaimed the man, and Baillot perceived that his subjugation was complete. He retired to the cabin, convinced that for the moment he had nothing to fear. Nevertheless he sat down somewhat gloomily in the dingy little place to reflect upon his certainly dubious position.

"Suppose I succeed in compelling this precious crew to take me to the island with my skin intact—a most unlikely supposition to begin with—how could I make good the escape of the women? Why in heaven's name did I speak of the island at all? Why did I not rather offer them gold to take me to Terciora? *Peste*, I am a fool. I am in their power. They will acquaint themselves with my purse whenever it so pleases them."

Just as he reached this disheartening conclusion he looked up and saw the dark face of the pirate, whose arm he had wounded with his pistol-ball, peering in at the door.

"Ah, my good fellow," he said, realizing with unpleasant distinctness that the fellow might have killed him with the greatest ease, "your arm. I am something of a surgeon, and can make shift to ease you of your pain, since there is no more skilled leech at hand." He said these words in French, bearing in mind the man's look when he had so addressed him upon deck.

"*Morbleu!*" ejaculated the man, holding out his injured member for inspection. "I can almost forgive you the pain, for the joy it gives me to hear once more the language of my own country. How may I call you, sir?"

"My name is Henri Baillot," replied the young man, examining the wounded arm with some anxiety. I fear that I shall make but a clumsy job of this; 'tis a bad hurt. But it serves you right for trying to poniard me! If you carry a stiff wrist for the rest of your life, my good man, you will not soon forget my name."

"Tell me, from what province are you?" said the pirate, staring hard at his amateur surgeon, who was endeavoring as gently as possible to dress a wound which

would have taxed the wits of a skilled surgeon. "—A
plague on my arm. I shall heal of it; I have had a
thousand hurts worse, they all come right after awhile. I
am no woman to mind the pain."

"I perceive that you are not," said Baillot, pausing
to tear his cambric handkerchief into strips. "I must
have hurt you confoundedly."

"But your province. Are you not from Béarn?"

"I am from Béarn; and what then?"

"Ah, monsieur, you would never remember Gaston
Goujet, and yet I lived many years on your father's estate. My father, Pierre Goujet, was the bailiff. I ran
away to sea when I was sixteen. You were then but a
child."

"What! Is it so?" exclaimed Baillot, "—Gaston
Goujet! 'Tis true that I had forgotten you; but my
mother has often told me how you rescued me from
drowning."

"Yes, *mon dieu*, it is true. You had escaped from
your nurse and were playing on the brink of a pool in
the forest. I stood behind a tree watching; suddenly
you reached forward too far and fell in with a scream.
The water closed over you. I stood still. I hated you.
Why should you live to be a lord, to ride fine horses, to
lie soft and eat luxuriously, while I could never be other
than what nature made me, fit only to receive the kicks
and abuse of those better born than myself?" The
man's face grew dark, and he turned a look of sullen
rage upon Baillot who was just finishing the bandaging
of his arm.

"It is completed, my good Gaston," said the young
man composedly. "You did not wish to save me,
but—"

The pirate sighed profoundly and shook his great shoulders. "I hated, yes, but thank God, I did not commence my career of murder then. You rose to the surface of the pool, and raising your hands, which gleamed white and dimpled in the sunlight, cried for help. I hesitated no longer, but plunged in and brought you safely to land. Your mother, sweet saint, loaded me with thanks and benefits. She idolized you; you were her only child. Had she lived all would have been well with me, but the following year she died. Your father was a hard man. I was caught poaching. He did not put me to death, nor even mutilate me, because I had saved his son's life, he said. But he caused me to be beaten, and again hatred broke loose in my heart, tearing me like a thousand devils. I ran away to sea, but kicks and blows followed me. Once the boatswain struck me across the face. I threw him into the sea that night. It was dark, the waves running mountains high. It was thought that he had been swept overboard. I alone knew better. On another vessel the captain was a foul-mouthed tyrant. We hung him to the mast. The ship became ours, but she was clumsy and slow, and we made haste to obtain a better by seizing this vessel. Her crew went over the side. The *Rouge et Noir* is a lucky vessel. I am no longer under the lash. I—But why do I tell all this to you! Why are you here, monsieur?"

Baillot had listened with profound attention to this recital. He saw that in this man lay his only hope of safety. He had been deeply affected by the look on the man's face when he had spoken of his dead mother, the lovely Comtesse de Lantenac, whose sweet face he dimly remembered as a vision of an angel. "Fortune has used me little better, my Gaston," he said. "I am a fugitive and a wanderer. Once more I appeal to you for aid. I trust you because you loved my mother."

"Yes, I loved her," said the man huskily. "She was the only human being that I ever loved. Nay, she was more than human, I swear; she was an angel of God. For her sake I will do what I can for you—the saints be my witness!" And he bent and kissed the outstretched hand of the young count.

"My father lived many years after the time you have spoken of," said Baillot after a pause; "naturally gloomy and taciturn he became more and more morose after the death of my mother. Like all who ever came in contact with her, he idolized her, and I believe he never loved any one else. At all events he seemed to care little for me. I was sent to Paris to be educated, and so grew up a stranger to home, and yet among those who taught me what honor was, what loyalty was, both to my God and to my country. I was under the care of an excellent man, a Huguenot. Under his roof I made many good friends, and I likewise got all the good that Paris could give with very little of the evil. After a time, through the influence of my father, I entered the navy, a career I had always longed for. I served until France was shaken to her centre by the Revocation of the Edict of Nantes. I was called upon to renounce the faith of my fathers; I refused and was condemned to the galleys. Just before the sentence was enforced, however, I made my escape. I made haste to look for my father, who was by this time an aged man; but I found upon my arrival in Béarn that he was dead of a stroke of apoplexy, induced by the quartering of a body of dragoons in his château. He had been buried secretly by night by one or two faithful servants. The château was still in the hands of the soldiery; they had sacked it from top to bottom, committing every possible outrage. Péyrade, the faithful servant of my father, who alone had stood by his death-bed, had in his possession certain papers with which my father had entrusted him for me, should I ever appear to claim them. Among them I found a title-deed to lands in America. Having no longer a home in France, a penniless outcast, hunted and condemned, I resolved to fly to the new world. I embarked as a common sailor on the bark *White Gull* from Southampton, whither I had succeeded in making my way. The rest is as I have said. I was shipwrecked with four companions on an unknown island. To rescue those companions and afterward to get to America is what I wish to do."

"But you have not yet told me how you came to be aboard the *Rouge et Noir*," said Goujet, who had listened to this story with an impenetrable air.

"True, I have not, and in order to do that, I must tell you how I came to leave the island." And as briefly as possible he outlined his mysterious removal from the château, his voyage and his stay in England, ending with the escape of the previous night. He did not, however, give the names of his abductors, and in the telling suppressed as much of the detail as possible. "I was told that I would find a skiff awaiting me," he said as he finished the recital. "I found it, and was conveyed to this vessel. You know the rest."

The pirate passed his hand slowly across his forehead as if in deep thought. "You took the wrong skiff," he said at length. "I killed the man who was waiting for you. I took him for an accursed spy. But what then became of Fisher?"

"He came to the beach just after we embarked," said Baillot boldly. "I saw him: I did not tell you."

CHAPTER XXIX

"Ay!" quoth Goujet with a short laugh, "you did not tell me, and yet it would have been better for you had you done so."

"Why?"

"I should have killed you, and returned for Fisher."

"Granting that you are correct in the statement, why would that have been better for me?"

"Because then you would have died quickly and easily. Now—unless I can make shift to save you from my shipmates—you will die in a different fashion and, *morbleu!* 'twill give you a bad quarter of an hour."

"You would not have killed me so easily as you think, my good Gaston, but on the other hand I might have been left to manage the boat alone, boarded the wrong vessel, and so have found myself among pirates with no ally and friend such as you to aid me. Tell me, am I not a better man than Fisher?"

"You are, I swear it. Fisher is all that you have said, and worse; but how did you know it?"

"I guessed it. I know something of the ways of 'gentlemen of fortune,' as you call yourselves. If then I am a better man than Fisher, I am also a better commander, and what is to hinder us from managing this crew?"

Goujet did not answer. He seemed lost in thought. At length he arose, and bringing down his uninjured

hand upon the table with a thwack, exclaimed, "It
must be done!—Ha! ha! 'tis a pretty mischance for
Fisher. His neck will doubtless stretch at the next
assizes. He will think that I did it out of revenge.
Ma foi! for once I was a better man than I might have
been, for I had no thought of playing him false. Let
the Englishman swing; he has deserved it, not once,
but a thousand times. I will tell you though that it
will be no child's play to keep the breath in our nos-
trils for the next few days. Do you know, that after
you threw me the second time and I promised to obey
—though, *mon dieu!* I did not mean it, save for the
instant—when you proposed to speak to the crew I
thought to myself, this fine loud-talking gentleman has
now but three minutes to live. For as sure as I stand
here, I believed that they would walk you over the
plank at the first word. How you managed to quiet
them I do not know, but they will not remain quiet,
mark me! There are at least two of them who will be
determined to be captain now that Fisher is gone. We
shall hear from them."

"Do not let us wait to hear from them. Do you
know which these are?"

"Yes."

"We will put them in irons at once."

"Easier said than done, my master. You are not
dealing with marines, who have but a single idea in
their stupid heads and that to obey. Every one of
these men is such as I." And the pirate shook his
great shoulders and looked—what he was, a creature
scarcely less dangerous than an animal possessed with
rabies.

"We must put them in irons," repeated Baillot,

"and we must do it now. The others will obey us. Who is the ringleader among the men?"

"An Englishman named Lock."

"Very well, I will retire to this cabin on the left, I am sleeping. Call Lock to the cabin. Talk with him of me. He will propose to assassinate me. Agree to this. Let him advance toward the cabin where I am; seize him from behind; snatch the poniard from his hand. I will do the rest. Should you fail to succeed," he added significantly, "you will not forget that I am armed, and that I never miss my aim."

"You do not trust me, master!" cried the pirate. "I will be true to you for the sake of your mother—I swear it. *Le bon Dieu* knows that I speak the truth for once!"

"I believe you," said Baillot simply, but in a tone which seemed to satisfy Goujet. "Now, I go," he added, " —I sleep; get you on deck and fetch Lock."

Goujet immediately disappeared.

He came back accompanied by the undersized man with the thick eyebrows, who had proposed to throw overboard the man who had so strangely claimed the command of the *Rouge et Noir.*

"Where is he?" he asked in a hissing whisper, as he entered the cabin.

"Asleep," replied Goujet, " —drunk," he added with a wink, producing as he spoke a black bottle and a brace of cups. "I plied him with this. Not a bad drink; try it, mate."

"Drunk?" said the other smacking his lips after emptying his cup at a single gulp. "Ha! as good as dead then. We will drop him astern. Who is he to force himself among us? I'll be blessed if ever I clapped eyes on him afore. I say, mate, you know I'm cap'n, don't you? You'll stand up for me—hey? You shall be second in command as you are now; more'n that you couldn't hope to be. If Mateo gets it—the bloody scoundrel!—he'll make you walk the plank. He swears he will, ay—and torture you into the bargain; he hates you,—since you know when." And the speaker paused to pour himself another cup of the liquor.

"I'm your friend, Goujet," he resumed whiningly. "Swelp me, I'm your friend, and if I'm cap'n, Mateo shan't touch a hair of your head. You shall do what you like with him; you shall hang him to the mast-head inside of an hour and no one to hinder."

Goujet gave a savage growl, like the beast of prey that he was. "That's all very well; but the other must be fixed first."

"Ay! Goujet, my good friend, so he must! Shall we hock him and drop him overboard now he is drunk, or save him for a little sport to-morrow? Let us save him; 'twill be a pretty way for me to begin—ay! and a warning to any who think to disobey me," he added with an ugly look at Goujet.

"The man is no coward," said Goujet slowly. "There will be plenty of sport later. Then there is Mateo. Best make a sure thing of it to-night."

"Poniard?"

"Ay. Do it now while he sleeps. No one so neat-handed as you, mate, for a job like this. He's yonder," with a jerk of his thumb over the shoulder.

Lock arose, a gratified grin overspreading his countenance at the apparent compliance of the mate, and began tiptoeing his way across the floor.

Goujet followed in a leisurely fashion, as if to see that the deed was properly accomplished, but just as Lock was about to enter the door, he sprang forward and snatched the weapon from his hand, exclaiming in a low mocking voice :

" Hold ! my would-be captain, this poniard of yours is not sharp enough to kill yonder gentleman !"

Lock turned in a fury, at the same instant Baillot sprang upon him from behind, mastered him with ease, gagged him securely, and after manacling him hand and foot, tossed him unceremoniously into the bunk.

" Now for the other," he said, pausing to recover breath.

" Ay," growled Goujet, " but let us finish with this one first." And he advanced toward the helpless man, brandishing the poniard savagely.

"What do you mean ?" cried Baillot, seizing him by the arm.

" To kill him of course. I will do it, master, a murder more or less will make little difference with my account."

" No, you shall not do this thing. He shall remain in irons—"

"—Until some one looses him, yes. I tell you he must die. Would he not have killed you ?"

" Yes, he would have killed me, and he doubtless deserves to die ; yet you shall not put him to death unjudged and uncondemned."

"Were he loose this minute, master, he would kill you, even though he owed you his life. Look at him ; liar—murderer—*rat !*"

Baillot shuddered in spite of himself at the look in the eyes of the man who lay bound. " Leave the

wretch as he is for the present," he said firmly. "Speak
to Mateo ; we will capture him in the same way."

Without another word Goujet left the cabin, to return
presently accompanied by another man. This worthy
was not over middle height but evidently of immense
muscular strength ; his hand was playing with the hilt
of a dagger as he entered, and he rolled his piercing
eyes suspiciously about the cabin.

"Sit down, mate," said Goujet, with a hospitable
wave of the hand, "and wet your coppers a bit, while
we talk of this queerish bit of business of losing our
cap'n and getting a fine gentleman in his place."

The Italian looked greedily at the bottle, but he did
not sit down.

"I look first in dese cabins," he said cautiously. "I
don' know where dat dam' Anglais be."

"Who, Lock?" said Goujet carelessly. "He's in
the fo'c'sle, trying to talk the men into making him
cap'n. What do you say to having Lock over our
heads?"

"I hate him!" hissed the Italian. "I kill him—
see?" And he described a significant gesture with the
dagger.

"You hate me too," said Goujet with a great laugh,
"yet I'm the only man aboard who can help you to
the cap'ncy."

"I—? hate *you ?—nevair !* But will you not be de
capitain yourself?"

"I? No, *peste !* I care too much for my ease ; I
am content as I am."

"Ah, you shall still be first mate, and I capitain—
no one so clevair as you, my friend, for first mate. I
do not hate you—no ! But Lock—ah— !" And the

Italian lay back in his chair and passed his dagger from ear to ear with a ferocious smile. "See!" he continued, "dat is what Lock do to you."

"Nothing like having a firm friend such as you, Mateo," remarked Goujet, filling the Italian's cup. "I shan't forget this of you. I never forget."

"Nor I, *nevair—nevair!*" murmured the Italian. "But what has become of the fine milor, who would be capitain? You have quiet him, is it not so?"

"Not without your orders, cap'n. He's asleep yonder."

"Asleep?—ha! He will not wake up—no. I will kill him. *But not until I have kill you, for to me you have lied!*" And with a snarl like that of a wild beast the Italian sprang at the half-crippled man before him.

Fortunately for Goujet he succeeded in jumping aside quickly enough to avoid the blow, which had been aimed directly at his heart. And before the Italian could recover himself for a second lunge Baillot had fallen upon him. Mateo turned with a yell, but Goujet pursuing the tactics which Baillot had suggested, caught him from behind, holding him about the body with a grip like iron, while Baillot disarmed him, not, however, without receiving a flesh wound in his shoulder which bled profusely.

"Shoot him, master! he has wounded you!" cried Goujet. "A *peste* on my arm! I can do nothing. Ha—the dog has bitten me!"

The Italian fairly foaming with rage had twisted himself about and buried his sharp white teeth in Goujet's wounded arm. The pain was intense, and for an instant the luckless Frenchman tottered as though he would have fallen. In that instant, however, Baillot had finished his conquest, and the wretch gagged and manacled lay helpless upon the floor.

"I suppose, my merciful master, that you will also preserve the life of this man?" said Goujet, looking down upon the prostrate Italian with unutterable hatred in his dark face. "Dog—coward!" he hissed through his shut teeth, and he kicked his helpless foe savagely.

"I might have killed him in self-defence, had that been necessary," said Baillot; "but, *voila!* we have conquered. He shall live."

CHAPTER XXX

"I SHALL take care that you do not repent your goodness, monsieur," said Goujet with a black look at the Italian. "But one of us must go on deck at once; we have been absent so long that some mischief or other will be brewing. Hark, what is that?"

Baillot, whose quick ear had already caught some unusual sound from above, sprang up the stairs two at a time, leaving Goujet to attend to the prisoners.

For a full minute that worthy stared hard at the yellow face of Mateo, fingering the handle of his poniard meanwhile with an air of relish. "Ah—my good capitain," he sneered, "my brave capitain, will you kill me now, or will you kindly permit me to live for a little?—'Tis no time for such nonsense!" he muttered as he rolled the helpless Italian over and over like a log to the cabin beyond. "The only safe man is a dead man; when my young lord has been a pirate a bit longer he will find that out for himself." He turned the key on his prisoners, after threatening them both with instant death should they attempt to remove their gags.

He then followed Baillot upon deck. The excitement had been caused by a sudden squall; the ill-disciplined crew demoralized by the continued absence of their officers, and absorbed furthermore by the plots and counterplots suggested by Lock and Mateo, had been

246

paying but scant attention to the safety of the vessel. Baillot had taken in the situation at a glance, and by a series of rapid commands, which the frightened sailors made haste to obey, had succeeded in making things snug before the tempest struck the ship.

" 'Tis only a stormlet, but, *morbleu*, enough to send us to the bottom, had it struck us with all our canvas spread," said Goujet in the ear of Baillot, as he stood with folded arms watching the sudden fury of the sea under the lash of the storm.

" The ship rides easily," observed Baillot.

" Ay, sir ! There's no stauncher, livelier boat on the seas than this little craft," said Goujet, rolling his eyes proudly about him. " We're well armed, eight guns— good ones, and a plenty of powder and shot. If you would content these fellows, give them enough to do— enough that is of fighting. But let them be idle !" and he shook his great shoulders significantly.

" We may be forced to defend ourselves," said Baillot in a non-committal tone.

" But you will not attack ; is that what you mean, master ?"

" Would you have me turn pirate in earnest, my Gaston ?" asked Baillot with a melancholy smile. " Is that a fit career for a man who is exiled from his country because of his religion ?"

" No, *mon dieu !* It is not. But what then shall we do ?"

" We shall do what we can. To-day alone is ours, to-morrow is God's."

" Ah, I see that you are the son of your mother," cried Goujet ; " and she was too good for this foul earth."

"I do not on that account intend to take the less care of myself," said Baillot. "You yourself have found that true this very night."

"Yes, yes, it is true!" murmured Goujet, hugging his wounded arm to his breast. "Why did you not kill me?"

"Because I saw that you might prove useful to me."

"And so I will; from this day forth and as long as I live, I am yours," exclaimed Goujet with a look of savage love, which was almost terrifying in its intensity. "Look you, I have sworn it!"

"Then you will not remain a pirate."

"*Bon!* I hate the life."

The gale had now swept to the northward leaving the sea agitated and foam-covered. Baillot at the earnest request of Goujet descended to the cabin, leaving the mate in command. Marvelling much within himself at the strange course of his fortunes during the past few hours, he wrapped his cloak about him and lay down to sleep. Awaking after a few hours of dream-haunted slumber, he sprang to his feet and ascended to the deck. Goujet was still pacing up and down; he turned on seeing Baillot, and approached him with a respectful salute.

"You have slept, master?"

"Yes, and am refreshed. I will remain upon deck now while you do likewise."

"The fog is as thick as gruel," quoth Goujet, lingering and seeming to devour the young count with the fire of his glances. "Ah," he cried, "you have the eyes of your mother!"

Baillot in his turn had been looking fixedly at the

haggard face of the man before him. It was a face seamed with the livid scars of many a battle, and lined with hatred, anger and fear. It was the face of one who has suffered the tortures of the lost. In a word, it was the face of a man without love in the world, and therefore without hope.

"You have suffered from your wound, man," he said kindly. "Go below and rest."

"Ay, I have suffered! But, *mon dieu!* What is a scratch like this! It is here that I have suffered!" and he grasped at his breast as if he would fain tear out the throbbing heart within, and hurl it into the sea. Then he turned suddenly, and plunged down the stairway.

"God!" murmured Baillot, "why are such beings born? To torture and be tortured in this life, and afterward—endlessly? I cannot believe it. There must be some other solution."

He now took a turn about the vessel, looking keenly at every part in the gray light of the dawn, which struggled through a dense mist. The wind had fallen, and the ship with most of her canvas set was plunging through the green water at a good rate of speed. Several sailors who were lounging about the deck looked curiously at the young man, and one of them touched his forehead with some show of respect. This man, after a whispered word or two with his companions, presently advanced boldly and planted himself directly in front of Baillot, a number of the sailors following close at his heels.

He was a gigantic fellow, as the young officer observed during the pause which followed, in which the sailor appeared to be endeavoring in a slow ox-like fashion to determine what it was best to say to the man who confronted him. Baillot further observed his great head thatched with a profusion of thick yellow curls like those of a child, also his light blue eyes, driven to a pin-point by the fierce sea winds, and looking, he thought, curiously out of place in the broad weather-beaten face. He perceived that the man had been put forward by his fellows as spokesman on account of his enormous strength. Glancing quickly over his shoulder he saw that a second grinning group had collected at his back. He was in a position of extreme peril, and fully realized it.

Without any appearance of haste or fear he shifted his position, so that he stood with his back to the rail, thus commanding a view of both groups of sailors.

"Jorgesen's too slow by half," growled one of the sailors with a ferocious oath. "Come, why don't you speak up, mate!"

"Where is our captain?" said the Scandinavian slowly, pushing up the sleeves of his jacket, and revealing great knotted arms, on which were depicted a number of cabalistic designs in the highest fashion of the tattooer's art. Baillot noticed these designs, and remembered them accurately afterward.

"I am your captain, man, for the balance of this cruise," he replied coolly. "Afterward you may choose whom you will, and go where you will."

"Ay, ay! But wot's to hender our doin' that now?" sang out one of the group on the left.

"Whar's Lock? Whar's Mateo?" bawled a chorus of other voices.

"What has happened to Lock and Mateo will happen to all of you, if you do not obey," said Baillot firmly. "Lock was second mate," he continued.

"Ay, and a pretty second mate he made!" growled the Scandinavian.

"I appoint you, Jorgesen, second mate in his stead."

"Who will be boson in my place?" asked the Scandinavian, evidently pleased with his promotion.

"Goujet shall determine that question. Now, my men," he continued, looking about him keenly, "this is going to be the best cruise you ever made—no rope's end, no abuse, and a plenty of plum-duff, as long as I am in command."

"Ay!" growled an oldish man, "and look you, no guzzling below in the cabin, while we go dry above."

Baillot was congratulating himself that the threatened storm had blown over as suddenly as had the squall of the night before, when some one repeated the threatening cry:

"Whar's Lock? Whar's Mateo?"

But the Scandinavian came unexpectedly to his relief in his new dignity of second mate.

"Never ye mind, ye lazy lubbers!" he bellowed in a voice of thunder. "I'm second mate here, I'd have ye to know. Get ye about your business lively, or I'll show ye a thing or two that undersized English dog couldn't."

The breeze was freshening, and the mist, rent in twain like a ragged robe, showed here and there through its openings vivid glimpses of sky and ocean. In one of these rents which opened upon the right of the vessel, Baillot on a sudden discovered the towering masts and gleaming hull of a man-of-war. At the same instant her lookout must have descried the pirate, for as the mist again closed over the sea in that quarter there came a long hail across the water.

"Clap on every rag of canvas!" commanded Baillot. "Call Goujet to the deck," he added.

The sailors hesitated. "Why not fight?" said one sullenly.

"Fight! With yonder man-of-war? She carries at least forty guns, man! We should be blown out of water like a kite!"

Again came the bellow of the speaking-trumpet. "She is hailing us to lay to, in order to board us!" growled the Scandinavian. "Guess you're right, sir. We're fitter for plucking a merchantman, than for trying a brush with a man-of-war."

The rigging was swarming with men by this time, and the vessel with every sail drawing, sped through the water like a thing of life.

"What has happened, master?" said Goujet approaching. "*Morbleu!*" he ejaculated, as the mist again lifted revealing the stately vessel. "If she gets a chance at us with her broadside we're done for!"

"We must get out of range before she can wing us," said Baillot; "'tis our only chance."

A shot which struck the water so near the ship that the spray flew into their faces, showed that the Englishman perceived their design of running away and meant to prevent it.

"A stern chase is a long chase," growled Goujet, "and I'm willing to bet my head that yonder lumbering hulk can't sail with the *Rouge et Noir*. What do you say to passing on the compliment with our guns, sir?"

"By all means, salute her as cordially as you please,"

252

said Baillot. "She intends business as you see." He lifted the glass which Goujet had handed him and anxiously scrutinized the vessel.

Then a cry of astonishment escaped him. He had caught sight of the gilded lettering which ran about her bow. What he read was this, *The Conqueror.*

CHAPTER XXXI

A VOICE OUT OF THE STORM

THE marine who was performing the duty of sentry about the cottage being, as a scientist would put it, a man whose nerve-fibers did not carry outside impressions with sufficient swiftness to the cortex of his cerebrum; in common parlance, being somewhat slow and stupid, stood for a moment staring open-mouthed in the direction from which had proceeded the crashing sound, which, as we know, was occasioned by the fall of the unfortunate Winters from the trunk of the pine tree.

Winters, luckily had been provided by nature with quite a different sort of mechanism; his nerve-fibers instantly telegraphed the mishap to his brain, and his brain responded by suggesting a retreat. Lying quite flat upon his belly he began to crawl serpent-wise, in a fashion which he had acquired in his youth from a close observation of the ways of the American Indian. So it chanced that by the time the slow-witted marine had bethought himself to fire his carbine in the direction of the noise, the quick-witted sailor was quite out of range, and approaching the edge of the thicket into which he had fallen. Once there he arose to his feet, and began to run swiftly toward the hidden retreat, swearing angrily to himself as he went.

"May I be everlastin'ly chalked for a loafin', fat-headed land-lubber!" he grumbled. "It's time I was buried, ay—buried an' et up by earthworms! Jack Win-

ters, I hope to the Lord you git shook off into the sea,
an' drownded the next time ye set foot on ship-board.
I'm ashamed of ye through an' through for a blarsted
butter-fingered, fumblin' old swab, ay, that I be !''

His indignation with himself however did not prevent
his getting over the ground with remarkable celerity.
So that by the time it had further occurred to the sentry
to arouse his superior officer and communicate to him
his suspicions, Winters had well-nigh reached the asylum
of the cavern. In fact he might already have been there,
but mindful of a painful sensation of emptiness in that
region of his body which should at this time have been
comfortably occupied in the digestion of his supper, and
chancing to pass through the orange orchard, where the
ripe fruit lay upon the ground in profusion, he stopped
for a moment to fill his pockets and the bulge of his
seaman's blouse with the juicy spheres.

"Poor provender for starvin' men," he muttered, as
he stuffed a dozen or so into the crown of his hat. "But
a blamed sight better'n nothin'.''

He found Constantin Dinant standing guard over the
grated door, and was instantly admitted.

"Where is de Langres?'' demanded the Huguenot
with visible anxiety.

"In the pine tree, unless they have hauled him down
by this time," said the sailor. Then with a groan he
added, "Consarn it ! kick me, will ye ; kick me from
here to the cave yonder. I need it, an' I'm blamed if
I don't think it would make me feel a sight better.''

"What do you mean, friend?'' asked Croissart.

"What do I mean? I mean that Jack Winters, able
seaman—*able* seaman, mind you—who ought to be able
to hang with his toe-nails to the under side of a pane of

glass, tumbled—ay, tumbled, like a blarsted, fresh-water lubber offen the trunk of that pine tree yonder into the bushes, an' was 'bleeged to sneak off to save his blamed old hide—that's what I mean. Lord! I'd take a tannin' with a cat-o'-nine-tails with as much pleasure as I'd eat supper arter such a cussed—"

"Hold, friend," said the old pastor severely, "your language is unseemly.—But what have you here?" catching sight as he spoke of the oranges.

Without a word the old sailor unburdened himself of an astonishing amount of the fruit, which he heaped upon the floor.

The Huguenot pastor regarded it with glistening eyes. "You are blaming yourself for your fall," he said, "and yet it may have saved our lives. We be starving men, and not strong to bear up, by reason of the fatigues and labors which have been our lot of late. Thank God for this mercy!"

In the meantime St. André de Langres, who had succeeded in reaching a place of comparative security in the lower branches of the pine, found himself in a sad quandary.

"If I advance to the shelter of the crow's nest," he thought, "the shock of my unexpected appearance would probably bring forth a shriek from one of the women, which would be fatal to all of us. If I remain where I am, I shall certainly be seen, if they bring torches underneath the tree."

He presently took advantage of the confusion which ensued in the camp to climb up somewhat further into the tree, where he hoped to be out of sight among the branches. His anxiety about Winters was intense, and still more unbearable was his fear for those who had been left in the tree-tops. He was shortly relieved in a measure from at least one of these anxieties. There was certainly some one in the retreat above his head, for he could hear a slight unmistakable sound as of one moving cautiously about. This was instantly hushed as two or three of the marines dashed forward armed with torches, and began a hasty search in the thicket at the foot of the tree. The search proving fruitless, St. André derived some faint satisfaction from overhearing the following conversation which took place between the sentry, Pierre, the sergeant, and lieutenants de Loignac and de Morney, who had been aroused from their slumbers in the cottage at the first alarm.

"What did you say the sound was like, you infernal blockhead?" said de Loignac, addressing the sentry.

"'Twas a crackling noise, sir," said the man, in evident terror of the scowling officers who confronted him, "—crackling, and yet at the same time heavy. It might have been a—a cow."

"You fired at it, you say?"

"Yes, sir, I fired at it,"—then with increasing cheerfulness, born of confidence—"It could not then, sir, have been a cow, else—"

"The devil take you to perdition—if he have use for such a fool in the infernal regions!" exclaimed de Loignac impatiently. "There was evidently no cow in the case, but only a very long-eared ass."

"Had it been an ass, sir, it would doubtless have brayed," quoth the sentry seriously.

"Quit braying!" shouted de Loignac, laughing in spite of himself. "What in thunder could it have been?" he demanded, turning to his companion, who was yawning dismally.

"*Sacre bleu!* How should I know? Perhaps one of those fool Huguenots spying about. We'll dispose of them along with the others to-morrow if they fall into our hands, if not—why, *voila!* we maroon them. · After we have burnt the cottages and destroyed the live stock, there'll be precious little left on this spot of earth. They can occupy themselves with burying what we leave behind; after that, *tiens!* Let them live till they die one by one. I'll not spend another hour here for the sake of catching the worthless beggars."

"Can we get off to morrow?"

"Why not? Our gracious master will hardly visit the spot to see whether all is to his liking."

"*Peste!* de Morney. You are imprudent," with a significant gesture toward the others of the group who were listening open-mouthed to this conversation.

"Let them dare!" replied de Morney, with a menacing scowl. "But, *diable!* I am sleepy. Post a double sentry, sergeant, and don't call us the next time you hear an owl hoot."

There was certainly cause for rejoicing in all this, thought St. André. The search given over, the island abandoned, surely they would be able to devise some way in which to live until such time as they should be rescued. "God will not forsake his children," said the young Huguenot with the devout faith of his people. His rejoicings, however, would have been changed to fear could he have heard the continuation of the conversation between the two officers, as they sauntered back to their quarters in the cottage.

"A devilish nasty business this, putting the convicts to death!" said de Morney. "By Jove, I'm not a professional assassin!"

258

A VOICE OUT OF THE STORM

"No," sneered de Loignac. "You're only a professional lady-killer and dandy."

"We're to settle that matter later, you know," replied de Morney, with an air of imperturbable good nature. "But, *ma foi!* I have a better plan; what do you say to leaving the convicts alive?"

"What?"

"Leave them alive, I say. You know they hate the Huguenots like poison. They'd fight like wild animals till they made an end of each other."

"They would, but we shouldn't be here to see."

"Pooh! One must provide for the amusement of others sometimes. Now I'm unselfishly inclined to give these poor fellows a little fun. Picture to yourself the Huguenots, thinking the coast clear, thrusting out their sneaking white faces from some rat-hole where they've hidden themselves, and getting a dose from the brawny fellows yonder. A pretty sight—eh? 'twould remind one of arenas, gladiators, wild-beast shows, and that sort of thing."

"But I tell you we shouldn't be here to see it."

"Why, my dear fellow, I'll leave you with all the pleasure in life. You shall witness the combat, award the laurel-wreaths, and—"

"Suppose *I* leave *you*—'tis your suggestion. Your lily fingers would wreath the laurel more deftly than mine; then you might perform the funeral orations when all was over. You were born a few centuries too late, de Morney. You should have been a Roman."

De Morney made no reply, but it was plain that he was furiously angry at the taunt.

De Loignac eyed him curiously for a moment, then he burst into a loud laugh. "If we should get sufficiently

259

angry to knife each other before we leave the island,"
he said at length, "it would please some people mightily."

"True," replied de Morney coolly, "and therefore I
am biding my time; 'twill suit me far better to finish
the matter later. Let us drop the subject.—You speak
in such a confoundedly common way, 'knife each other!'
I am no bandit."

For some hours nothing further occurred to disturb
the encampment about the fire. The two sentries
marched back and forth monotonously; the convicts
tossed and muttered in their sleep; and the young Huguenot, not daring to drowse on his giddy perch, sat
open-eyed, thinking of many things. The hours betwixt
midnight and dawn dragged slowly by. Towards
morning a thunder-shower came up, the wind blew violently, so that the great trees groaned and twisted, and
lashed their giant branches to and fro. The low black-
bellied clouds belched forth great sheets of flame and the
sound of the thunder was deafening. Then followed
the rain, a drenching, smothering downpour.

St. André had ventured by this time to ensconce himself upon the stairway which led up to the singular structure above. He was greatly worried lest the crow's
nest should be too frail to endure the fearful stress of the
wind. He could distinctly hear the creaking of the timbers and the cracking and straining of the fastenings. It
was very dark. The fire which had been smouldering
dully was almost extinguished by the pouring rain; he
could hear the impatient mutterings of the men below.
Finally taking advantage of the darkness and the all-
pervading noise of the storm, he crept cautiously up the
ladder He had almost reached the platform when he

paused for a moment; he was sure that he could hear the sound of a voice in low rapid speech. He went on a few steps, his head was now on a level with the crow's nest. He had not been mistaken; there was a voice, he caught the words.

"—We know that we are as safe in this wind-tossed tree-top as under the peaceful roof of home. But oh Lord, —merciful Father, we be but women; have mercy upon us, and abate the violence of the storm, we beseech thee!"

His heart leapt to his throat. It was his mother's voice! She was praying in the extremity of her terror. How well he remembered her white face when she had reassured him, a trembling child, amid the terrifying grandeur of a thunder-storm. "Are you not afraid, mother?" he would say; and she would make answer, "The body of my flesh trembles before the majesty of the power of God. But surely there is nothing for his children to fear; we are as ever under the shadow of his wings—safe."

The sound of the praying voice continued, "My son, O Lord! thou knowest where he is; he is thine. If he be living, grant him peace and an unfaltering trust in thy sure providence, though the ways of his life look dark above him as the clouds above our heads. Restore him to us in thine own good time, we beseech thee!"

"Mother!"

"I heard a voice—out of the storm!" said Madeline with a faint sob. "It was—oh mother—it was the voice of St. André!"

"I have come back to you," said St. André softly. "Do not be frightened! I am alive and well. It is God's good time!"

261

CHAPTER XXXII

IF anyone of the little party in the tree-tops thought again of the storm, which was still raging about them with unabated fury, it was only to thank God for it, since the shock of the thunder and the booming of the rain served to cover the sound of their rejoicings. After the wanderer, who had been so strangely restored to them had told his story, they had time to think of the brave old sailor, to whom curiously enough all owed their present comparative safety if not their lives.

"They did not capture him," said St. André, "of that I am sure, for I heard all that passed. I trust that he is with the others in the cave. These men will leave the island to-day," he added, "then we shall be safe for the present."

"Ah, thank God!" sighed Madeline. "But I can never forget these frightful days; since the good sailor —our last friend save Cato here—disappeared, we have existed in one long agony of fear."

"Fear of which I am heartily ashamed," said Madame de Langres wiping the happy tears from her eyes. "Why, why are we so ungrateful, and suspicious of God's purposes? I shall never be so again."

"I am afraid that I shall," said Madeline, smiling to herself in the dark, as she leaned her head against her brother's shoulder. "I am too much like a very bad child, and I forget so easily ; but I believe that the Father loves us in spite of our follies."

The storm had now abated so that they were forced to stop talking. Cato with the noiselessness of a mouse had overhauled their stock of eatables, and de Langres seeing the food remembered that he was starving.

"I fear that I shall make great inroads upon your slender store," he said in a whisper; "I have eaten nothing for six-and-thirty hours."

"No fear of that," said Madame de Langres, leaning forward to caress with a trembling hand the long unkempt locks which hung about the young man's haggard face. Her maternal soul was wrung within her at sight of the change which a few short months had wrought. And he, on his part, was not less moved by the tear-dimmed eyes, and whitened hair of his mother. His pretty little mother, he had been wont to call her in the happy peaceful days of the past. "She shall be happy again," he resolved; "that shall be my care."

A general commotion in the camp below, now announced the beginning of the day's activities. The convicts were aroused, counted, and provided with their miserable rations. Madame de Langres shuddered as she looked down at them, and tightened her grasp on her son's hand. He had been one of them. He too had been driven forth as a beast to labor. Ah, God was good ! She would remember !

The officers now came out from the cottage, talking and gesticulating violently.

"Fetch pitch and tow, and whatever you have that is inflammable," commanded de Loignac, "and set these cottages afire. We must get away to-day; we have already outstayed our time. The loss of those accursed Huguenots put us back at least two days.''

"Do you purpose to abandon the island without finding them, sir?" asked Pierre respectfully.

"What business is that of yours," growled de Loignac; "is it your place to question? What say you, de Morney, shall we leave our valuable sergeant along with the convicts to continue the search?"

"It might be well," replied that gentleman, who was gently whistling a tune from the latest opera. "He has given us considerable trouble from time to time. It would teach him a lesson—though to be sure he would hardly have opportunity to avail himself of its valuable effects on his character."

"What—what do you mean, honored sirs?" stammered the sergeant, whitening visibly beneath his tan. "I have not meant—I am sure that I have tried to do my full duty."

"Yes?" sneered de Morney, "*Voila!* Continue then to obey. Here you, Gaston, fetch out our toilet-cases and the portmanteaux from the cottage. Take them to the ship; tell the captain that we shall come on board presently. If he has not already laid in sufficient fresh water, fruit and vegetables for the voyage, he must do so at once."

"And the convicts, sir," said Pierre, who had apparently recovered himself. "What shall they do?"

De Morney glanced carelessly at the group of men, some forty in all, who stood at a little distance under guard of the marines. He twisted his mustaches thoughtfully, as he studied one by one the cruel, beast-like faces. "The convicts?" he said slowly. "Attend

sergeant !" and he whispered some order into the ear
of Pierre.

"Ay, ay, sir !" said the sergeant stolidly. Then he
turned to the marines. "March them toward the château !" he commanded.

More marines now appeared bearing combustibles, and
shortly to the great regret of the anxious watchers in
the pine trees, the cottage which had sheltered them so
pleasantly during the past few months lay in smoking
ruins. A little further away among the trees, arose a
second smother of smoke and flame which announced
the demolition of the laborers' huts, together with the
barns and out-buildings. And now cries of pain, and
the wild lowing of cattle proclaimed that the domestic
animals, which had so long dwelt in peaceful happiness
amid the groves and meadows, were being driven out
and ruthlessly slaughtered. Madeline could hardly re-
strain her indignation when one of the marines roughly
caught and held up at arm's length the little spaniel,
which she had been forced to leave below.

"What about this little beast !" he shouted ; "shall
I kill him ?"

"Of course," said Pierre ; "you know the orders."

"Hold hard, fellow !" cried de Morney, who was
personally superintending the slaughter. "Let me have
a look at the beast. No—" he said after a careful examination of the dog, "this is a valuable animal ; I shall
keep it."

It was now late in the afternoon. St. André had
kept a close watch upon the ship, and about five o'clock
he announced that the preparations for departure were
unquestionably complete. Boats, laden with fresh water,
fruits, and the choicer parts of the slaughtered animals,

had been plying between the island and the ship all day ; but these had all been drawn up to their places, and there was no further sign of human presence upon the island. "; I believe that they are all aboard," he said, dropping the glass.

"Now de Lord be bressed !" exclaimed Cato loudly. "I ain't dared breeve for mor'n a week. Halleluia ! Amen !" The old man brought out the last two words with astounding emphasis, and had opened his mouth for a continuation of his fervid rejoicings, when Madeline seized him by the arm.

"Hush ! I am sure that I heard some one talking !" All listened intently.

"I think you are mistaken, my child," began Madame de Langres, with a relieved look on her worn face. Then she stopped suddenly.

There was an unmistakable sound of human voices ; presently two men came into view. They were instantly recognized by the watchers as the officers in charge of this singular expedition. They were evidently engaged in taking a last survey of the island preparatory to abandoning it ; two armed marines followed them at a little distance.

"I tell you," declared de Loignac, as the party paused for an instant under the pines, "that I heard a voice shouting *amen !* If we could but root out those palavering hypocrites, together with that mythical Englishman before leaving the place—I say mythical, for I believe that the whole story of his find was a lie invented by those two scoundrels, Pierre and Gaston, for the purpose of covering their cursed carelessness."

"A clumsy enough lie !" replied the other, lighting a cigar.

"Clumsy enough, yes; but lying—that is to say artistic, soul-convincing deceit, the variety that carries compelling belief in its train—is one of the fine arts. One could scarcely expect a clod like Pierre to have mastered it."

De Morney emitted a cloud of tobacco smoke before replying, then he laughed sarcastically. "You should add, my friend, that the art of lying is a special gift bestowed by the prince of darkness upon his votaries,—the father of lies is, I believe, a good orthodox name for his infernal highness—and further, that one gains skill and address therein by practice and by a faithful and devout attention to the secret spiritual admonitions of *le bon diable* and his emissaries."

"You should have been an abbé, de Morney. Your exposition is positively edifying. But, *morbleu!* speaking of the devil—what is that?"

De Loignac as he spoke had glanced up carelessly into the branches above his head. Now it chanced unhappily that the storm in its fury had torn away a part of the great tree; de Loignac had therefore caught a glimpse of the black face of Cato as he leaned over the side of the crow's nest, horrified at the scandalous talk of the two officers. He had instantly withdrawn his head upon hearing the exclamation of de Loignac, and crouched behind the shelter of the low railing, absolutely paralyzed with fear. Madame de Langres and Madeline convulsively clutched each other by the hand, and listened breathlessly for the next words from below.

"What do you mean?" said de Morney, looking up in his turn. "I see nothing. No, by Jove! there is something curious up there. It can hardly be the convicts; but suppose we try the effect of a shot in that direction."

Snatching a carbine from one of the marines he raised it and fired directly upward. The shot passed through the floor carrying away a fragment of Madeline's gown and buried itself in the trunk of the tree.

The young girl sank back half-fainting against her mother's shoulder, but not a sound escaped her lips.

"What did you see anyhow?" inquired de Morney, after he had paused a moment to observe the effect of his random assault.

"I caught but a single glimpse," confessed de Loignac, "but it looked to me like the face of a black man, with monstrous staring eyes."

De Morney burst into a laugh. "Did you never see a monkey, man?—one of those man-faced apes I mean."

"Do you suppose it was that?" said de Loignac doubtfully. "I couldn't swear that it was not, though so far I have seen nothing of the sort on the island. It looks rather unnatural up there to me," he continued, staring fixedly into the branches. "I believe I'll send one of the men up to see. I say, you Vonard, get up that tree in a hurry and see what's above."

The marine handed his carbine to his fellow without a word, and divested himself of his jacket.

St. André arose to his feet noiselessly, and looked about him, then he stooped over the shivering, crouching negro. "Have you any weapon?" he whispered in his ear.

The negro looked up. His face was ashen; he seemed unable to speak.

"Answer!" said St. André, with a menacing gesture, "or by the Lord, I'll throw you down to them!"

This threat acted at once as a mental tonic; raising one shaking hand, the unfortunate Cato pointed to the cupboard. St. André reached it with a single noiseless stride, and discovered therein a sharp two-edged knife, a brace of which Winters had taken the precaution to bring from the wreck of the *White Gull*, and one of which he had thoughtfully placed among the stores of the crow's nest. Cato had too evidently made use of this knife in his culinary operations, and St. André passing his thumb along the edge of the blade, frowned darkly.

"But I will kill him!" he whispered between his shut teeth. "I will kill them all!" He looked at his mother and Madeline, and felt the strength of ten men animate his body, as he thought what would follow should they be captured.

The marine had by this time reached the lower branches of the tree where he discovered the stairway which led up to the retreat above. He uttered a slight cry of surprise, then instead of advancing, began a swift retreat.

"What are you coming down for, coward?" shouted de Loignac.

The man had by this time reached the ground. "I thought it more prudent to consult you, sir," he said in a low voice; "there may be a dozen armed men concealed above." And he proceeded to acquaint the officers with what he had seen.

CHAPTER XXXIII

"A PEST on you for a cowardly fool!" began de Loignac in a violent rage. "Had there been armed men up there, we would have heard of it before this. The stairway is no new device, man. Get you up quickly, or I shall assist you in a way that you will not relish."

The marine with a sullen look prepared to obey. "Give me your pistol, sir," he said. "I shall not be able to carry my carbine."

De Morney who had calmly continued to smoke during this conversation tossed the fragment of his cigar aside. He had in the meantime been studying the structure in the tree-tops from various points of view.

"I don't blame the fellow for not wanting to go up," he said at length; "and I am not sure but that we are exposing ourselves needlessly to stand here. Suppose we hold a council of war yonder. A party of marines with axes would be more to the point, I fancy."

"But the men are all on board," objected de Loignac impatiently, "and we must get off by the next tide."

"There's no 'must' about it, to-morrow morning would do quite as well. If Vonard finds a wasps' nest aloft, and gets badly stung, *voila !* the wasps' nest must come down!"

Vonard by this time had reached the wooden ladder, and holding the pistol in one hand, began the ascent.

St. André crouched behind the railing.

Step by step the marine advanced. He was afraid, as was evidenced by his slow, hesitating approach. St. André remained motionless until the man had reached the platform, where he stood for a moment looking about him in surprise, then his eye fell upon Cato; he advanced with a cry, raising his hand as if to fire.

This was what St. André had counted upon. He sprang up with a bound, knocked the pistol out of the man's hand, then seizing him under the armpits hurled him violently over the ledge. The unfortunate marine uttered a loud cry, and spread abroad his hands in a vain endeavor to save himself; crashing twice or thrice with a dull thud upon the intervening branches he fell down—down—down, striking the ground with a horrible sound at the very feet of the two officers.

De Loignac started back with an oath, but de Morney turned the body over with his foot, using it gingerly lest he should soil his polished boot.

"He is quite dead," he said coldly at length, "—neck broken for one thing. Will you take my advice now, or will you send up the other man?"

"I will go up myself!" cried de Loignac; "the fellow was a slow-witted fool!"

"Ah," said de Morney nonchalantly, lifting his eyebrows, "then is our duel off? I rather regret—"

"What do you mean?" interrupted the other roughly.

"Nothing, only that there are better ways of dying than this," and he again carelessly nudged the body of the dead Vonard with the toe of his boot.

De Loignac tugged savagely at his mustaches. "Come on," he said at length; "we will return to the ship for assistance."

"And leave the occupants of the tree to escape in our absence?" said de Morney, shrugging his shoulders.

"Some one must go. There are only three of us—"

"Send the marine. You and I will make an ambuscade to pick off any who may try to descend."

"*Bon!*—But what is that? The signal gun! one—two—three—*four! Immediate return!* What can it be?"

"We must return and see."

"And leave the tree unguarded?"

"*Certes*, it may after all be only an ape. The creatures are immensely strong, and inconceivably quick."

"And Vonard, poor devil, was inconceivably slow. We must take him."

"Pah! we shall soil our hands."

"Let Gaspard take him over his shoulders."

So in this fashion, to the great surprise of St. André, who was watching their movements with feelings which may be better imagined than described, the three set forth. After what seemed an age he saw their boat creeping like a snail across the water in the direction of the vessel.

He had not been able to hear the latter part of the conversation, and fancied that they had only returned for men to cut down the trees. He therefore approached the women, who were still crouching in a state of semi-insensibility behind their screen of blankets.

"How did you get up here?" he demanded of Madeline?

"By a rope-ladder," replied the young girl faintly. Then raising her head, "Are they there still?"

"No, they have gone; but only to fetch axes to cut

272

down the trees. We must hasten! Where is the rope-ladder?"

"At the foot of the stairway, I suppose. Mr. Winters drew it up."

"Yes, I understand. I will let it down. Give mother something to revive her. Be quick!"

Descending the stairway, the young man found the rope-ladder, coiled up and tied to the limb, just as Winters had left it. He unfastened it, descended and made it taut at its lower end, then he hurried back to where the women were awaiting him; glancing at the ship, he was amazed to see it with every stitch of canvas spread, apparently getting under way. He caught up the glass in astonishment.

"There is another ship," said Madeline breathlessly. "I see no boat; can it be that they have left, not meaning to return?"

"They have been forced to leave!" cried St. André, dropping the glass. "If I am not very much mistaken yonder sail is that of the enemy; there is also another which I can see by the aid of the glass, possibly the consort of the first. At all events the French ship has deemed it prudent to withdraw."

"Then we are saved!"

"For the present—yes," replied St. André slowly. "But there is one thing concerning which I must satisfy myself before you descend. I should have taken the risk had it appeared that they were to return—but now—" He paused for a moment and knit his brows thoughtfully.

"What do you mean?"

"I mean the convicts," and the young man turned to descend. He paused, however, with his foot on the

18   273

first step of the stairway to say, "I shall haul up the rope-ladder again for the present; I will return as soon as I have reconnoitered a little."

"Oh, brother!" begged Madeline, clasping her hands in sudden terror, "suppose the convicts—"

"You are already forgetting, little sister," said St. André with a grave smile. "I am armed and they are not," he added, pointing to de Loignac's pistol. "Courage! I shall be with you before you have time to fear."

The young man prudently resolved to first visit the cavern, and acquaint his companions who were imprisoned there with the course which events had taken. But Winters had already seen the departure of the vessel from his post of observation, and burning with impatience and anxiety, was on his way to the great trees to look after the safety of those whom he had left behind when he descended upon the tour of investigation which had been fraught with such momentous results.

He was accompanied by the five Huguenots, and when St. André spied them, all six were bending over some object which was lying upon the ground. As the young man hurriedly approached them, he perceived that the object of their attention was the body of a man lying flat upon his face.

"God be thanked, you are safe!" exclaimed the Huguenot pastor devoutly as he caught sight of St. André—"and the others?"

"They too are safe," replied the young man.

"Are they—?"

"Yes, my mother and my sister," said St. André.

"Wonderful providence of the Most High! Truly

274

the Lord reigneth; He delighteth himself in mercy, Alleluia!"

"This 'ere man ain't dead," put in Winters, with his accustomed irrelevancy. "I can hear him breathe."

St. André looked attentively at the body. It stirred slightly; he stooped and turned it over. "It is the convict who threatened to betray us!" he exclaimed. "Where are the others?"

Winters jerked his thumb over his shoulder by way of reply, and St. André following the motion, was horrified at the sight of an indiscriminate heap of dead bodies, lying in ghastly confusion in a hollow place at the foot of a knoll; this hollow was literally brimming over with blood.

"Shot!" explained Winters briefly. "—This fellow wa'n't killed outright an' dragged himself away. He'll live if we take care of him. Shall we do it?"

The Huguenot pastor frowned. "Do you ask that question, son of Belial," he said severely, "after the wonderful display of divine mercy and providence which we have just witnessed? Were it not for the intervention of the potent arm of the Almighty you also would be lying dead in yonder pool of blood."

"Wall," said Winters scratching his head reflectively, "I might, then agin I might not. When folks talk about proverdunce that way, a thankin' God that they was presarved when other folks wa'n't, I allers think about that sayin', 'The early bird catches the worm;' thar's the worm, you know—an' like as not an all-fired good industrious worm—as gits caught. In this 'ere case, we're saved, the fellows yonder are shot, what's the reason?"

"They were sinful men—" began the Huguenot.

"So be I!" cut in Winters, grinning cheerfully. "You jes' called me a son of Belial; an' here's this old cuss on the ground, the wust one of the lot, as 'ud knife us all if he got a chance an' it was to his betterin'."

The Huguenot pastor looked down at the face of the unconscious man. "It may be," he said thoughtfully, "that even we may prove humble instruments in God's hand to snatch this poor sinner as a brand from the burning. But we must first attend to his physical hurts. Alas! that all is destroyed; we have now neither food nor shelter."

"Thar's the cave, parson," said Winters; "as for victuals, we'll find a plenty. But these 'ere bodies must be got underground as soon as possible. It won't do to have the women-folks see anything of the sort."

"I will return to the tree and reassure them of safety," said St. André.

"Thar's a heap to do for everybody," quoth Winters. "If you've no objections, sir, I'd like to git up that tree myself. I want to take a partin' look at the ship through the glass, an' notice which way she's headed. If they ain't made ducks an' drakes of the yacht—as I make no doubt they have—we'll be settin' sail ourselves some fine day."

"She's headed nor' by nor'west," said de Langres, "but visit the crow's nest by all means; my mother and sister are longing to see you with their own eyes. They have not forgotten to whom they owe everything; nor have I," he added, grasping the old sailor by the hand.

"Why, blow me, sir, I ain't done nothin' wuth mentioning," replied Winters; "couldn't do less anyhow; I made that there crow's nest as much for myself as for anybody. I kind of blundered into a good job, that's all. The parson here'll explain how 'tis that a son of Belial—that's me—sometimes does blunder that way." The old man's eyes glistened as he spoke, and he drew his jacket-sleeve across his eyes. "Guess I'll git along," he added, "whilst he's explainin' of it. I don't know how it is, but too much religion allers makes me sassy."

CHAPTER XXXIV

AT St. André's request nothing was said to either of the women concerning the massacre of the convicts. "They have had horrors enough to bear," declared the young man.

The presence of the wounded convict the women attributed to an accident, and addressed themselves with zeal to the task of nursing him back to health. The man had shortly recovered consciousness, but seemed disinclined to speak, which was thought to be one of the unfortunate effects of his wound.

Madeline was delighted with the cave, for as the story of the mysterious dead man had also been suppressed, the place had no unpleasant associations for her. "What a charmingly mysterious place," she had exclaimed, when introduced to the cavern by its outer entrance. "What could it have been used for; perhaps to bury treasure in, who knows?"

The young girl with her accustomed light-heartedness had already recovered her spirits. "How can I help but be happy?" she cried. "St. André is restored to us, and that dear old Winters, besides our pastor—and who could have dreamed of that? I believe that those wicked men will never return; why should we not remain here, and rebuild the cottage?"

But St. André shook his head. "This is not a place in which to remain," he said gravely.

278

As for Winters he was more bent than ever upon leaving the island. "I ain't for sayin' now, in view of
what's happened, that I wish we'd gone to begin with.
We was kep' for a purpose, as the parson says, an' it
looks reasonable. But it seems to me that as soon as we
can git the yacht in order, we'd best git out of here."
The others agreed with him.

The yacht had fortunately escaped the hands of the
destroyers. It had evidently been visited, and after a
wanton overhauling which left its interior in the wildest
confusion, had been set on fire. But for some reason or
other the fire had gone out after doing but little damage.
Luckily no one had taken the pains to make sure of its
destruction, so that to the great joy and relief of Winters he had found the little vessel comparatively uninjured.

"I'm for holdin' a special praise-meetin' over this little craft!" he cried joyfully. The old man had adopted
the religious tone of his companions with a fervor which
brought a smile to the grave faces of the Huguenots
more than once, commingled as it was with his own peculiar and picturesque profanity. "I'll be blowed if
this ain't—taking it all round—the han'somest thing
the A'mighty has done yit for us poor miserable sin-
ners! I tell ye, prayin's the thing; I'm in for it from
now on! While your askin' for one thing, an' like as
not forgittin' all about suthin' more important, the Lord
jes' throws that in, so to speak. He ain't forgot it.
No, sir!"

The Huguenot pastor soon ceased to rebuke the old
man for his somewhat dubious sayings. He had begun
to understand the simple, childlike and yet wonderfully
shrewd mind of the sailor, and took a deal of quiet pleas-

ure in sounding the depths of his character. He had thrown himself with fervor into the work of refitting the vessel and had thus further advanced himself in his good graces.

"You say that you are an Englishman, friend," he said one day, as the two were busily at work repairing the rigging of the yacht. The sailor had been expatiating at length upon America whither all the Huguenots hoped to arrive at no distant day. "I should have said that you were an American, though I confess to knowing very little about them."

"Wall, I *was* born in England an' no mistake, so I'm an Englishman all right, but I'll tell ye how it was. My father was born in the colonies at Plymouth; he stayed there fightin' Injuns an' raisin' corn till he was 'bout twenty years old, then he went back to England, an' stayed a spell. While he was thar he married his second cousin, an' I was born—in England. Arter that they both came back, an' I was raised in Ameriky. I took to the sea, married an English wife, an' I've been knockin' about ever since—a hard case too most of the time. Reckon I got too much preachin' when I was young. Got set in the stocks once for laughin' out loud in meetin'. The parson he'd preached fur two hours 'bout hell an' damnation, an' all that sort of thing—it never sca't me much anyhow. An' I set there watchin' a fly as was crawlin' up onto the slippery bald head of an old man right in front of me. He was asleep, though he set up and pertended to be listenin' with his eyes shet. He kep' a reachin' up for that fly sort of oneasy like, an' the fly he dodged as cute as a pin. I reckon the devil got arter me, for I laughed right out loud, an' as I say, got set in the stocks fur two hours for an example. I was about fourteen then, an' I took to the sea that very night.''

"Now if you had listened to that sermon——" began the Huguenot gravely.

"Oh yas, if I had listened to that 'ere sermon,'' interrupted the sailor, "I shouldn't have seen the fly; I'd have kep' still 'stead of ha-ha-in' right out in meetin'—— Lord! how they all stared! Prob'ly I should have stayed in Ameriky till I died—might have died young too, along of the Indians. Then whar'd you an' Miss Madeline an' her ma, an' all the rest of ye be?''

"The ways of the Lord are unsearchable and past finding out,'' quoth the pastor meditatively.

"Jes' so,'' commented Winters. "I s'pose one thing 's proverdunce 's much as another. I had to laugh out loud in meetin', an' git set in the stocks, an' knocked about the world, so 's to be on hand for this 'ere job, don't you see!''

"Well, I hardly know about that, friend. Scripture speaks concerning the *over-ruling* providence; that is to say, God is able to subdue even wickedness to his glorious purposes, as in the case of the crucifixion of our blessed Lord.''

"Now you're a gittin' out of my soundin's; it's time to tack, I reckon. What do you think about our friend the convict,—Bovet, he says his name is? Somehow I don't feel altogether safe 'bout him. He's too quiet by half, an' there 's a look in his eye that I don't like.''

"I hardly know what to say in answer to that question,'' replied the Huguenot thoughtfully. "I have endeavored to talk with the man twice or thrice, but he had very little to say for himself. I had hoped that mademoiselle might influence him; he seems disposed to listen to her more attentively than to anyone else."

"Humph!" ejaculated Winters, pulling away at the cordage with a grim expression upon his countenance which might mean anything or nothing. "Wall, sir! I'll tell ye what I think," he burst out at length. "I think the fellow is a brute beast; a heap more to be feared than any tiger that ever sneaked in the jungle. If I had my way about it, he'd 'a been whar he belongs 'afore this time, an' that ain't in heaven. But since we've gone and done the good Samaritan act, and got him all nussed up, I reckon we'd better do two things, first, make him work day times—"

"But he still complains of pain in the region of his wound," objected the old minister mildly.

"Yer granny!—'xcuse me, sir—he's jest a playin' off. He's all right, an' able enough to work. The second thing I was goin' to mention is, that I think as how he ought to be chained up nights. What's to hinder him from murderin' every mother's son of us while we're asleep?"

"What object could the man have in so doing?" questioned the Huguenot, looking troubled; "his own safety certainly depends in a measure upon us."

"Does a mad dog think? does a tiger reason things out, sir? I tell ye he ain't human, an' he ain't fit to be loose."

"I believe that you are wrong, friend," persisted the Huguenot. Nevertheless he observed the man, Bovet, that night more narrowly than he had done heretofore. The party, now consisting of the six Huguenots, Winters, Cato, and the two women, making with the wounded convict eleven persons in all, were gathered about the cheerful blaze which it had become the custom to light every evening near the entrance to the cavern.

"We can git off by—say the day after to-morrow," Winters was saying cheerfully. "The parson an' I have got things into pretty good shape aboard the yacht. How have you folks come on with your dried meat, and yer cooked victuals?"

"Mighty well," said Cato triumphantly, to whose experienced hands had been entrusted the victualling of the ship. "Mighty well, an' what's better, we done dug into some of the cellars under the ruin to-day, and found dey was a plenty ob good victuals there yet that wasn't touched by fire nor powder."

Constantin Dinant, whose eyes were thoughtfully fixed upon the man Bovet, was startled to observe the look of wolfish greed which leapt into his eyes as he listened. "Is it possible that the fellow understands English?" thought the minister to himself, feeling somewhat uneasy at the circumstance. The conversation had often been carried on in that language in presence of the convict, for the benefit of Winters to whom French was unintelligible. He now remembered that Winters had repeatedly said before the man, "He won't bother us long— He's the sort to be wanted 'most anywhere," and other remarks of like import. He continued to stare reflectively at the convict, whose small, savage eyes were now fixed upon Madeline with an expression which obviously rendered the young girl uneasy, for she arose at length and crossing to the opposite side of the fire, seated herself near her brother, who was occupied in reading from a small volume which he had found in the cabin of the yacht. The convict smiled, an evil smile, and dropping his head muttered something to himself.

"What are you thinking about, friend?" demanded the pastor, suddenly rising, and standing before the man. He asked the question in English, and the startled look in the eyes of the convict convinced him that he was perfectly understood.

"I—ah—*Je ne vous comprends pas, monsieur.*"

"You are not telling the truth," replied the Huguenot quietly. The convict made no reply, but a murderous fire blazed up in his eyes for an instant, then died away dully.

"*Je ne vous comprends,*" he repeated with a stupid air.

Constantin Dinant turned away, thoughtfully drawing his long silvery beard through his hand. He was decidedly uneasy; deeply versed in the ways of men, with all his far-reaching benevolence he was not lacking in shrewd caution. "Friend Winters is right," he said to himself, "the man is dangerous. I should like for the moment to be able to look behind those green eyes of his." Even as he thought thus within himself that mysterious sixth sense, whose verity has always been rejected as a species of irreligion, flashed so dark a picture before his mental vision that he shrank back appalled. "Lord, why do such visions of guilty passion afflict my soul?" was the mental prayer with which he strove to combat the God-given warning. Yet was he sufficiently moved thereby to approach St. André and request a few moments' conversation aside.

"I am going for fresh water from the spring," he said aloud with a genial smile.

St. André sprang up instantly. "You wished to

284

speak with me?'' he said in a low tone as the two walked away together.

"Yes, I wish to advise that hereafter—as long as we remain upon the island—the women shall pass the night in the crow's nest, as our good friend Winters calls it; you also to guard them.''

"Why is that, sir?'' asked the young man in surprise. "We shall not be here more than two nights longer, and we have removed all of the blankets, together with the hammocks, to the little nook which I have arranged for them in the cave.''

"I know all that, my son, and yet I want you to do it. I fear the man, Bovet, I hardly know why; Winters also distrusts him, and he is a man of remarkable sagacity. He advises to chain him up at night, but we could not do that, it savors too much of the ways of the flesh in dealing with erring humanity. But there could be no harm in taking reasonable precautions, such as removing the women to the tree-tops, *and drawing up the rope-ladder.*''

"It shall be done,'' said St. André looking troubled. " I hope I am not doing wrong in wishing that the bullets of the marines had been better aimed in his case.''

The old minister made no comment upon this speech; he had himself been visited with a similar regret on more than one occasion. "Do not let him know of the change,'' he said simply.

Neither Winters nor the Huguenot pastor slept much during the night. There was something profoundly disturbing in the mental atmosphere, which both men felt acutely. The convict lay a little to one side on the bed which he still preëmpted. He slept soundly to all appearances, so did the others. Shortly after midnight,

Winters who was mentally cursing himself for his wakefulness, heard a slight sound. He sat up and instantly struck a light which he had taken the precaution to have at hand.

"What is it?" whispered Constantin Dinant, starting up at the sound of the flint.

"Nothin', it seems," replied Winters, looking about him. "I thought I heard something—but he is asleep. Consarn it, I am goin' to sleep myself!" he added, apparently much out of temper, and extinguishing the light he lay down once more in his place. He was presently snoring.

About an hour afterward the convict again moved cautiously in his place. This time no sound of striking flint and steel reached his ears. He arose noiselessly to his feet, then paused an instant to listen. He could hear nothing save the heavy breathing of the sleepers.

He smiled to himself in the dark, then reaching under the cover of his bed drew out a long knife.

"Now my fine sailor friend," he said to himself, "and my whining, hypocritical, long-faced comrades—convicts all, I will show you how you shall die without a sound! The girl shall be mine, and I—lord of the island!"

CHAPTER XXXV

In the excitement of the hours which followed neither Baillot nor Goujet gave a single thought to the two men, Lock and Mateo, whom they had left bound and gagged in the inner cabin of the *Rouge et Noir*. As time passed on the sufferings of the luckless captives became almost unbearable. Mateo at length succeeded in freeing his tongue from the gag, and his shrieks and imprecations were something frightful to hear. To his surprise, however, no one heeded him, every soul of the crew being on deck and absorbed in the race between the *Rouge et Noir* and the man-of-war. The English ship continued at intervals to fire her bow guns at the flying brigantine, which responded heartily from her stern; neither did much damage, and Baillot observed with satisfaction that the distance between the two vessels increased rather than lessened with every passing hour.

The prisoners below, hearing the guns, and feeling the trembling of the ship as she drove violently through the water, partly guessed at the state of things.

"Cowards!" hissed the Italian through his closed teeth, "why do dey not fight? Dey should die rather than run were Mateo capitain!" Then he beat his manacled hands together violently and shouted. "Villains! Dogs! Pigs! Come quick, loose me!" ending with a long inarticulate howl of rage.

He had repeated this performance perhaps a score of

287

times, without other result than an increase of his already intolerable thirst, when he heard a fumbling sound at the door outside, which Góujet had taken the pains to lock.

"Open, dear, good friend!" shrieked the Italian, thinking best to change his mode of address. " For de love of all de saints, for de love of heaven, open! I am perishing!"

"But I cannot open; the door is fast;" answered a soft whining voice which Mateo recognized as belonging to a Genoese lad, whom he himself had picked up in port a few months previous, and who officiated on board the *Rouge et Noir* as cook.

His eyes gleamed with satisfaction. "That you, Tito?" he asked in Italian.

"Yes, master. How can I open? Shall I call some one—the mate Goujet, or the new captain?"

"A thousand devils! No! 'tis they who have bound me. Listen, fetch Salmo, together you can force the trumpery door. Quick now! and let no one hear you." Having delivered these commands, Mateo sank back, smiling grimly to himself as he thought what he should do, once loosened from his hateful bonds. He could hear Lock moaning and snuffling dismally from his bunk; his face grew thoughtful. Should he loose him also? Upon mature reflection he decided that he would. Together they could rid themselves of the usurper and of Goujet. "I can settle my little business with the Englishman," he said, "when he is no longer useful to me." Arriving at which satisfactory conclusion, he awaited with all the patience at his command the return of Tito. This was so long delayed that he began to fear lest something had befallen the lad. "The purblind imbecile !'' he muttered to himself. "He has been caught by that villain Goujet,—ah, I could grind him between these teeth like an almond!'' Then he beguiled the moments by stringing together the several oaths of which he was master in Italian, English, French, Portuguese and Spanish, in all of which languages he was sufficiently proficient to swear fluently.

At length he heard steps and voices in the cabin without. There was a violent wrench at the door, a snapping of hinges and screws.

"*Diavolo !* but I am glad to see you !'' he cried, as the door finally yielded. "You Tito, fetch me drink ; I am perishing with thirst. Have you a file, Salmo? I must get loose of these cursed handcuffs.''

"Who has done this thing?'' said Salmo, setting to work with a will at the rusty irons.

"The usurper, who else ? He shall die for it—'' hissed the captive. "The saints interest themselves in me now !'' he added devoutly. "A score of wax candles at the shrine of my patron saint, Giuseppe, if I get loose before they find it out.''

"Never fear, they are too busy watching the English vessel,'' quoth Salmo.

"Is that what they are doing ? Why do they not fight ?''

"Fight with a vessel of war ? You have not seen, my Mateo. We must run and that is all, else we shall dance at the end of a rope ere long. I tell you the new captain understands the matter of handling a ship. *Rouge et Noir* sails like a witch for him.''

"The new captain ! You dare to say the words in my presence? Dog !'' and in a violent rage Mateo struck at the man who was doing his best to liberate him.

19   289

Salmo leapt to his feet with an oath. "The new captain!—Yes! I say it in your presence. And who are you to strike me? ay—and to call me dog! Can a dog use the file? Can a dog liberate you? Can a dog give you drink?"

"No—no—no—good Salmo," whined Mateo, perceiving his mistake. "I meant nothing, I assure you —nothing at all! I am mad with pain and thirst. For the love of heaven now, do not desert a countryman in his extremity!"

Salmo looked at him coldly, but did not resume his labor with the file. "Who is this!" he said, peering in at the bunk where Lock still tossed and moaned uneasily. "See, I will unloose you," he added, removing the gag.

"Water!" gasped the wretched Englishman faintly.

"You shall drink first; the dog wills it," said Salmo, showing his white teeth in a wicked grin, as Mateo writhed in speechless anger. And taking the bottle from Tito he held it to the lips of Lock, who drank greedily.

"Good, sweet Salmo, forgive me! Tito, dear child, give me to drink!" pleaded Mateo, goaded to a frenzy by the cooling glugity-glugity-glug of the liquor as it passed rapidly down the Englishman's capacious throat.

"Am I a dog?" cried Salmo fiercely, "answer me!"

"No—no!" moaned Mateo. "You are a saint—an angel, if you will only give me to drink. I suffer the torments of the damned, I tell you."

"Drink, then," growled Salmo, "but call me dog a second time and you shall go where you shall plead in vain for a drop even of water to cool your accursed tongue."

"Now listen!" exclaimed Mateo, casting aside the bottle after taking a lengthy draught, "both of you work like mad to rid us of our fetters. We are four; we can make ourselves masters of the vessel; the others will obey us. Lock shall be capitaine, if he wills, I care not.—I swear I do not. Only two to put out of the way—only two; the rest will obey us."

"But you cannot handle the vessel as does this man —Baillot, he calls himself," objected Salmo sullenly. "And if we are taken we hang. 'Tis no time for a mutiny."

"As you like, good Salmo. Let him be till this thing is past. But afterward—surely afterward you do not desire him?" Then as Salmo still hesitated he added with a dark look, "You have also forgotten something, my Salmo; you have forgotten—but no? you remember once more!"

Salmo had turned pale; he picked up the file and without a word applied himself to the task of severing the irons with such vigor that in a very few moments Mateo was at liberty.

"Ah!" he whispered to himself, as he paced noiselessly up and down the narrow confines of the cabin, stopping now and again to chafe his stiffened limbs. "Free once more!—Give me your dirk, my Salmo? No? You will not? This poniard will answer," and he plucked one from the wall. "Do not fear me," he continued in a tone as gentle and soothing as that of a woman. "I would not hurt one little black curl on your head, for all you were so cruel to me just now. You do not know Mateo. All is forgotten between us; we are brothers, my Salmo! And Tito here also; thou art a good child, Tito. Fetch us something to eat, little one, Salmo will finish the irons on the Englishman. As for me I am too weak. I must save myself that I may have strength to kill."

"If you kill the man now you make a fool of yourself," said Lock, speaking for the first time.

"What you say?" snarled Mateo, pausing for an instant in his stealthy shamble to glare balefully at the Englishman.

Lock's hands were free now, he reached out for the bottle. "That cursed gag set me on fire within," he remarked, wiping his lips with the back of his hand. "I don't intend to spare the villains," he continued; "but I have a better plan than yours, and a safer. If you will listen to me we shall succeed, if not we shall be dead men before the sun sets. That Goujet is the very devil—and the devil with one arm is stronger than both of us. Hold your infernal chattering tongue if you can till I get through," as Mateo snarled impatiently. "This fellow—Baillot you called him—knows of a treasure."

"Lies!" burst out Mateo.

"But, sink me, suppose that he is not lying; suppose that there is such a treasure? If we kill him now we cannot get it; we do not know where it is. Let us submit to the man until we see, and *then*—What do you say?"

"If he have lied all the crew will turn against him," said Mateo slowly.

"Of course! We shall lose nothing by waiting and we may gain a pretty pocketful. They shall die afterward fast enough; we shall be avenged, and the vessel will be ours. You and I will cast lots for the captaincy, the one who loses shall be first mate."

"But Goujet—"

"Must not clap his eye onto us till we have made all smooth with this fellow Baillot. He's a soft one and will believe whatever we tell him."

"A soft one, you call him?" muttered the Italian, surveying his bruised wrists with a savage grin. "But we must hide, Tito will make us a place. When Goujet goes below we speak to dis capitaine, is it not so?"

"Yes, that is it. We are very sorry—eh? and are going to be very good from now on."

"Si—si. Vary good, I will talk. You shall see what I say."

While this pair of worthies were arranging matters to their satisfaction below decks, Baillot and Goujet were bending all their energies to the difficult task which lay before them.

"A few more minutes will put us completely out of range," remarked Baillot, glancing anxiously aloft at the straining canvas.

"Better go to the bottom with all on board than fall into their hands," growled Goujet who was serving the cannon. "I'd like to get a shot through one of those big sails of theirs," he continued. "Ah! that hit them at last."

"Yes," replied Baillot quietly, "and they have hit us in the hull. Look to it at once; we want no further ballast in the shape of water in the hold."

Goujet disappeared. This was the opportunity for which Mateo and Lock had been waiting; they immediately issued from their hiding-places and approached the young officer.

"My vary good capitaine!" whined Mateo, plucking him gently by the sleeve.

Baillot turned suddenly. "Ah!" as he recognized the swarthy face before him. "How did you get loose? Goujet must look to your case."

"Mercy, good signor!" said the Italian, rolling up his eyes beseechingly. "We are ready to obey. You forgot us; we were dying of thirst."

"True!" exclaimed Baillot, "I did forget you— *Peste!* I would not have treated a dog to such torture. Who loosed you then?"

"Tito, the cook. He is but a child; I am his friend; he obeyed me. See, you will believe me that I obey, for I might have kill you but now!" And the wily Italian displayed the poniard which he had thrust into his belt.

"You got the better of us, cap'n. Sink me, if I don't know when I meet a man of parts," put in Lock. "I'm blest if I want a better cap'n than you, sir. You can count on Peter Lock from now on, and I ain't the worst man aboard either; ask Goujet. Say! You'll speak a good word to the mate for us, won't you, sir? He'll be for hocking us and dropping us over the side."

Goujet had by this time finished his examination of the hull, and bethinking himself of the prisoners, stopped to take a look at them. Finding the broken irons on the floor of the cabin, he came rushing up to the deck filled with the gravest apprehension for his master's safety. He stopped short on beholding the two ruffians apparently engaged in amicable conversation with Baillot.

"What the devil!" he exclaimed under his breath.

"Our prisoners have escaped, you see," said Baillot, eyeing them doubtfully, "but as they declare that they are ready to submit to discipline, we may as well let them be. They were dying with thirst. You see we forgot them, man ; think of the torture of a gag all these hours !"

"*Mon dieu*, they are lying, master! Don't leave them loose as you value your life. Let me drop them astern for the Englishman to fire at !"

" The Englishman must needs fire at something astern of us," said Baillot, "for we are fairly out of range at last ; if we can keep this speed for a few hours longer we are safe. What about the shot below our water-line?"

" It did no damage to speak of, sir," replied Goujet. " I set the carpenter to work to make all secure against a possible leak. But these rascals are like to be worse than ten leaks," he added frowning. " You don't mean to leave them loose, do you, sir?"

" As long as they obey orders—yes," said Baillot firmly. " You, Lock, are degraded from being second mate for the rest of the cruise ; Jorgesen has your place."

The Englishman's small green eyes flashed ominously, but he made no reply beyond a sullen nod of the head.

" Remember," continued Baillot sternly, " that the slightest disobedience will put you into irons again. Next time we shall see to it that you are bestowed where your friends cannot assist you."

" De capitaine shall be obeyed ; I am as the dust under his feet," declared Mateo, showing his white teeth in an amiable smile. "Ah—you do not know Mateo, you shall see how I shall lofe you !"

"You *lofe* me too, don't you?" sneered Goujet.

" You ? *Si, I lofe you like dis!*" hissed the Italian, springing forward with a cry.

There was the keen flash of a poniard, and a sharp cry from Mateo as he whirled over the side of the vessel.

"Lower a boat instantly!" shouted Baillot.

"You are mad, sir! Should we stop to lower a boat all would be over with us!" cried Goujet, grasping him by the arm.

"Fool!" muttered Lock, as he watched the black head of the Italian bobbing up and down among the waves as he swam after the vessel in the vain hope of saving himself. "Why couldn't he have stowed his temper. I could have killed the fellow when he told me I was degraded, but—I can wait. He laughs best who laughs last, say I!" And he waved his hand with a mocking gesture of farewell to his unfortunate companion.

The Italian perceiving that no effort was to be made to save him, with a last desperate struggle raised himself out of the water and shrieked some futile imprecation after the flying vessel; the words mingled confusedly with the sounds of the hurtling water and straining cordage, then the black head disappeared beneath the waves.

CHAPTER XXXVI

BAILLOT drew his cap low down on his forehead and strode away. He was sick at heart. Goujet, observing his face, followed him.

"You are sorry to see that man perish, is it not so, master?" he said; "but what could I do? He was a beast—a tiger, the author of a thousand murders, and yet the death he died was the death any honest sailor might covet. Had he lived we must have died, for he loved you even as he loved me, and you saw how well that was. The villains had concocted some dark scheme ; we still have Lock to deal with."

Baillot made no answer.

"Ah!" said Goujet drawing in his breath quickly, "you hate me because I have done this thing. *Mon dieu*, I wish he had stabbed me!" and he bent his head in deep dejection.

Something in his tone and look aroused Baillot out of the black mood into which he had fallen. It seemed to him that he saw a sparkle of moisture in the man's fierce eyes.

"You could not have done otherwise, under the circumstances, my friend," he said slowly. "Thank God, my Gaston, that you still live!" He was amazed to note the change which these few words produced in the man's face ; joy and hope swept across it like a burst of sunlight over a stormy sea. In truth a miracle had

297

been wrought in the soul of this strange being. The love which he had given to the dead mother of Baillot —such love as a mortal may give to an angel—though buried deep under long years of hopeless sin and misery, had sprung up anew at sight of her son. It is not easy for us to comprehend that Love is the supreme energy of the universe.

Something of all this was evident to the mind of Baillot; he was vaguely cheered and strengthened by it. "You love me, my Gaston," he said simply.

The man responded by a look, but such a look. One may surprise a like expression of devotion in the brown eyes of a faithful dog, as he rests his head on the knee of his master.

"Cap'n," said the new second mate Jorgesen, approaching respectfully, "if our main-sail remains spread many minutes longer, something will happen."

"Make things snug at once, sir," replied Baillot, shaking off in an instant the last remnant of his depression. He perceived in the black cloud which lay upon the water at the northward, death or safety.

Two minutes more and the storm had struck them, a swift darkness illumined now and again by the downward stroke of cimeter-like lightnings. These flashes revealed the English ship, already far to the leeward, with every sail clewed down, her tall naked masts bending to the fury of the wind. Then the rain like a close curtain shut them in.

All night the vessel drove onward in the teeth of a howling gale; when morning broke clear and sparkling, the sun shone brilliantly on broken masses of flying cloud and avalanches of glittering spray, but nowhere did it reveal to the anxious eyes of the lookout the enemy who had pursued them so fiercely the day before.

The voyage proceeded smoothly from this time, the weather remained favorable, and they made good progress toward Terciora. Baillot spent much time in anxious thought; he finally took Goujet more completely into his confidence, and told him bit by bit the whole story of the island, and of the shipwreck.

"You couldn't help yourself, master, I see that," said the mate seriously. "Once aboard this precious craft you had to do the best you could on the moment. It was a miracle, that I didn't make an end of you at the first; I was a bloody villain," and Goujet shook his grizzled head slowly. "Do you know what I think?" —lowering his voice almost to a whisper—"It was your mother; she knew about me and about you. It all happened that I might find you."

"So you believe in spirits," said Baillot with a half-smile.

"Believe in them? *Mon dieu !* yes. Do not you, master?"

"I believe that my mother is in heaven, but I cannot think she is forced to visit the earth on my account."

"You are wrong there, master," said Goujet solemnly. "She keeps a close watch over you. I know because—"

"Because of what?"

"Because I have seen her."

"You were dreaming, man."

"No, master, I was as wide awake as I am this minute. Listen ! You were studying the charts in the cabin, I was on deck—"

"When was this?"

"Yesterday, just before sundown."

"Well?"

"I was on deck," continued Goujet; "suddenly I missed Lock,—I don't trust the man, he means mischief —so I quietly slipped down the stairway. You sat studying the charts—you remember, sir?"

"Yes, but what of that? Lock was nowhere about."

"I know it, sir. I didn't say that he was. I found afterward that he was in the fo'c'sle. But I saw, standing behind your chair looking down at the chart over your shoulder—just as though she was interested in it too, your mother. Yes, you may look surprised; you don't remember her, sir, as I do. She looked just as she used to do. As I stood in the door she raised her head—she must have seen that I saw her from the way I stared, for she smiled at me—then with just a little wave of the hand toward you she seemed to melt away into the air."

Baillot said nothing to this extraordinary story. He had the unwillingness, amounting almost to determination, possessed by most healthy well-balanced minds, to believe anything bordering upon the supernatural.

Goujet looked at him keenly. "You do not believe that I saw her," he said. "You think I dreamed it, or that I have invented the story. Well, I have done neither, but one cannot force one's self to believe, I know that well.—But tell me, master, how you propose in the first place to find this man, José de Miguel? And after that you have found him, what shall you say to him, since you do not even known what this mysterious island is called?"

"I have thought of all that," said Baillot, knitting his brows. "And it does not trouble me so much as does the question how to manage the rescue of Madame de Langres and her daughter with such a crew as this.''

''Have you any money, master?''

''Yes, I have money, plenty of it—that is to say a thousand pistoles.''

''I have half as much myself. We must get rid of this crew, that is we must abandon it, and if possible buy another vessel.''

''I had thought of that,'' said Baillot, ''but how? I have promised the treasure to these men—a thing I had no right to do, by the way, since it does not belong to me.''

''*Diable!* It belongs to you as much as to any one,'' cried Goujet with a shrug. ''To find is to own with a gentleman of fortune,—nay more, to seize is to own.''

''But we are not gentlemen of fortune—as you are pleased to call pirates, my friend.''

''What then is Louis XIV.?'' said Goujet with a short laugh. ''What has become of your ancestral domains, my master?''

The young man flushed hotly, then he said, quietly enough, ''Two wrongs do not make a right. If the king has seized upon that which is not his own, it does not follow that I may do the same.''

''Live and let live, master, say I. Let us reach Terciora first, then we shall see.''

Land was sighted not many days after; it proved to be the most northerly of the three groups into which the Azores are divided. Terciora belongs to the central group, and thither without loss of time, except to take aboard fresh water, the vessel proceeded. The crew had conducted themselves in a tolerably peaceable manner up to this point, but Baillot fancied that he 'could detect signs of growing impatience among them, as the voyage neared its close. When the brigantine was fairly anchored to the leeward of the island of Terciora, Goujet deemed it wise to make some further explanation to the crew who were sullenly eyeing the shore.

"What do we stop here for?" demanded Lock suddenly. "Is this the island where the treasure is to be found?"

"We stop here to obtain a chart from a man who knows the place," said Goujet boldly, but rather injudiciously, as he perceived, no sooner were the words out of his mouth.

"Then our captain "—with an offensive emphasis on the word captain—"does not himself know the place, and we have been tricked into a month's voyage with neither booty nor pay to reward us? Answer! what does this mean?" A low threatening murmur from the crew followed these words. Lock had fixed his small savage eyes upon Goujet. He perceived his embarrassment and burst out again more defiantly and loudly than before. "There is some deep-laid plot here to ruin us all. It is all a lie about the treasure; I knew it from the beginning. Who is this man, Baillot, whom you yourself brought aboard, and whom you call master? *Master!* Is that the way for such as we to address any man? I tell you, mates, this Goujet is a traitor!"

"Have it your own way," said Goujet doggedly, planting himself, however, in an attitude which announced his determination to defend himself to the last gasp. "Have it your own way, my hearties. You have behaved yourselves well up to now, and our captain said to me only last night, 'The men have done well,' he says, 'and do you divide amongst 'em this gold to make merry with, while we victual the ship, and get everything handy to finish the cruise.' Here you, Jorgesen, divide this; and mark me, this ain't a beginning of what's coming to you later if you keep on behaving yourselves. Ask Lock what *he's* got for you. The whining sawed-off liar !''

Jorgesen came forward and received the canvas bag which clinked musically as it passed into his hands. The crew gathered around him instantly, like bees about a pot of honey.

''Good ! as long as it lasts,'' muttered Goujet, ''but it won't last long.'' Then he hurried down to the cabin, where Baillot was making ready, with a somewhat cloudy and anxious brow, for his expedition ashore in search of de Miguel.

''*Ma foi !* Master, we must slip away as fast as possible,'' he said, ''and it is a chance if we ever come back. I have quieted them for the present with my five hundred pistoles, but 'tis only a mouthful for such as they.''

CHAPTER XXXVII

WHEN Baillot reached the deck, he found the ship surrounded by a swarm of small boats, laden with tropical fruits and nuts, which the sailors were purchasing with lavish prodigality. A number of them approached him and asked for leave to go on shore with a show of civility that surprised him. Goujet's pistoles had appeased them for the moment; as long as the gold pieces clinked musically in their pockets, they had but one desire in the world and that was to spend them.

The island of Terciora, with its mountainous slopes embowered with orange and lemon-groves, the white walls of its detached villages and huts gleaming through the masses of greenery, presented a most charming appearance. As Baillot knew, the inhabitants were mostly Portuguese, an idle and unambitious folk, who were content to scarcely stir the surface of the rich volcanic soil, which would have yielded ample harvests to more industrious husbandmen. Arrived on shore, he made immediate inquiry for one José de Miguel, and was directed to a village about a mile inland.

As the two men tramped silently along, the hot sun beating down upon their heads, Goujet wiped his face, all shining with perspiration, and stole a keen look at his silent companion.

"I say, master," he said at length, "this island you've been telling about is a mighty strange place.

I've cruised a deal about these parts, and I never heard of it before. You don't suppose now, that the shipwreck gave you a touch of the fever, and that a part of all this was a kind of—that is a sort of—that is—"

"*Peste*, man! Do you take me for an escaped lunatic?" cried Baillot, stopping short, and eyeing his companion somewhat suspiciously. "What I have told you is no figment of a disordered imagination, but plain, everyday fact, little as it may sound so. Return, if you will, to the *Rouge et Noir*, I can and will go on alone."

"*Mon dieu*, no, master! I didn't mean that. You can't get rid of me so easily. I am going to stick to you about as tight as your shadow from now on—at least till I see you settled a bit better than you are at present. What I was going to say is this, if the man we're in search of don't know anything about the place, or won't tell, which amounts to the same thing, there's a ship in the harbor now—or what answers for a harbor —flying the English flag. She's bound for the English Colonies in America. Now what's to hinder you from just stepping on board of her, and getting off to the new country. With a thousand pistoles in your pocket. you could make yourself a grand seignior over there. Come now, sir! Why not? Let those shipwrecked folks shift for themselves; perhaps they have gone from the island already. You may lose your life cruising about after them, and then like as not miss them. They are nothing to you anyhow; I can't see as you are beholden to them. You did your full duty when you stuck by them through thick and thin; you didn't leave them, you were carried off. That ends your duties to them, now don't it, sir?"

Baillot listened to this tirade in perfect silence. He too had noticed the merchantman flying the English colors. "How do you know that yonder vessel is bound for America?" he said at length, stopping a moment in his rapid walk to take another look at the ship.

"Because I asked, sir," said Goujet, delighted at what he supposed to be compliance with his suggestion. "She sails three days from now, or as soon as her timbers are repaired. She was touched a bit about the tops in the storm."

"Three days!" repeated Baillot thoughtfully, "then if we can get off to-day we might possibly be able to get back before she leaves!"

"Get off to-day!" exclaimed Goujet ruefully. "Then you will not give up this mad scheme?"

"No, my friend, I will not. I would not sail to-day in yonder ship were she loaded with pistoles, and every coin of them to be mine on landing."

"*Ma foi!*" murmured Goujet thoughtfully, half-closing his fiery eyes and surveying the dark, determined-looking face before him. A new light was breaking in upon him. "Then this mademoiselle is very beautiful, *n'est-ce pas?* She must needs be, to become the Comtesse de Lantenac."

"Goujet!" cried Baillot, wheeling suddenly about, "I have a mind to knock you down! Because I must do my plain Christian duty you think——"

"*Morbleu*, master, do not be angry with me and my poor thoughts! I meant no harm. It is not so then, the lady is old and ugly, and monsieur will rescue her because it is his 'plain Christian duty.'"

"A plague on you for an impertinent rascal, Gou-

jet!'' said Baillot, a smile passing over his face in spite
of himself. "No, she is not old and ugly. She is as
beautiful as an angel, as brave as a man, and as pure and
good as was my mother. I do love her, and I will find
her if it takes the last drop of blood in my body!''

"It is well said, master. You shall not be sorry
that you have told me,'' said Goujet softly. The two
strode on in silence, and were about to enter the straggling street of the village when they encountered a
half-grown, gipsy-looking lad who was whistling and
singing alternately as he loitered along, a basket of
oranges poised carelessly upon his head. He stopped
short on beholding the strangers and stared at them
curiously.

"Can you tell me which is the house of José de
Miguel?'' said Baillot, flinging a small coin in the
direction of the lad, who caught and deposited it
deftly in some mysterious receptacle of his parti-colored
rags.

"*Si, seignior!*'' replied the boy eagerly. "I myself
will conduct you. 'Tis only a few steps.''

Following the boy the two Frenchmen presently
found themselves in the courtyard of a flat-roofed,
adobe house, rather more pretentious than some of the
neighboring huts. A grape-vine laden with half-ripe
fruit shaded the enclosure, and beneath its shelter, apparently unmindful of the dozen or so swarthy, half-
naked children who played noisily about, sat a man.
He was immensely fat, and of a greasy, swarthy complexion; his black hair falling in scanty snake-locks
upon his broad shoulders, half-concealed the gold hoops
which swung from the thick lobes of his ears. For the
rest he seemed asleep, for his eyes were closed, but the

regular puff, puff, of his long-stemmed pipe showed that this was not the case.

" *Padre !* " exclaimed the lad, running up to this somnolent figure, " *Padre !* here are seigniors !"

With a sort of inarticulate grunt, and a slow wave of the hand, the man opened his small, beady black eyes, and fixed them upon the two men, who advanced in response to his gesture.

" You are José de Miguel ?" said Baillot interrogatively. The man replied by another grunt which might mean yes or no, and calmly continued his smoking, again allowing his eyes to close slowly.

" I have business with you, José de Miguel ; attend me, for I am in haste !"

The man waved one hand slightly in token that he understood, but he neither opened his eyes nor removed the pipe from his mouth.

Baillot stopped for a moment in perplexity, and surveyed the impassive figure before him with something of anger. " You are uncivil, sir," he said at length, hoping to arouse him. " I tell you that my business is weighty. You will do well to attend."

The man did not stir, but Baillot observed that he had opened his eyes again, and was staring at him fixedly.

" I have come for directions and a chart which you have in your possession," he continued boldly, " for the finding of a certain island not many leagues distant. I do not name the island, but you know what place I refer to. There is a certain château thereon, and many other curious things. I must go there in order to remove four shipwrecked persons who were left there some two months or more ago." He paused when he had said this, and waited for de Miguel to answer.

Except, however, for a slight acceleration in the puffs of smoke which issued from his pipe there was no change in the aspect of the figure in the chair. He still stared unwinkingly at the face of the young officer, which gradually assumed the hue of anger under the cold impudent look of the small black eyes.

"Have the goodness to inform me, sir, if you comprehend what I have said to you?" said Baillot at length. He had spoken in excellent Spanish heretofore, he now changed his mode of address to French.

"I understand—your words," grunted de Miguel, again closing his eyes, "but not their meaning."

"Can you understand this?" said Baillot, producing a handful of gold pieces from his pocket, and clinking them musically.

The effect was magical. The beady black eyes flew open at once. "Here Juan!" he called loudly, "lazy dog, why do you not fetch seats for the seigniors?"

The lad who had been hanging about the doorway, watching the scene with an interested eye, hastily fetched a couple of rude benches from the interior of the hut.

"Be seated, seigniors!" said de Miguel blandly, with a wave of his hand. "You have a paper to show me, is it not so?"

"I have nothing to show you except this," declared Baillot firmly, producing another handful of the coins from his pocket.

The eye of the Portuguese gleamed covetously for a moment, but he lay back in his chair and resumed his smoking, without having spoken a word.

"The paper of which you speak is unimportant," urged the young man in a fury of impatience. "You are well aware that the place has been abandoned."

Goujet meanwhile had arisen from his bench and was amusing himself with the children, who seemed to take to him amazingly. He finally seated himself upon the ground quite at his ease, and was exhibiting to half-a-score of admiring black eyes a marvelous watch, which it is to be feared had not come into his possession in the ordinary and legitimate manner. The lad, whom his father had addressed as Juan, was to all appearances as much fascinated by the shining object as the others; he drew close to Goujet and listened open-mouthed to the explanations, which that worthy was giving in excellent Spanish, with a pause now and again to observe the progress of the halting conversation between de Miguel and his master.

"I am prepared," Baillot was saying, "to pay well for the information."

De Miguel's sole reply was one of his non-committal ejaculations. "This is not the man we are looking for, master," said Goujet, rising suddenly and thrusting the watch into his fob. "He is rich, he wants none of our gold. We have only to sail in a certain direction that I know of for three days, and we shall find the place." He said this at a venture, as one will fire a careless shot into the air, but it did amazing execution.

"Juan!" cried de Miguel in a voice of thunder, "What you doing here! Have I not told you to carry those oranges? You shall presently miss a large portion of your hinder skin, for I will take it from you!"

"I didn't tell him, father," whined the lad, taking up his basket, "I didn't say—"

"Hold your tongue, son of perdition!" roared de Miguel, the great veins standing out upon his forehead in a manner alarmingly suggestive of apoplexy.

"We shall go on, shall we not, my lord?" continued Goujet, grinning delightedly. "We must look at that sloop also, you know."

"You wish to buy a vessel, excellency?" said de Miguel with a sudden access of politeness. "I shall perhaps be able to serve you. I have a most beautiful, ah, a most charming—"

"I must first obtain the charts," interrupted Baillot. "It is true that we already know much about the island, I myself have been there only a short time ago. But I wish to lose no time in returning thither, my errand being solely to remove the persons of whom I spoke to you."

"What persons do you refer to?" asked de Miguel, resuming his former impenetrable air of dulness.

"There were two ladies, a colored man, and an English sailor, Winters by name," replied Baillot, deeming it best to be perfectly frank with the man. A gleam of intelligence passed swiftly over the face of the Portuguese which did not escape the notice of Goujet.

"Were there no others?"

"There was no one else. The island was deserted as I have told you, when this shipwrecked party arrived."

De Miguel dropped his head, he seemed to be thinking deeply.

"The chart!" exclaimed Baillot impatiently. "Will you give it me?"

"Come back to-morrow at the same hour."

"But I want it now—to-day. I must have it."

"Come back to-morrow at the same hour."

"I will give you a hundred pistoles—two hundred—"

" To-morrow at the same hour," repeated de Miguel doggedly.

" Come, master !" whispered Goujet, " there is nothing to be gained by talking with the old rascal further. Let us go."

CHAPTER XXXVIII

GEORGES MENDON OF PARIS

"If I am not mistaken, master," said Goujet, as the two walked slowly away, "we shall shortly find ourselves betwixt the devil and the deep sea. What with our crew expecting plunder, and that old serpent yonder who is meditating some villainy or other—Hold, I have a plan!"

"What is it?" said Baillot gloomily.

"Buy, rent or steal a small vessel of some sort, then kidnap that little rascal of a Juan and force him to show us where the place is; he knows, I'll be bound."

"A bold enough plan, but—"

"But what?"

"There are a dozen reasons why it might not succeed. In the first place, while the boy undoubtedly knows something about the place—has been there perhaps, once out at sea without chart, he could do nothing. Again he fears his father, he would refuse."

"He shall shortly fear me more."

"Let us wait until to-morrow," said Baillot wearily, "de Miguel may be inclined to accept some of the gold pieces by that time."

"Yes, and in the meanwhile perhaps a dozen other things may happen. *Mon dieu!* but it is hot."

"Yes," repeated Baillot, mechanically raising his hand to his head, "it is hot, and my head—" He

313

spoke in a dull hollow tone, and Goujet looking at him
attentively observed that he reeled like a drunken man.

"*Diable!*" he exclaimed under his breath. "He is
ill! Sit down here in the shade, master, and rest a
while." Baillot apparently did not hear, he walked a
few steps further, then staggered and would have fallen,
but for the faithful Goujet who caught him in his
arms.

"What shall I do?" he muttered, looking about him
in perplexity. "I will take him here," beckoning to
a ragged peasant who had stopped to stare at them curiously. The two carried the unconscious man into a
small hut near the roadway, and laid him down on the
cool earthen floor.

"Here you, fetch water—brandy, quick!" called
Goujet distractedly to the dark-eyed mistress of the
house, who had paused in her occupation of sorting
lemons at this sudden intrusion into her domicile.

"Is it the rum then, and at this hour of the day?"
she said indifferently enough. "Why do you bring the
man here? My husband will not be pleased."

"The devil take you!" roared Goujet. "Don't you
see that the man is ill? He is a great lord and can
pave your dirty floor with gold. Take this and attend
him at once!" And he flung the woman one of the
few coins which he had left.

The sight of the gold had the usual enlivening effect;
the woman hastened to fetch water with which she proceeded to bathe the unconscious man's head, while
Goujet forced open his clenched teeth and poured a
spoonful of brandy down his throat.

Under this treatment the patient after awhile opened
his eyes and groaned. Fortunately he had not been

smitten with a genuine sunstroke. Had that been the case the career of the last Comte de Lantenac might shortly have ended in a nameless grave. The mental strain of the past few months had been terrific; this together with the almost tropical heat, and the disappointment which he felt in having failed to obtain the chart, had combined to bring about the unfortunate seizure. In a word he was overtaken by a calamity to which all flesh, however heroic the spirit within, is liable. As he opened his eyes he dimly recognized the face of Goujet bending over him, but he felt the most profound indifference as to what might thereafter happen.

During the hours that followed, the dark anxious face of Goujet, the broad jovial countenance of Winters, the sweet looks of Madeline all mingled in a dim and frightful phantasmagoria, through which he was vaguely conscious of figures coming and going, of low-toned conversations, which he partly comprehended and feverishly wove into his fantastic imaginings. It was not until the third day after, that he woke in his right mind, to find himself lying on a not uncomfortable couch in a small dark hut, none of the details of whose interior he remembered to have seen before.

As he lay quite still, his eyes roving in idle and indifferent curiosity about the cobwebby rafters of the roof, he became aware that some one was near him; he turned his head feebly, and beheld Goujet. The pirate was sitting on a low bench, his arms hanging at his side, his head leaning back against the wall. Baillot observed still further that he was sleeping, for his eyes were closed, while his mouth remained half-open. The whole figure of the man expressed extreme weariness, as of one who has unwillingly succumbed to an exhaustion which he can no longer combat. Before him stood a bottle half-full of some dark liquid, beside it a cup, also a wooden bowl carefully covered. While the sick man's eyes were slowly taking in these details, and the brain behind was weakly trying to grasp the situation, Goujet suddenly awoke. He gave a sudden start, and shook his great shoulders with a frown, as if displeased with himself for having slept. He then took up the bottle and eyeing it critically, proceeded to measure out with extreme nicety a portion of its contents, this he carefully mingled with water in the cup, then rising, tiptoed toward the couch. Observing that the eyes of his patient were open, he paused, and said very softly,

"Master, do you know me?"

"Know you, of course; why not?" said Baillot with some irritation. "But where am I? What is the matter with me?"

"Ah, thank God!" exclaimed Goujet with real fervor. "Take these drops, then sleep, afterward you will be yourself."

Too weak to protest, the sick man swallowed the draught, then closing his eyes sank into a deep dreamless slumber.

When he awoke the second time it was toward evening. Feeling considerably refreshed and strengthened he looked about him with some curiosity. Goujet was no longer sitting beside the couch, in his place was a woman, clad gaily in a yellow gown striped with red, an attire which set off admirably the rich dark hues of her velvety skin. Her black hair was braided under a gay little cap of red and gold, while from the tips of her small ears depended long earrings, reaching almost to her shoulder. Her slender brown hands were crossed idly in her lap; as soon, however, as she perceived that her patient was awake, she sprang up with a delighted little laugh.

"Ah, seignior," she said gaily, her head on one side, her white teeth showing through the parted crimson of her lips, "you are awake at last—such a sleep! But it is good—very good. Now you shall eat, I have a broth most excellent, made exactly as the wise seignior from the ship yonder bade me. 'Take two young fowls,' he said, 'and cook them gently many hours, and of the liquor that remains give him, when he shall awake, some great spoonfuls, adding also of salt a little.' See!" she continued, "I will feed you. You have not the strength, is it not so?"

"Where is Goujet?" said Baillot.

"Ah, you mean the good seignior who takes care of you. It is true that he has scarcely left you for a single moment. Such devotion never have I seen, he has neither slept nor eaten.—Does the broth please you, my lord?"

"It is excellent," replied Baillot who had taken the spoon from her hand and was eating with a very good appetite. "But Goujet, where is he?"

"But a short time ago José de Miguel stopped to make inquiries for you, and the seignior went away with him; he left me in charge; he will be back directly."

"José de Miguel!" repeated Baillot meditatively, "and what might he want?"

"It was about a ship, for I heard the talk between them. José de Miguel is rich—very rich indeed. He has business with many strangers; I myself have seen them. Much gold—ah, I could never tell you how much—passes into his hands. You also came here to see him, is it not so? You will do well to listen to me, the man has dark ways with him—yes, it is so. I tell you because I care not for de Miguel; I have my own reasons also." The speaker tossed her pretty head and frowned till her black brows met in a straight line above her flashing eyes. "Ah!" she continued, drawing a deep breath and permitting the dimples to steal slowly back into her brown cheeks. "You would never believe how wicked he is! I say my prayers out of pure fright every time I see his fat black face—the saints forgive me! But my husband can take care of me. You have not seen my husband? As tall as yourself, seignior, and perhaps more handsome." She paused to survey her patient, her head on one side like a meditative bird. Giuseppe is displeased that you are here," she continued, laughing softly. "He is perhaps jealous! But of that I am glad—yes! He would not be jealous if he did not love me. Betta's husband does not care a pistareen for her. He says Betta could have taken better care of you than I. It is not true. He only wanted the gold. As for myself I care not for gold, though it is true that—"

"You shall have money to buy some new gowns, and—"

"A necklace?" broke in his hostess eagerly.

"A necklace, certainly, and anything else that you wish," said Baillot a little wearily, "but will you not go to the door and see if Goujet is coming?"

"He is not coming yet," said the young woman returning to the bedside. "He will come soon. You have had visitors—yes, the doctor from the English ship, twice, thrice, and with him once came seigniors, one very tall man with a great beard, snow white. They wished to carry you away on their ship, but the seignior—Goujet you call him?—would not permit of it. He said you would not wish to find yourself carried away.—Already I hear the steps of one. It may be that he comes."

"Ah, master!" said Goujet as he entered the hut. "You look yourself again. *Mon dieu !* but I feared the worst one day. Had you died then, all would have been over with me ; they might have dug for us one grave. But that's past now, thank God ! I have a lot of news for you, if you are fit to hear it."

"Fit? Yes, and anxious to hear it ! My tongue aches with questions, but—" and he glanced significantly at the woman, who was looking at them with an air of childish curiosity, though as the conversation was carried on in French, it is doubtful whether she understood a word of what was spoken.

"Go outside now, mistress," said Goujet, with scant ceremony. "I will look after my lord for the present. To begin with," he continued when they were alone, "the *Rouge et Noir* is gone."

"Gone !" exclaimed Baillot. "When and where?"

"The very day after we landed, but where—of course I know not. I only hope 'tis far enough off from these parts. That first night when you lay like a log because of the medicine you had taken, I stole out, got into the skiff and rowed out to where our ship lay. I had taken the precaution to muffle my oars, so I slipped around under her cabin ports without a bit of a splash to betray me. I heard a great noise of shouting and swearing from within, and swinging myself up by a rope that hung over the side I managed to get a peep inside. There sat Lock and two or three others, roaring drunk, the floor covered with broken bottles and a dozen full ones atop of the table.

"'What are you going to do with that lying knave, Goujet, when he comes back?' sings out one of them. 'Walk him over the plank lively, with enough shot on his heels to keep him down till the day of judgment,' says Lock, 'and as for the sneak that brought us here, drowning's a heap too good for him, we'll—' but I won't tell you what he said, sir. The low-lived murderer! I had a mind to shoot him through the port, but I thinks to myself that I might get caught if I did, and that would leave you to shift for yourself, which you weren't in a condition to do just then. So I got down off the rope, but before I took leave of them I just played a little trick that I learned when I was a boy. You should have seen the rascals when a deep hollow voice apparently from under the table said, 'You are doomed men, if you lay but a finger on him who was your captain, or on Goujet.' Up they jumped as pale as a cloth, swearing fit to lift the ship out of the water, and whilst they were all raising a great hue and cry, tumbling one over the other to get to the deck, I slipped away. The very next morning before sunrise they were off."

"Good, so far," commented Baillot. "What next?"

"The lady of the house has perhaps told you how I had the surgeon from the English ship to see you. I met him down at the port. He was for carrying you off with them, said you wanted good care for a month."

"I am all right now," cried Baillot. "'Tis lucky you didn't allow it."

"I knew you'd say so—if you ever spoke again, which didn't seem likely at one time. Two of the passengers came with him one day, they were of the same mind, but I wouldn't give in. They asked a lot of questions, but I didn't give them much satisfaction ; I didn't know what they might be up to. Told them your name was Georges Mendon, that you were an agent for a company in Paris. Threw them off the track whatever mischief they had in mind."

Baillot laughed weakly. "Did they look like rascals?"

"You can't always spot a rascal, sir," replied Goujet sagely. "I've learned that ; a piouser, milder-looking man than our late captain, Fisher, you wouldn't want to see, but he was the very devil. At all events they've gone too, sailed yesterday. Now the best thing I have to tell you is that old de Miguel has come to time."

"Ah ! Then you have the chart?"

"Not yet. You see the money was in a belt about your body, and I didn't want to meddle with it, but he'll hand it over anytime now. I had to go high for it though, five hundred pistoles."

"Good ! it's worth it if we may be sure he's not lying."

"I've fixed that," said Goujet grinning. "He's to go along, and if he is lying why he'll suffer for it, that's all."

"But a ship?"

"He's got one, a little beauty. I saw him chaffering for it with one of the very men who came here to see you. They were evidently the owners. He bought it of them and will let us have the use of it for ten days, for three hundred pistoles. Not a livre less, though I've been beating him down all I could ; that only leaves you a couple of hundreds."

"It is enough," said Baillot thoughtfully, "but now let us sleep, to-morrow I must be up and about this business. God only knows how important may be a single day to those on the island."

\

CHAPTER XXXIX

WE left our friend Winters sound asleep with his companions in the cavern on the island, while over them in the darkness hung the baleful figure of the convict, armed with the knife which he had secreted, and with which he meant presently to make an end of every creature on the island except himself and Madeline, whom he had chosen as the companion of his guilty solitude.

But the Huguenot pastor, Constantin Dinant, was not asleep. He had not slept during the night; he had beguiled the long hours with prayers, none the less fervent because they were inaudible.

"Why bemoan a sleepless night?" he was wont to say. "These are the hours that God snatches for us out of the thirsty waste of our lives, wherein to give us the living water. Rejoice then, when sleep forsakes thine eyes, for it is a sign of favor. Surely communion with the King of kings is better than the unconsciousness of sleep, which is ours in common with the meaner animals."

In accordance with these favorite precepts, the good man was lying with clasped hands—beneath which however lay the flint and steel, of which he had taken possession when he perceived that Winters slept. "From the evil devices of men, do thou preserve us, oh Lord!" he was saying. "Give thine angels charge concerning this little company!" When suddenly a strange sound came to his ears; it was not a loud sound, only a gentle gurgling, as if something had been poured out from a flask. Instantly he sat up and struck a light, calling at the same time in a loud tremulous voice upon his companions.

"What is it, sir?" cried Winters starting to his feet, while the others—all save one, sat up and began sleepily to rub their eyes.

"Nay! I know not, perhaps I have aroused you from your slumbers without a cause," began the good pastor, "but I thought the Lord said unto me, arise! and I—"

"No, by the Lord, you did not arouse us without a cause!" cried Winters, who had snatched the torch from his hand, and instigated a hasty search about the place. "Look!" All gathered about and gazed in horror upon the body of one of their number. The man had been stabbed through the heart and had died instantly, as the peaceful expression of his face bore witness.

"Now where is the hell-hound that has done this thing?" roared Winters, snatching up a heavy club from the ground. "He shall die, and that without mercy!" As he flashed the light of the torch into the dark corners of the place a crouching figure leapt out. Winters sprang to one side, barely escaping the murderous lunge of the knife.

"Consarn ye, ye miserable varmint!" bellowed the old sailor, fetching a tremendous blow at his assailant; the creature dodged and doubled, then with a long howl like that of a maddened wolf darted down the passageway that led to the château.

"Pursue and slay!" shouted the aged pastor, his blood thoroughly on fire with righteous wrath. "The sword of Gideon and of the Lord!"

Accordingly the whole company, armed with whatever they could lay hands upon in the confusion of the moment, followed the flying figure of the convict. Unfortunately a gust of wind which drew adown the draughty passage extinguished their torch and they were suddenly left in total darkness.

"The flint—the flint!" cried Winters. From somewhere at a little distance there came a mocking laugh, which echoing along the low-vaulted roof of the passage and ringing in their startled ears, froze the very blood in their veins.

"Back—back to the cavern," whispered Dinant. "Woe is me! I have left the implements behind."

Several minutes were consumed in finding the flint and steel, and when the light of the torch once more flared upon the pale anxious faces of the Huguenots, there seemed to be a general disposition on the part of all of them to consider the situation with a little more care.

"I tell ye we must sarch out the bloody villain and put an end to him!" declared Winters stoutly. "As long as he's atop of the 'arth he'll be doin' mischief to somebody."

"The Lord delighteth not in a bloody man!" quoted the minister solemnly. "—I repent me of my thoughts towards the man, for I would have slain him willingly but now. Yet has the Lord again spared his life for some purpose of his own; it may be that he will yet repent him of his evil ways. Let us leave him alive to a life of solitude on this island, where surrounded by the impassable boundary of ocean, and the silent forms of the dead, he may finish his allotted time. God will not neglect to avenge the death of his servant who has departed from us this night."

Such also was the judgment of the others.

"Surely you do not desire the death of this poor misguided wretch," said the pastor mildly, turning to Winters, who plainly showed that he was dissatisfied with the decision. "It would only add blood to blood; it would utterly fail to restore life to yonder pale form. What profit would there be for us to slay the man, and what harm to leave him alive in this desolate spot?"

"That's all very well, parson," replied Winters. "I ain't in favor of killin' as an occupation, an' I never done much of it, but if a man ever desarved to be put to death it's the varmint what's in hidin' yonder. Don't it say in yer Bible, 'Whoever sheds blood, by man shall his blood be shed?' An' as far as this bein' a desolate spot, a desolate spot it is, an' mighty unpleasant for a man to stay in all by himself, but we was shipwrecked here—leastways the women, Cato an' myself, as well as him that's gone—an' what's to hinder somebody else bein' cast up here in the same way? Wouldn't it be ruther hard on 'em to meet with a man-eatin' tiger loose about the place?"

"A most unlikely happening, friend," said the Huguenot, shaking his head, "and hardly sufficient reason for us to risk our lives in endeavoring to ferret out this dangerous man, who is undoubtedly secreted in the ruins, from whence it might prove most difficult, if not dangerous, to dislodge him."

"Now you're talkin' sense," said Winters. "I'm willin' to admit that it 'ud be no fool's job to git at the rascal; 'bout as easy I reckon as to find an Injun or a rattlesnake, once they've set about it to hide.—Wall, I'm willin' to leave the cuss, if you all say so; but I'd a sight ruther the breath was outside of him fust.''

Strangely enough, when the women were acquainted with what had occurred, Madeline was found to be of the same opinion.

"I can't bear to think of going away and leaving him here," she said with a shudder. "Suppose some one should come?"

"As our good pastor says, my child," said her mother gently, "it is extremely unlikely that such a thing will occur. What could anyone want in this most God-forsaken spot?"

"You have forgotten M. Baillot," said Madeline, blushing rosily. "I am sure that he will return to search for us."

"I have given up all hope of that long ago. He would have returned ere this had it been possible for him to do so. I fear that his fate will remain forever hidden from us."

"He will return, I know—I feel it!" declared Madeline passionately, but the blush died away from her cheeks.

"Of whom are you speaking?" said St. André. "What! are you not satisfied with having recovered your brother that you must lose your roses at the thought of this missing sailor?" he asked, looking keenly at the girl's downcast face. "But come," he added gravely, "we are about to commit the body of our unfortunate companion to the earth, after which we shall get away from this accursed spot with what speed we may."

The service at the grave of the dead Huguenot was a brief one, for the tide which must bear their little craft out into the ocean was about to turn, and all was ready for the start. The grave had been dug near the tomb where the angel of marble still kept guard, for, strangely enough, this spot alone had escaped the hands of the despoilers. The body swathed in a blanket, which the survivors had taken from their slender store, was laid in the hole which had been dug for it, the earth was quickly replaced, a brief prayer was breathed by the aged pastor, and all was over. Immediately afterward the little company in silence and sadness wended their way toward the shore.

Up to this time nothing had been seen of the convict; he had doubtless lain concealed in the ruins of the château, keeping a close watch upon the movements of the party. No sooner had they embarked than he ran out upon the bank of the lagoon waving his arms violently above his head.

"Don't leave me here! in God's name, don't leave me here!" he shrieked. "Don't you know that they will all be with me? I shall see them night and day. They are laughing now to think that I shall be here alone in their power. Don't you see them yonder?" and the wretch pointed frantically in the direction of the ruin.

"Poor sin-laden soul! The hand of the Lord is heavy upon him," said the pastor, averting his eyes with a gesture of farewell.

"Come back, come back—kill me—kill me! don't leave me here alive!" screamed the convict, as the ship moved further and further from the shore.

A solemn silence prevailed on board the yacht, a

feeling that they were executing a terrible but just sentence upon the murderer filled the hearts of all. The vessel presently neared the point of land which defined the entrance of the stream into the lagoon; the convict had traversed the intervening space with great leaps and bounds, and stood awaiting them, still screaming loudly to be taken on board. As the yacht slowly rounded the point, only a few feet of water between her side and the shore, Bovet, who had ceased his shrieks for the moment, made a wild spring, and to the astonishment and alarm of all landed squarely on the deck. Before he had time to recover himself, Winters had fallen upon him like a whirlwind, and hurled him violently over the side. He sank instantly and was seen no more by any of them.

Madeline burst into tears. "Why, oh why," she sobbed, "must such dreadful things happen? Surely we must be made of stone to hear such cries, and yet suffer the petitioner to beg for our mercy in vain. In the sight of God our own hearts may seem as dark—nay indeed, are we not all guilty of the death of yonder unfortunate man?"

"Peace, maiden!" said Constantin Dinant soothingly, laying his large withered hand upon her bowed head. "Thou hast no cause to reproach thyself; though doubt not, that thy tears of pity are such as angels must often shed when looking upon this fallen earth of ours. Raise thine eyes, daughter! and take a last look at this place where amid such signal judgments upon wickedness, have been wrought out such mercy and blessing for us all."

Somewhat comforted by the words of the good man, Madeline obediently wiped her eyes and fixed them upon the shores past which they were gliding slowly. The sun just rising shed a glory of dazzling light upon the green meadows embowered in trees, upon the watery path of the stream before them, and shot long rays of splendor toward the distant purple of the sea beyond, upon whose trackless wastes, with neither chart nor compass to guide, the little company were about to entrust themselves. As she looked, her heart grew light in her bosom. Somewhere beyond that dim blue verge lay life, and happiness, and safety.

CHAPTER XL

"WE'LL steer nor' by nor'-west, since that was the direction in which the French ship started off, though, dash my buttons! I hain't an idee whether that'll take us anywhar in particular," declared Winters, when he had succeeded with the assistance of his inexperienced crew, in hoisting sail, and making things what he called "snug and in sea-goin' shape" about the yacht.

During the process, which was accompanied by many blunders, as indeed might have been expected, the old sailor more than once lost his temper, and consequently indulged in much profanity of a strictly nautical kind. He "blarsted his buttons," and "shivered his timbers," called the crew "consarned fat-headed land-lubbers," and "blowed old swabs," till at length the good pastor felt called upon to remonstrate mildly.

"Don't forget, friend Winters," he said with impressive solemnity, "that we are helpless in the hands of the Almighty, without chart or compass, and in this frail craft about to tempt the perils of the deep; such a display of temper is assuredly most unseemly."

Winters paused a moment in his hasty tramping up and down the deck—where indeed he was doing the work of half a dozen men—long enough to deliver himself of the following characteristic remarks.

"If we was a puttin' out to sea in the biggest ship

33¹

ever built, with the smartest crew 'at ever signed articles, I reckon·we'd be just as much in the hands of the A'mighty as we be now. If the Lord only holds his hand stiddy we're agoin' to be all right. As fur my temper, do you 'spose for a minute that God A'mighty 'ull lay that up agin the hull of us? He aint so all-fired small an' mean as that, I'll bet. And havin' made the sea and all sea-goin' critters, he's got a sight more notion than you have of the aggravatin'ness of tryin' to sail a tight little craft like this, with a lot o' land-lubbers.''

After which there was nothing for the good old Huguenot—who was troubled with what he found at times to be a most inconvenient sense of humor—save to turn away to hide the smile, which crept over the would-be severity of his countenance.

The Lord did "hold his hand stiddy," for the weather remained fair, with a constant light breeze from the south, which sent the little vessel speeding over the water in the most amazing style. The impromptu crew, especially Croissart and young de Langres, soon became fairly apt in the handling of the sails, and received many compliments from their instructor.

"I tell ye, my boy," said Winters patronizingly to St. André with a resounding slap upon his shoulder, "you've got a sight too much stuff in you to stay land-lubber fur the rest of your days. A few more cruises 'ud make a consarned good sailor out of ye. What be you goin' to do with yourself anyhow ?''

"My fortunes have taken such surprising turns of late," replied the Huguenot with a smile, "that I hardly know. A year ago, I should have said that my station in life demanded of me only a just administration of my

332

estates in Languedoc, suitable care of my mother and sister, and loyalty to the king. A day changed all that ; my property was swept away, my liberty gone, my family lost to me, and I a nameless convict, with no better prospect before me than a life of joyless toil with a shallow grave at its close. Again I find myself free and reunited to those whom I love, but as yet I have had little opportunity to plan my future. Let me once put foot onto dry land in safety and I shall be better able to answer you."

" Ay ! spoken like a land-lubber. Why do you talk so much about dry land, man ? It's too blamed dry to suit me. Now if we strike the Azores all right—as we likely shall by to-morrow morning, for I've seen land-birds in the rigging this very day—we could do an amazin' good trade fetchin' and carryin' atween the islands with this little craft ; an' mebbe later we could sell, an' git hold of suthin' bigger. What would you say to that ?"

" My mother has in her possession title-deeds to lands in America," said St. André thoughtfully, " and both she and my sister are most anxious to get there as soon as possible."

" Whar might your lands be, if I may make so bold as to ask ?" said Winters.

" In the neighborhood of Boston, I believe," replied St. André. " I never gave the matter much consideration, since our ever seeing the place seemed at one time so unlikely. Are there many savages thereabouts ?"

" Wall, not now, that is to say, the varmints don't dare interfere much with the towns. Course you see plenty of 'em ; and further in, they're thicker'n rattle-snakes. Your land might be wuth a consid'able if it's

in the right place, an' agin it might not be wuth the
paper it's writ down on.''

The next morning they sighted land. As may be
imagined this was an occasion for the liveliest rejoicings.
Even the pale face of Madame de Langres wore a
smile ; as for Madeline, her joy knew no bounds, she
even sang a gay little French ballad, as she stood by
the rail looking at the long low cloud in the distance which Winters assured her was the wished-for
haven.

''Is it not wonderful,'' she asked with sparkling
eyes of the pastor who stood by her side, ''that we
should have come straight to the land over these trackless waters with nothing to guide us?''

''Not more wonderful, my child,'' he replied earnestly, ''than that yonder bird should wing its unerring
way through the boundless heavens. We are too prone
to pray, scarce believing that we shall receive. So
faithless indeed are we, that we receive with surprise
and almost incredulity the answers we seek.''

Making in the afternoon of the same day the islands
of St. Mary and St. Michael, where they obtained
fresh water, they passed on the next day to the central
group of the Azores, where they hoped to find a ship
bound to some friendly port. In this hope they were
not disappointed, for sailing to the leeward of the island
of Terciora, the sharp eyes of Winters quickly perceived
a large vessel flying the English colors.

''Here we be, miss !'' he exclaimed, ''and yonder's
the good flag of England. The worst that'll happen
'ull be that you'll have an extra v'yage.''

''Oh, I hope we shall not have to go back to England !'' said the young girl, clasping her hands in

her earnestness. "I am so tired of ships and of the ocean."

"I ain't a goin' to say one word agin that sentiment from a tender little thing like you, miss," said the old man with an indulgent smile. "A nice snug little cottage is the place for women-folks; an' a good stout man to go out in the world an' do the wrastlin', whilst you keep the hearth bright and cheery fur him— hey?"

As soon as *L'Espérance* was snugly anchored, a deputation consisting of Winters, Constantin Dinant and St. André de Langres visited the English ship; they soon returned with the cheering intelligence that the good ship, *Royal Mary*, was bound to the English Colonies in America, and that their whole company could be accommodated on board. Indeed an officer of her crew accompanied them on their return to the yacht, bearing a hearty invitation from the captain of the *Royal Mary* to the ladies to come at once on board.

Winters, who had unexpectedly found the berth of second mate at his disposal, was especially jubilant. He had at once abandoned his notion of continuing to sail the yacht, and proposed to sell her and divide the proceeds equally amongst the party.

"The money ought all to belong to you," declared Madeline, "for you certainly saved the vessel when you concealed it so cleverly."

"That may be, miss," replied the old man. "But Jack Winters ain't a forgittin' who's prayed him out o' perdition, an' like as not saved his life by a hitchin' it onto a gospel craft what was bound to git to port, when this blamed old derelict would ha' gone to the bottom along of its own sins." By which he merely intended to intimate that the Huguenots should share in the proceeds of the sale. His generosity, however, was premature, as we shall see.

The following day as Madeline sat upon the deck of the *Royal Mary*, with her mother and several English ladies, also passengers, she perceived that another vessel had approached and was about to cast anchor.

"Look," she cried, "there is another ship !"

"A pretty boat, I'm sure!" exclaimed one of the English women, a plump, rosy, smiling dame, known as Mrs. Buxton. "I think sailors are monstrous interesting. What do you say, my dear?" addressing Madeline. Then without waiting for an answer she rattled on. "I told my husband before we started that I was sure the voyage would be the death of us all, but it hasn't. Now that old sailor who came aboard with you, what a queer-looking old guy he is to be sure, but *that* kind and good, your mother was saying. But look, some of the sailors from the ship yonder are going ashore ! I wish they had stopped nearer so we could see them ; if I had the captain's glass now—I wonder if he wouldn't loan it for a minute." And the excellent woman bustled away.

Madeline had remained quietly in her place, watching without very much interest the distant ship. Her canvas had been neatly clewed down by this time, the sailors looking not much larger than mice, as they clambered briskly down her shrouds. Now a long boat laden with men shot away from her dark sides, and after an interval of several minutes, a skiff containing two figures crept out a little way from the ship, then paused for an instant, while the man in the stern arose in his

place, evidently to shout out some order to those on the
deck of the vessel. The sound of his voice crept across
the water and echoed faintly from the lofty sides of the
Royal Mary. The young girl started to her feet with a
low cry, while the color sank away from her cheeks,
leaving her deathly pale.

"What is it, my child?" asked her mother in alarm.

"I thought—I fancied—did you not hear, mother?
And oh, where is Mrs. Buxton—the glass—the captain's
glass." And she broke through the little group which
surrounded her with a haste quite unlike her usual gentle
movements.

Madame de Langres looked after her in astonishment, then she too turned her eyes upon the skiff,
which was rapidly skimming over the water shoreward.

"What has agitated your daughter, madame?" inquired an elderly woman who so prided herself upon
the elegance with which she spoke the French language
that she never failed of an opportunity to display her
knowledge of it, the shrinking horror with which her
murderous onslaughts upon the language were received
having no effect whatever upon her.

"I hardly know," replied Madame de Langres
civilly. Then she arose from her seat, with the manifest intention of finding out.

"Shall I not accompany you, *cher Madame?*" said
the lady, rising with alacrity. "I have some *tres excellent* salts should the young lady feel ill."

"Thank you, I do not think she is ill," said Madame
de Langres rather coldly, as she walked away. She encountered Madeline herself about half-way across the
deck, and drew her into the shadow of a drooping sail.
"What ails you, my child?" she inquired anxiously.

"You must not forget—" with a glance towards the group which she had just quitted, "that you are once more in the world, and that curious eyes and ears are at hand."

"I know whom you mean, mother," replied Madeline petulantly, "that odious woman who insists upon speaking to us in French—it makes me shudder to see her open her mouth. But I cannot find Mrs. Buxton or the captain anywhere, and I do so want the glass for just an instant!"

"What an extraordinary idea; you surely do not mean that you think—"

"I mean that I believe the man in yonder skiff to be—ah; there is Mrs. Buxton!—Dear Mrs. Buxton did you find the captain? Have you the glass?"

"My dear young lady," replied the English woman smilingly, "I have found that the captain has been on shore for the last two hours. Everybody is on shore who owns a glass, it appears, so we shall have to content ourselves with our eyes. The bosun just told me that he believes yonder stranger to be a pirate. Is not that romantic? 'She's got a mighty suspicious look to her, ma'am,' he said, with such a picturesque hitch to his trouser band. Why *do* sailors always hitch up their trousers do you suppose? But perhaps they have no suspenders—though why they shouldn't I can't think. I mean to ask my husband to find out." With all of which the good woman herself was so taken up, that she quite failed to notice the disappointed look that crept over the ingenuous face of the young girl.

Madeline did not see the skiff return to the distant brigantine, though she watched anxiously through the glass which St. André procured for her. What she did

see was half a dozen or so of swarthy, rascally-looking
fellows attired in red jackets and caps disporting themselves about her decks, which certainly went a long way
toward confirming the bosun's opinion as reported by
Mrs. Buxton.

Two days later just before the *Royal Mary* sailed, the
little company once more assembled on her deck.

"Don't feel too badly about that matter of the
yacht," St. André was saying to Winters, who was evidently much disgruntled about something. "In a way
the fellow was right."

"Right? the black-faced greasy scoundrel! I wish
I could have spoken his gibberish, that's all. If you
can't make a man understand ye when yer mad, it beats
anything I know of for aggravatin' ness."

"What was it?" asked Madeline, smiling in the old
man's wrathful face.

"Why we found somebody as wanted the yacht,
wanted it bad too. A Portuguese fellow de—what?"

"De Miguel," said St. André.

"Yes, de Miguel—Wall, the fellow, jes' as we was
about to close the bargain, said as how he had found
out where we got the craft, and that if we didn't *leave it
with him*, he'd have us clapped into irons. We inquired
around, an' found that he could ha' done it too; it
seems 't he's the biggest frog in the puddle in these 'ere
parts. So there was nothin' left for us to do, but jes' to
give in, for considerin' all the circumstances it wouldn't
do for us to git into irons jes' now."

"I should think so!" ejaculated Madeline, who had
grown pale at the thought. "I am sure he is welcome
to the yacht if he only leaves us in peace."

"St. André and I saw rather an interesting person to-

339

day," remarked Constantin Dinant, by way of diversion. "It seems that Smith, our ship's doctor, has been attending a patient on shore for the past few days; he asked us to step in and see him this morning. He was a singularly handsome, refined-looking, young man, with a face something after the style of the portraits we see of Julius Cæsar, only infinitely more noble in type."

"Did you speak with him?" asked Madeline in a rather unnatural voice, fixing her large eyes anxiously upon the speaker.

"Oh no, my child, he was unconscious—had been so for some days, I believe; but we asked his name."

"And it was—"

"Georges Mendon, a Parisian agent for rum in the islands," replied the old man quietly. "But see! they are hoisting anchor. Now, all hail for America, the glorious land where we may worship our God in freedom and peace!"

And so, embarked upon summer seas, their troubles over for at least some brief space, we may leave our friends while we follow the fortunes of Henri Baillot, Comte de Lantenac.

CHAPTER XLI

"You are exorbitant in your charges for the use of the vessel, friend. I have already paid you five hundred pistoles for this scrap of paper, which you dignify by the name of chart, and—"

"You shall give it back to me if you like not my price," said de Miguel, doggedly. "I will take it now, and as for using my ship!" He snapped his fingers derisively and shrugged his pudgy shoulders in a way which signified that he was very well aware that he—José de Miguel—was complete master of the situation. Then apparently bethinking himself that there might yet be more pistoles to be obtained from this free-handed stranger, he resumed the soft whining tone which he habitually made use of.

"Besides, gracious seignior, you have not yet beheld this little ship. I have this very day paid for her in gold"—with a melancholy shake of the head—"more than three thousand pistoles! Is not that a great price for a poor man like José de Miguel? It would have been impossible for me had I not received the five hundred pistoles for my chart, which—may the Holy Virgin forgive me! for to do it I had no right in the world. José de Miguel's heart is too soft, ah, seignior, that is where the trouble lies. When I see a fine noble gentleman like you, seignior, anxious to rescue shipwrecked folk— who are doubtless awaiting succor with sufferings which

341

one can hardly imagine—delicate women too !—ah, my
heart bleeds for them ! There is nothing José will not
do for a lovely woman, everybody about the island
knows that." The speaker paused for a moment to take
breath.

Baillot smiled slightly as he listened to the worthy
man's eulogy on the fair sex, and at the same time re-
called the expression on his little hostess's face when
she had spoken of him. "You paid, you say, three
thousand pistoles for the vessel," he said, "and charge
me three hundred for ten days; at that rate you will
soon recover your money."

"Ah, but gracious seignior, you are forgetting that I
bought the vessel solely on your account; what does
José de Miguel want with a ship? I am content to
stay at home with my family, as you found me. Then
too, the risk, seignior. Suppose you lose the vessel,
where then should I find myself? Only three hundred
pistoles, it is nothing at all I assure you."

"You would not care for that," quoth Goujet, who
was following close at their heels, and on whom not a
word of the conversation had been lost, "for you would
be either drowned or shipwrecked, and in either case
pistoles would not interest you."

"Surely you will not hold me to that? I told you
that I would go, it is true, but of what use would you
find an old man like me? I cannot sail the vessel, and
I hate the sea," the last words were addressed in a con-
fidential tone to Baillot, but Goujet was not to be ig-
nored.

"Hate the sea, do you?" he remarked in a con-
temptuous tone, as he quickened his steps till he was
abreast of the other two. "Well, I should suppose so

342

by the cut of your jib, but that can't be helped, sir, you're going along, and don't you think otherwise for a minute."

De Miguel scowled blackly, but he said nothing in reply. The three men had by this time reached the shore where they presently embarked in a skiff.

" The vessel is yonder," said the Portuguese sulkily.

"Of whom did you purchase it?" asked Baillot, with a start of surprise.

De Miguel had been expecting this question, and he replied at once with that glib mixture of truth and falsehood of which he was consummate master.

"Of whom did I purchase her, noble seignior? Of two French gentlemen, whose names I did not ask. Truly it mattered not to me what they were called."

They had now approached quite near to the vessel in question. There was no mistaking that slender, low-lying hull, those tapering masts. Even before he had caught a glimpse of the gilded letters that ran about her bow, Baillot was certain that it was no other than *L'Espérance*, which lay gently rising and falling on the glassy green swells.

"Two French gentlemen," repeated de Miguel loudly. He had been studying the face of the man before him, and had made a shrewd guess at the thoughts which were thronging his brain. "They have been trading back and forth between the islands for a year or more—so they told me. And indeed I have seen the vessel before she became my property. A tight little craft, and of unusual build for these parts. I have wondered where she was built and how she became the property of the men who sailed her. But—" and the speaker shrugged his shoulders, "it was not my busi-

ness to know. For my part I do not ask many questions; it does not profit, for why? A man may lie with
his tongue. Far better is it to watch and consider and
see for one's self. For myself I speak only the truth;
I am sincere; I am open. All the world knows my
heart." And the speaker smote upon his breast and
smiled, a fat, oily smile which somehow was not pleasant to look upon.

"He is telling the truth for once, master," whispered Goujet, "for I saw the men, and heard them
speak, they also came to see you while you lay ill in the
hut."

They had now boarded the yacht; Baillot looked
eagerly about for some token which might tell of its late
occupants. He presently saw, however, that the vessel
had been completely stripped of all its former luxurious
fittings. Its cabins had the appearance of an ordinary
coasting schooner of the better class; the bunks were
furnished with bedding not too scrupulously clean, and
the galley with common coarse crockery and pewter
vessels, which had evidently seen long and hard usage.
In short, there was nothing about the craft to indicate
that de Miguel had not told the exact truth in regard
to her. Baillot turned away with an impatient sigh.

"The seignior is not pleased?" cried de Miguel, who
had been inwardly congratulating himself on the shrewd-
ness which he had displayed in the refitting of the vessel, an operation which had cost him a long and hard
night's labor. "And why? Is it not a beautiful vessel, and well furnished, and swift?—the seignior cannot
conceive of anything more swift! I have also caused
most excellent supplies to be placed on board. And I
have bespoken a crew of sailors, brave and expert."

"I will look to the crew, my man," remarked Goujet, who had been examining the little vessel with the eye of a connoisseur. "We shall not require more than two hands besides ourselves. You, Monsieur de Miguel, shall be our passenger. As to the ship, master," continued Goujet, "one could hardly find anything better than this little craft for our purpose. The *Rouge et Noir* was a vessel that could show a clean pair of heels to almost anything afloat, but, *morbleu!* I believe this craft could beat her. Why not get off with the next tide? A day at sea will do more for you than all the doctor's stuff that ever was brewed."

"Yes, by all means!" said Baillot, bringing himself back with some difficulty to the matter in hand. "Let us get off with all the speed we may. As for taking this man along, I—"

"You—*insist*, certainly," interrupted Goujet with a warning look. "Quite right too; a little cruise, Monsieur de Miguel, will not only serve to whet your appetite for the delights of your own roof and the endearments of your family circle, but it will also, if I mistake not, materially benefit your liver, in perhaps relieving you of an excess of bile. Ah, you comprehend!" as de Miguel groaned dismally. "A little *mal de mer* is most excellent for a person of your habit, most excellent, I assure you."

"The devil take you, sir!" quoth de Miguel, goaded into frankness for once.

"Quite right," said Goujet approvingly. "I have every reason to suppose that your kind wish will be realized at some future time. In the meantime if we do not fall into the hands of pirates by the way, we shall have a most enjoyable voyage together."

At the mention of pirates, de Miguel rolled up his eyes with a faint ejaculation, expressive of the deepest alarm.

"A not unlikely happening, eh, my lord?" continued Goujet remorselessly, yet with a touch of real anxiety in his tones, which did not escape the attention of Baillot.

"It will not be amiss to go suitably armed," he said, looking thoughtfully out to sea, where several sails were visible.

"I am so ill, noble seignior, when on the sea," whined de Miguel, "that I should be of no use to you— no use whatever; why not take some one younger, my son Juan, for example; I should have no objection to permitting it. He could fight pirates now; he is young and active, and—"

"You must go," interrupted Goujet loudly and decidedly, "to look after this valuable bit of property, if for nothing more. How do you know we're not pirates?" he added wickedly. "Do I not look like one?"

"You do—you do!" cried de Miguel, starting back. "I will not go with you. I will not let my vessel to such as you. I swear I will not! Let me go!"

"Hold!" said Baillot sternly. "You are not dealing with that man," and he darted an angry look at Goujet, "but with me. I am a man of honor and so, I believe, is Goujet, though it pleases him to make very sorry jests. You shall accompany us, since it was in the bond; and here is the sum specified, three hundred pistoles. We get off at once, *at once* you understand."

Somewhat mollified by the sight and feel of the gold pieces, which he fingered lovingly, as he stowed them

346

carefully away in his capacious wallet, de Miguel bowed cringingly. "The sum specified for the letting of the vessel for the space of ten days or less," he murmured softly, "and I thank the seignior for the same. The provisions"—here the speaker paused to cough discreetly—"will of course be paid for later ; likewise the hire of the seamen—a mere trifle of course, hardly worth mentioning."

As Baillot attempted no remonstrance, and Goujet remained sulkily silent, de Miguel gathered courage and continued in a somewhat louder tone, "One hundred pistoles—perhaps, for the victualling of the vessel ; a mere bagatelle, is it not?—Ah ! such luxuries, seignior, as I have provided ; I know the taste of such gentlemen as you. Fifty more—probably, for the hire of the seamen ? Not much, you say?" Baillot had not spoken. "You are right ; I shall get no gain out of this thing, it is true. I am too generous, always too generous—prodigal even. That is why I am a poor man. At my age, seignior, it is not pleasant to feel the hot breath of the wolf at one's door. And the little ones too, ah me ! ten of them, and more coming, always more coming. I—"

"A pest on your brainless chatter, man !" interrupted Baillot with a frown, "I will hear no more. I will pay you the balance when we return to this place, only on condition that you hold your insufferable tongue."

"But, master !" protested Goujet in an energetic whisper, "a hundred pistoles for the victualling ! Consider, I beg of you ; for fifteen I could—"

"Nay ! I care not, it would take time, and that is more precious to me now than I can tell you. Engage two or more of the fellows who are waiting in the boat there, then go ashore and fetch a supply of arms. Here is my purse. Do the best you can, for you see the supply is running low.''

"*Morbleu!* I should think so,'' muttered Goujet, as he swung himself over the side of the vessel, "and if that old fox gets his clutches onto another pistole, I hope I may be boiled in oil for at least a hundred years!''

.The remaining preparations were quickly made, and with wind and tide both in her favor, *L'Espérance* began her swift flight back to the island, from which she had just come. Goujet, quite in his element, was soon cracking alarming jokes with the two Portuguese seamen, pausing now and again to bestow a sly thrust upon de Miguel, who was coiled up into a wretched heap in the stern.

"You look pale about the gills, my friend,'' he remarked, planting himself directly in front of the unhappy man. " Not exactly pale, either,'' he continued, putting his head on one side and assuming an air of mock sympathy, "but a sort of a pasty, waxy, yellow; the sort of complexion pirates can give a man when they get to touching him up with their cosmetics a bit. How about those pistoles, got them safe?''

The wretched man clutched convulsively at his pockets and groaned aloud.

" What!'' cried Goujet, apparently much surprised, "you don't mean to say that you've brought them along? But why? You'll not need money on this cruise; money won't prevent your liver from turning over three times; or your stomach from dancing to the tune the ocean sets for it. And when you get so ill that you don't care what becomes of you, what then?'' and he

348

bent a fearful stare on that portion of de Miguel's person where was bestowed the wallet containing the pistoles.

"I must go below," stammered the unfortunate man, writhing beneath his tormentor's pitiless gaze. "I am too ill to remain here; I shall go to the cabin at once," and he staggered to his feet with as much dignity as he could muster.

"No you don't, you old swine!" growled Goujet, stepping in front of him. "My master has hired this vessel for ten days, and paid you three hundred pistoles for it. Not a drop, not a sup, do you get, not a bunk to lie in, without paying for it. And provisions come high on this craft, and bunks come high too; no one knows that better than you."

De Miguel's jaw dropped. He almost forgot to be seasick for a moment. "What—what did you say?" he stammered. "You—you *asked* me to come! you—you *insisted* that I should come! I didn't *want* to come. I won't pay, you scoundrel." And he dropped back and groaned aloud.

Goujet grinned. "You needn't pay now," he said soothingly. "I'm not so hard at a bargain as you. One hundred pistoles for your passage, say—a mere bagatelle, eh? I knew you would say so! and for your meals while on board, fifty pistoles—not much, you say? but I am so generous, so prodigal!"

"I—I—will tell the good seignior how you maltreat me, you black devil, you!" began de Miguel vociferously, then as the vessel gave an uneasy lurch, he clapped his hand over the pit of his stomach, and fairly blubbered. "The Holy Virgin and all the saints will punish you!" he howled betwixt his sobs, "and I hope you may burn in purgatory a million years!"

CHAPTER XLII

MORE FINANCIAL TRANSACTIONS

"WELL, master!" said Goujet in high good-humor. "I've come up with that old rascal at last."

"What have you done with him?" asked Baillot sternly. "Remember that you are aboard no pirate craft now, my man."

"*Mon dieu!* No, I shall remember that fast enough. I have only helped the old gentleman into his bunk to get rid of his *mal de mer*," chuckled Goujet, prudently resolving not to acquaint his master with his late financial transaction. "But *voila*, this little ship! I have never seen her like for sailing. Have you now, master?"

"I've sailed in her before," said Baillot, looking about him gloomily. "This is the very vessel that we met adrift off the island."

"But how came she into the possession of those men?"

"That is what I have been asking myself. If you had not seen them, I should have thought the Portuguese lied to us, and that Winters had successfully carried out his plan of taking the party off the island by means of the yacht. Here is the ship, at all events, but much changed since I saw her last."

"But may not the sailor—Winters you call him—have carried out his plan and afterward sold the craft to the men of whom de Miguel bought her?"

350

"The rascal said they had owned her more than a year, that much at least is a lie. If I could but compel him to tell the truth!"

"I could compel him," said Goujet, an ominous glitter in his black eyes. "There is more than one way to get at the truth, master; the sight of a red-hot poker now—"

"You would torture him? For shame, man!"

"'Twould be but a taste of what he will get in the hereafter," said Goujet apologetically, "and perhaps would count off just so much from his reckonings in purgatory."

"His punishment is none of our concern, friend. Doubt not that God will deal with him according to the measure of his sins. Let us beware only of adding to our own."

"Ay! spoken like a Huguenot," muttered Goujet. "But he shall at least pay roundly for his ten days in our good company."

Baillot was silent for a time, then he turned suddenly. "What think you of yonder sail, man?"

Goujet looked him squarely in the eyes. "You have already thought, master," he said, "for myself I need only to look once to see that yonder vessel is the *Rouge et Noir;* and what then, if *L'Espérance* can sail the faster?"

"We will at least sell our lives dearly," said Baillot. "I am going below," he added shortly, "do you keep a keen lookout."

"No need to bid me do that, master," replied the other, looking slightly offended. "I am glad you are going below. You need rest; you are not yet perfectly recovered."

But Baillot was not going below to rest. He was haunted by the conviction that de Miguel had lied to him ; full of this idea he began a thorough search in the cabins for some token that his instinct had not deceived him. For some time his search was in vain, and he was about to give it up with an impatient sigh, when in a dark corner of the inner cabin he caught a glimpse of something that glittered dimly. He picked it up, it was a jewelled comb of quaint design which had belonged to Madeline de Langres. He had no doubt about it ; he remembered just how she had used it to fasten the abundant braids of her hair.

After a moment's hesitation he sought out de Miguel.

"Ah, seignior," exclaimed that worthy pathetically, "you take compassion on my sufferings. You have come to tell me that it is not true. A hundred pistoles —holy heavens ! a hundred and fifty pistoles, and I can eat nothing !"

"I don't know what you are talking about," said Baillot coldly. "Hold your tongue, if you can, and listen. I just now found this ornament in the corner of my cabin. What does it mean ?"

"What does it mean, seignior ? Blessed Mary ! How should I know ? What is the object—a comb, is it not so ?"

"But suppose that I know to whom this comb belongs ; suppose I tell you that it belongs to the lady whom I wish to rescue. I believe that you have lied to me, rascal ; she has already gone, and you know it ; this ship is but just now come from the island, and you bought it from Winters."

De Miguel stared at the angry face of his questioner in silence for a full minute.

"Speak, scoundrel!" thundered Baillot, "or by heaven, I will turn you over to Goujet to deal with; he may find a way to get the truth out of you."

"How can I answer you, seignior, when I am so ill," whined de Miguel, wincing at the mention of Goujet. "You have no heart, or you would not speak in that harsh tone to one who has done nothing to harm you. As for calling me a liar, why—" and the speaker assumed a ludicrously threatening air, "no man can do that safely. Now listen to me, I know nothing of this trumpery ornament. The worthy white-haired gentleman might have had his daughter or his mistress aboard, or—" as Baillot interrupted him with an impatient ejaculation, "it may have dropped from the hair of the signorina when she was on board the vessel before."

"Ah, rascal! You have betrayed yourself. You knew then that this vessel belonged to the island!"

"I never said that I did not, seignior. I know far more about the island than I shall tell you," replied de Miguel calmly. "It is as I have said; I bought the vessel from the two French gentlemen; I saw no women; I know nothing more," and the speaker closed his eyes resolutely, as if he had said his say.

Baillot regarded him angrily for a moment. "Very well," he said at length. "You may be sorry, and that right soon, that you have not told me the truth. I shall go to the island now at any hazard." And thrusting the ornament into his pocket, he left the Portuguese to his meditations.

That these meditations were of a most unpleasant nature would have been evident to one looking on; the unfortunate man groaned and twisted, prayed and swore alternately. "Holy Virgin!" he whimpered, "what

did he mean? Can it be that we are already in danger
of pirates? Ah! it is so, I feel it—I know it! What
then shall I do? They will steal my pistoles! and that
beast would deprive me of a hundred and fifty more.
Why are such crimes permitted? Ah, I could choke
him, I—I—could—But no, I am in danger, I must not
permit such evil thoughts. May all the saints bear me
witness, that until I get once more on dry land the
man is forgiven as I hope to be forgiven. Yes, it is so.
But suppose I should tell him all. We might then go
back. But he would force me to give up the pistoles,
and that I cannot do.—Ah, I am so ill, I shall not live
to see the land, I know I shall not. Stay, I *will* tell
him! I care not—for the—pistoles. Seignior! Good,
merciful, gracious, noble seignior! I will—No, I will
not—I cannot!" and his voice died away into a low inarticulate mumble.

Meantime Baillot was moodily pacing up and down
the deck, pausing now and again to take a look through
his glass at the distant brigantine. He was thinking
over what de Miguel had said. Was it possible that
the ornament had been dropped during their first
voyage? No, he was sure that he had seen it afterward—during their sojourn in the château. Granted,
could she not have visited the yacht subsequently?
He drew the little ornament from his pocket, and such
a picture of the delicate, bewitching face of its owner
rose before his mental vision that he involuntarily smiled.

"The brigantine keeps about the same distance from
us," said the voice of Goujet suddenly.

"The brigantine? ah—yes. You are right."

"Either she cannot catch us, or she has some other
scheme or deck."

"It may be that she sees better game," said Baillot; "she may take us for a fishing craft."

"We expected to find treasure, you remember. She may leave us unmolested till we make ready to leave the island, and then—*voila!* descend on us like a hawk upon its quarry. If we find the women, that might prove—"

"Enough!" cried the young man fiercely. "Before yonder villains shall lay hands upon the women, I myself will kill them!"

"And you would do wisely and well," commented Goujet gravely. "But," he added briskly, "a thousand things may happen. 'Tis always what one does not prefigure to one's self that becomes reality; I know that well enough. And 'tis rarely the worst comes to pass without a slice of better fortune thrown in to balance it!"

The next morning after a night of steady sailing before the constant wind, the brigantine was visible upon their weather bow in very much the same position as that of the night before, except that she was several miles nearer.

"*Morbleu!*" growled Goujet, staring at her through the glass, "she has crept up on us in the night. All hands! Shake out every stitch of our topsails, and be lively if you don't want to swing from a pirate's yards before sunset."

A fragment of this speech reached the ears of the wretched de Miguel, who, after a fearful night, had painfully crawled out from his bunk, and now lay prone upon the deck, his head pillowed upon a rough jacket which one of the sailors had placed for his convenience.

"Pirates, did you say, good seignior," he whined abjectly, raising his ghastly countenance from its rough pillow. "Pirates? But where?"

"Right over yonder, my invalid friend," said Goujet, looking down at the figure at his feet with a curious mixture of contempt and pity on his dark face, "with their eyes glued to this pretty little craft of ours. Ever met any pirates, eh?" as de Miguel groaned louder than ever.

"How do you know that yonder ship is a pirate?" demanded the Portuguese tremulously.

"How do I know it's a pirate?" repeated Goujet. "How do I know that it's daylight, that the wind holds, that you are an accursed scoundrel, or anything else that's perfectly evident? I'll tell you how I know, my friend," he continued, sinking his voice ominously. "That vessel yonder, with her black hull, her raking masts and her peculiar rig—square in front, do you see? And her mainmast fore and aft rigged—that brigantine, I say, is as familiar a sight to me as a cup of grog, and why? Because I've sailed in her for the last three years, and a bloody record she has. Why man, they make no more of walking a prisoner over the plank than of eating their duff!"

The Portuguese lifted himself on one elbow. "Then you are a pirate?" he said eagerly.

Goujet scratched his head reflectively. "Well, I hardly know," he remarked doubtfully, staring curiously at the swarthy face before him. "Why yes, *morbleu!* I am!" he declared, slapping his leg violently as a sudden light broke in upon him. "A pirate and a bloody one you may believe; I don't know how I've kept my hands off you so long."

"Ah, then you can save me ! Dear, good, gracious pirate, pity—pity the father of ten helpless babes, and more com—"

"Shut up, and get down to business; if I speak a good word for you to yonder messmates of mine when they nab us, how much is it worth to you?"

"I will give you fifty pistoles; I have no more, I swear it. I—"

"Hand out your wallet; I'll count the contents for you, you are too ill, I see it," said Goujet, grinning remorselessly. "You won't, eh? All right, then take your chances with the pirates, but don't blame me when you find yourself on the way to the bottom with a hundred weight of shot on your heels."

"Mercy—mercy, seignior ! Take the wallet; if there be more than fifty pistoles—why—I have forgotten how much there is !" and the wretched man wallowed in the extremity of his anguish.

"Fifty—one hundred," counted Goujet aloud. "Yes, it is evident that you forgot, for I find here three hundred pistoles, the same three hundred my master gave you yesterday. Now your life, how much is it worth to you, friend? Fifty? Bah ! I snap my fingers at you. One hundred? I would not open my lips for that sum. Say three hundred now and I will listen."

"Three hundred ! Ah, how can I?" wailed his wretched victim. "It is all that I have in the world, may the saints bear me witness, and I a poor old man with ten—"

"Do you think the gentlemen yonder will leave you in possession of your gold?" sneered Goujet. "No, they will relieve you of all such worldly anxieties before they—"

357

"Take it—take it!" groaned de Miguel, hiding his face with his hands, while tears of anguish actually rolled down between his fingers.

"What is all this about?" said the stern voice of Baillot. "Have you not tormented this unhappy wretch sufficiently?—What is this? his purse? Ah! Goujet, Goujet, you cannot easily relinquish your calling. Restore it at once, I command you. Then come with me, I have something for your private ear."

Goujet sullenly tossed the purse toward the Portuguese who clutched at it joyfully. But as he was crossing the deck a few minutes later, he heard the voice of de Miguel calling him softly.

"What do you want?" he said gruffly.

"The purse—take it, you must have it!" whispered de Miguel beseechingly, "but remember to do as you have promised!"

Goujet hesitated a moment, then with a sidelong glance at Baillot he thrust it into his pocket. "I never refuse gold when a gentleman offers it to me so politely," he growled, "and I will remember the bargain—though *morbleu!* 'tis not likely to go any easier with you on that account."

CHAPTER XLIII

TOWARDS evening of that same day, the irregular out-lines of the island came into view. The *Rouge et Noir* still hung upon the horizon in very much the same position as when she was first sighted.

Goujet shook his head. "They are bound to over-haul us before long," he predicted. "If we could but make the secret entrance you speak of, master, 'tis just possible that we might shake them off; but I don't hope for it, they would anchor and send a boat ashore and search till they found us. Suppose we go on and thus throw them off the scent; I believe they would find it difficult to overhaul us."

"They would not try," said Baillot. "They would land on the island, and if the women are still there, and comparatively unprotected—" the speaker paused, then added in a firm voice, "We will stop now."

"Let us at least lay off and on for a few hours, we may perhaps be able to enter the channel unperceived," suggested Goujet. And to this course, after some hesitation, Baillot consented. He was on fire with impatience, and would have landed without regard to the possible intentions of the pirates had the matter been left entirely to his own judgment.

Under the wary hand of Goujet the little vessel executed a number of manœuvers, calculated to mislead the enemy, who did not fail in the meantime to lessen the distance between them by several miles. Towards nightfall the yacht sailed around the island, whose wooded heights now intervened to cut off the sharp eyes aboard the brigantine, and favored by the inflowing tide, slipped quietly in toward her old moorings.

As Baillot stood in the bow the memory of that other evening rushed back upon his mind. Now as then the brilliant hues of sunset gleamed upon the glassy surface of the stream, birds called to each other amid trees and thickets, and the heavy odor of flowers drifted past like clouds of incense. Goujet stood at his side quite silent, looking curiously about him ; the two Portuguese sailors chattered together in the stern, while de Miguel, who had somewhat recovered himself, stood apart, smoking in sullen silence. Suddenly the yacht rounded the point, and a cry of dismay burst from Baillot as his eye fell upon the disconsolate heap of ruins which crowned the heights above the lagoon. He turned instinctively to de Miguel, who was regarding the place with his usual inscrutable air.

"What has happened here?" he cried. De Miguel's sole reply was a shrug and a deprecatory wave of the hand. "Ah, you knew of this. How did it happen? Who has been here?"

"How should I know, seignior," replied the Portuguese. "Am I a saint in heaven that I should behold all that passes upon the earth? I swear to you that I have not stepped my foot off the island of Terciora for a year past ; I know nothing of what has taken place here. Perhaps there has been an earthquake."

"Yes, that is possible in these latitudes," murmured Baillot to himself. "My God! What has become of her !"

"There is at least some person on the island, master," said Goujet, touching him lightly upon the shoulder. "See!"

Baillot looked eagerly, he thought he could make out the outlines of a human figure in the gathering darkness. "Winters, ahoy!" he shouted, then as no answer came back, "Hola! there, Cato! Winters! 'Tis a friend."

Still there was no sound of voices, no stir in the dark shadow that lurked in a corner of the rocky stairway leading up to the ruined terrace. "You are mistaken," he said turning to Goujet. "There is no one there; 'tis but a shadow."

As if to contradict this statement, the shadow in question started up and flitted along the stair toward the terrace; at the same instant there fell upon their ears a singular and indescribable sound, ending in a long, blood-curdling, wailing shriek.

Baillot stood for an instant perfectly motionless. The two sailors shaking as if with the palsy had drawn close to Goujet, calling aloud on all the saints to protect them. But it was upon de Miguel that this discomfiting incident produced the most startling effect. The half-smoked manilla had dropped from his fingers at the first mention of human presence, but as the echo of that strange cry died away among the ruins, he darted forward, his eyeballs starting out of his head, his ghastly face drawn almost out of semblance to that of a human being.

"God in heaven!" he cried in a husky, unnatural voice. "'Tis he! I betrayed him—I alone knew." Rushing past the astonished beholders he precipitated himself violently down the stair into the cabin, the door of which they could hear him double-locking after him.

"Whew!" said Goujet, who was the first to recover himself, "our friend has something on his conscience. *Voila !* he'll have to unlock that door, we'll hardly be able to give up both cabins to his convenience. What now is your thought, master, of a shadow that can make such disagreeable noises?"

"The explanation is only too evident," said Baillot gloomily. "Some horrrible disaster has befallen all the party save one; that one has become a maniac."

"I fear that you are right," said Goujet with a rueful shake of his grizzled head. "We must at all events find out; the poor devil may recover his senses if he be taken from this dismal spot. *Morbleu !* master, figure to yourself what it must be to be mad and alone in a place like this!" Then as Baillot answered him never a word but still stood staring into the darkness, he continued in a matter-of-fact way, "'Twill be altogether best to land, since our late messmates may drop down upon us at almost any moment. On shipboard our chances would be—" and he snapped his fingers expressively—"but among the nooks and crannies of yonder ruins we might defy them. I will undertake to unearth our passenger," and whistling cheerfully he clattered down the narrow stairway and assailed the closed door of the cabin with no gentle hand.

"Open the door, you rascal," he shouted. "There's nothing above to hurt a mouse! What do you mean by locking yourself in the captain's quarters, you dirty lubber, you? Open this instant or I'll kick down the door, and its probably worth fifty pistoles—and you a poor man with ten small children and more coming. Open, I say!"

Then as there was no reply whatever, he proceeded to put his threat into execution, the door giving way with a crash before the enormous strength of his shoulders.

"Where are you, villain!" he said, peering curiously about. "Ah, *voila!*" as his eye fell upon de Miguel who was crouched in a shivering heap in one corner. "What are you afraid of, imbecile? At the worst 'tis but some poor madman, crazed by the solitude of this infernal place. Come now, get you up on deck; we are going on shore to camp." And he laid a compelling hand on the shoulder of the Portuguese.

"No, no!" wailed de Miguel, "I will not go on shore. I will stay here—though God knows, perhaps he will find me here also!" and he gazed about him with a vacant stare.

"Come, come, man! you have been ill, and you were a bit shaken by that crazy loon among the ruins; it was not a pleasant sound I'll allow, but there's no occasion for a fuss like this. You see"—added the speaker with a grin—"those pirates I was telling you about are not more than a mile away by this time; they know well enough where we've gone, and it won't be many hours before they clap eyes onto this vessel. It won't be healthy for us to be aboard along about that time; we'd stand about as much chance as a bluefish before a shark. The ship you're bound to lose, my man, but you may make out to save your neck if you aren't too much of an ass."

De Miguel apparently did not hear what was being said, he was still muttering unintelligibly to himself. Goujet stared at him curiously.

"I say, my friend!" he said at length, "what is this you're jabbering about? Who is *he?* And what do you suppose *he's* going to do to you, supposing it was *he* we heard caterwauling above?"

De Miguel eyed his questioner dully. "Don't you know that I can't tell?" he asked, with some surprise evident in his voice. "They would kill me—yes, by inches," and he shudderingly relapsed into silence.

"It's pretty evident that you've lost whatever wits you may have had. Stay here, if you want to, I don't care a pistareen. We are going ashore, and we're going now."

"Don't leave me!" cried de Miguel, sinking to his knees and catching at Goujet's trousers. "Don't leave me here alone," his voice raising to a shriek. "I am a rich man, I will give you five hundred—stay—a thousand pistoles if you will take me away from this accursed spot. Good friend, kind seignior, you have a good heart and you love gold. Listen!"

And indeed Goujet was listening with all his ears. "A thousand pistoles!" he exclaimed under his breath. "You don't mean that now!"

"But, yes, seignior. I do mean it. And you shall have this vessel also, I swear it. Think what a fine little business you could do in your line!" The speaker's voice had resumed something of its natural oily and persuasive tone by this time. "Come, seignior," he whispered, "I could put you onto something very desirable, very lucrative—ah, you don't know!"

Goujet burst into a great laugh. "Don't I?" he exclaimed. "Well, I ought to if I don't, I've seen the way you manage a bargain. But I've other business on hand for the present. I'll take you away—for the consideration mentioned—to-morrow, if the pirates haven't found us by that time. Come now, be lively! We must get out of here."

Without a word de Miguel sprang past him to the deck. The two sailors had already scrambled over the side, and were busy making the ship fast to the pier, but they returned instantly to the deck in response to de Miguel's shrill whistle. He talked with them earnestly for a few minutes in some language which Goujet did not understand.

"What do you mean, men," exclaimed Baillot, "by leaving your work to attend another's commands?"

De Miguel uttered a short sharp command in the same unknown tongue, and the two sprang over the side and resumed their occupation without even so much as a glance at Baillot.

"Perhaps I had best demand an explanation of this singular occurrence from you, Monsieur de Miguel," said the young man, turning to the Portuguese. "How does it happen that you give counter-commands to sailors on my own ship?"

"Your own ship!" repeated de Miguel with an offensive laugh.

"Yes, my own ship, sir, in that I have paid you three hundred pistoles for the use of it. It is mine for ten days."

"And where might the pistoles be at this moment?" said the Portuguese, planting his legs far apart and staring insolently into Baillot's face.

"How should I know, fellow," replied Baillot, whitening with anger. "I paid you; you do not pretend to deny the fact, do you?"

"You paid me, truly," said de Miguel, snapping his fingers contemptuously. "But within twenty-four hours what happens. Your worthy friend here, your mate—I know not what you call him, I shall call him another name, not a pretty one; shall I tell you what it is? Your *accomplice*, that is what I please to call him—gets the three hundred pistoles away from me when I am weak with illness, and moreover will not permit me to lay my head in a bunk till I have paid him one hundred and fifty more. What then? Is this *your* ship? Are these sailors under *your* command? Bah, I spit in your face! you are nothing but a dirty pirate, you and your—Help! Murder!"

"Let him be, Goujet! Take your hands off him! Now answer, is what he said true?"

"Yes," said Goujet sullenly. "It is partly true; but did he not cheat you, master! What right had he—"

"Hold, friend! he did not cheat me if I agreed to his terms. I did so, you remember. You have humiliated me more than I can tell you; if what he had said was false, I should have given him reason to remember that he had called the last of the de Lantenacs—a— thief! but now—"

"Oh, master, master, don't look at me like that! don't hate me! I don't care for the gold, let him have it! I did it for you. I—"

"Restore the gold, and say no more about it, but remember in the future that whilst we are together the world will judge me through you."

"God forbid!" ejaculated Goujet fervently. "Here take your money, dog, but do not forget that the bargain is off between us."

"I shall have no need of your assistance, seignior," said de Miguel with an unpleasant smile. He seemed to have forgotten his fears, and leaned upon the rail blowing light rings of smoke from his lips with an air of insolent triumph. Goujet looked at him keenly but he said nothing; several new and unpleasant ideas had come into his head.

"There are three of them," he whispered to Baillot, "and that fellow means mischief of some kind. Let us get on shore at once. But we must keep a sharp lookout; these Portuguese are the very devil once their resentment is aroused."

CHAPTER XLIV

THE RUINS

"We will go now," said Baillot after a pause. "Come," he added, addressing de Miguel with no trace of anger in his voice. "You will accompany us?"

"I prefer to remain on board, honored seignior," said de Miguel with an insolent smile. "Between pirates on land and pirates on the sea there is, I believe, very little choice."

"I shall kill him—I must kill him!" whispered Goujet, his voice skaking with rage. "He has insulted you."

"He has but spoken as you gave him reason," said Baillot wearily. "Come, I care not what he says, let him remain if he will."

"The sailors must go with us," said Goujet savagely. "Move lively now, my men; carry these things up the hill."

But the two sailors seemed not to have heard the order; they stood, stolidly smoking their short black pipes and exchanging an occasional sentence.

"Did you hear what I said to you?" said Goujet in a loud voice, which in spite of himself betrayed his anxiety.

De Miguel who was still leaning over the rail, watching the scene with malicious enjoyment, allowed his amusement to carry him still further at this, for he laughed aloud.

Baillot had already climbed half-way up the ascent to the ruined château. He did not care whether the sailors came with them or not; he had forgotten the pirates; the insolence of de Miguel was something that he had no mind to consider. In a word, he was for the time being oblivious to all earthly considerations save those concerning the companions whom he had last seen alive in this mysterious place. Were they alive still? The awful catastrophe which had taken place, and to which the shapeless ruins above his head bore witness, was it of nature, or had the hand of man produced it? What was the formless shadow whence had proceeded the eldrich shrieks?

Deep in thought the young man kept steadily on his way without once stopping to look behind; he had almost gained the terrace when the short sharp crack of a pistol from below aroused him from his anxious revery. He stopped to listen; a second, then a third report followed, then he saw someone running toward him with great leaps and bounds. It was Goujet.

"How now, sir," he said sternly, "what has happened?"

"Do not stop to question me. Up to the ruins as quickly as possible!"

Once on the terrace, Goujet paused for an instant to look back, there was neither sound nor motion from below. "The cowards," he exclaimed between his shut teeth, "they will not dare to pursue us!"

"What has happened?"

"Those dogs of sailors refused to obey me, and de Miguel laughed in my face. I told him that in case the

24 369

rascals did not obey I would shoot them—which is quite proper, as you know, master, in a case of mutiny. Then he spoke to them in that infernal gibberish, which I believe to be Malay, the language of the devil, and one of them drew a pistol and fired at me. Luckily he missed; it didn't take me long to return the compliment with rather better effect; the fellow dropped like a log, I didn't wait to pick him up and find out where he was hit.''

''And the third shot?''

''Was fired after me by de Miguel; it winged me too, I believe. Yes, here in the shoulder. A mere trifle, though; don't trouble yourself, master. The worst of it is, that I was forced to leave everything behind. We shall pass a sorry night with neither fire nor food. For myself I care not, but for you—''

''It matters not, if the rascals do not carry off the vessel.''

''That is what they mean to do,'' quoth Goujet. ''But their only possible chance is to get away to-night; and with but one man to work the ship, and the tide still running in! Bah! Let them try it!''

It was now quite dark and although Baillot was burning with impatience to begin his investigations, he perceived that this would be impossible before daybreak. He therefore seated himself upon the terrace, his back against the wall, and wrapping his cloak about him, prepared to pass the night in this position. Goujet after some hesitation followed his example.

''Are you asleep, master?'' he whispered after an interval of silence.

''No.''

''Did you hear that noise?''

"Assuredly, I have good ears."

The noise in question was a strange one ; it recurred at intervals. Swish ! swish ! swish ! the interruptions of the swishing sounds being filled in with a low, incoherent murmur.

"What do you think it is?"

"Owls, perhaps ; perhaps the madman."

"The mad shadow, you mean. We saw no man."

"True !"

The two relapsed into silence again, dozing fitfully, but always sleeping, as the old saying has it, with one ear open. After a time the strange noises ceased, and complete silence, broken only by the sound of the night-wind as it wailed through the eyeless windows, brooded peacefully over the dismal ruin, and the uneasy sleepers on its threshold. Toward morning Baillot opened his eyes and started up ; he fancied that he had heard somewhere near them a stealthy sound, as of one walking on the stones with bare feet. But though he listened breathlessly, the sound was not repeated, and the impenetrable darkness gave no sign that a still blacker shadow was lurking under its cover. At the first streak of dawn he sprang to his feet, and looked keenly about him ; below he could dimly make out through the misty uncertain light the masts and rigging of the yacht. There was nothing to be seen on the terrace nor on the stairway ; but the light, which was momently growing brighter, revealed more plainly the havoc wrought in the once stately château. Yawning rents in the smoke-blackened walls permitted glimpses into its interior, which had evidently been gutted by fire, though here and there a bit of rich drapery fluttering in the breeze, or a half-ruined cornice which had escaped the fury of the devouring element, gave a look of ghastly brightness to the place, as of a corpse decked out with tinsel and ribbons.

The ruin however possessed little interest for Baillot. He had not forgotten how Winters had wished to remove to the more modest quarters afforded by the cottage, and he still hoped that he might find his companions there alive and well. He bent over Goujet, who was really sleeping now, as his relaxed limbs and heavy breathing bore witness.

"Awake," he cried in the sleeper's ear. "Come, it is day!" accompanying his words with a vigorous shake.

"Ah—yes—certainly—that is. Is the yacht gone?" cried Goujet, springing to his feet with alacrity as his senses came back to him. "*Bon!* I see her there. We will now descend and see what has happened."

"Not until we have looked about the place," said Baillot firmly. "Come, I am going now."

"But, master, the pirates may be here at any moment. We must at least secure materials for a fire, and some provisions."

But Baillot paid no heed, he was already half over a pile of broken stone and débris.

"*Morbleu!*" muttered Goujet, looking after his retreating figure ruefully. "We shall not then breakfast this morning! We did not sup last night! But what is food when a man is in love? *Hélas!* to be tied to a man in love is like being hitched to the tail of a comet. I am not in love; but I must go after him, I suppose." And casting one last, longing look in the direction of the landing, where the yacht with no sign of life about her white decks, lay quietly rising and falling on the

light ripples of the lagoon, he followed rapidly on after
the active figure of the young count.

"And how will all this end?" he grumbled, as he
hurried along, stopping to snatch at some half-rotted
fruit as they passed through the orchard closes. "If
the mademoiselle and her lady mother are here, what
shall we do with them? If they are not here, what in
heaven's name shall I do with him? He will be ready
to die with grief. In any case there is that rascal de
Miguel to deal with, to say nothing of the pirates. If
only I had let them carry him aboard the English vessel when he was out of his mind there. *Ma foi*, but it
would have been a good thing! What does he see now
I wonder; he has stopped short." And the faithful
fellow quickened his pace to a run.

"What is it, master?" he said.

The young man only groaned aloud.

Goujet looked about him carefully and presently his
eye fell upon the ruins of the cottage showing black
and dismal in the bright light of the dawn. "Do
you mean that you hoped to find them yonder?" he
asked; then as Baillot did not answer, he continued,
"There's been some sort of queer work here, I should
say. What now may this mean?" indicating as he
spoke a long rough hillock of freshly-dug earth, in the
top of which a couple of iron spades stood up stiffly
while near at hand lay several rusty pickaxes.

Baillot shuddered. "It looks," he said in a smothered voice, "like a great grave." And in this conjecture he was right, it being the spot where the Huguenots
had buried the unfortunate convicts.

Goujet was privately of the same opinion, but he did
not say so. "Let us make haste," he said briskly,

"and look the place over thoroughly while we are about it; it will not take long. I am beginning to hope, my lord, that your notion was the right one, and that your party made good their escape some time ago, as was evidenced by finding mademoiselle's ornament in the cabin of the yacht. We will return, and it shall go hard with me if I do not in some way force that scoundrel de Miguel to tell us the truth of the matter—that is, if you will permit me to try my own way with the fellow."

Baillot's dull eyes kindled. "I care not what you do with him," he cried hotly. "He has dealt foully with me; I am persuaded that he knew of this thing,— that he knows—what has become of her."

"Never fear, master," said Goujet confidently, "we shall find them yet. For my part, I think it is a good thing that they are not here; we shall go away with a good conscience, and—"

"We shall perhaps leave them—if they are there," said Baillot, relapsing into hopeless gloom, and indicating the rough hillock with a gesture full of horror.

"Do not let that trouble you, master. No one would have the heart to murder two helpless women. We shall see, and in the meantime what harm to hope for the best that may very easily have happened? That sailor, Winters, was a shrewd fellow now from what you have told me, is it not so? Very well then; many things may have taken place, but with a brave quick-witted man to protect them the women have doubtless escaped long before all this," indicating with a wave of his hand the ruined buildings and the ominous mound at their feet.

"It is true that he was most anxious to take to the yacht as soon as we found that the island was deserted," said Baillot musingly, and with a slight relaxing of the set lines of his face.

Goujet who was watching him closely perceived this with satisfaction. "And why did you not do so?" he asked.

"Why did we not? Would to heaven that we had! There were no charts, and I objected on that account; the women also were unwilling—"

"But don't you see, master," broke in Goujet eagerly, "that after your mysterious disappearance the women would be very much frightened, and then the sailor would have no difficulty in persuading them to leave the island? Now this fire, and also this mound, is of very recent date, for there is no vegetation about, and in this climate there would be in a very short time; also the yacht was uninjured. There is no doubt about it; they left soon after you did."

Baillot did not reply, but Goujet's arguments had evidently carried some degree of conviction, for he walked more briskly and looked about him with less of gloom and sadness.

The circuit of the island was soon completed. They saw nothing to throw any additional light upon the matter; the ruined barns, and the festering remains of several of the domestic animals only confirming them in their conviction that the devastation and death evident upon every hand was the deliberate work of man's hand.

"Now if we can but slip away and get well out to sea before the *Rouge et Noir* gets wind of our whereabouts, we shall be able to make good our escape,"

Goujet was saying as they caught sight of the yacht. But the words were no sooner out of his mouth than he followed them by a shocking oath. "We are too late," he cried. "The rascals have landed!"

CHAPTER XLV

"We must look lively now, for some of the devils have started up the hill," said Goujet in an anxious whisper. "The yacht's lost anyhow!"

Baillot stood composedly watching the scene with a curious expression upon his face. Half a dozen of the pirates were examining the rigging of their prize, while a second group were gathered closely about some object on the deck. This it presently appeared was a man; the man was de Miguel. Even from the distance at which they stood they could hear the bursts of derisive laughter with which his captors were receiving his evident supplications.

Goujet smiled grimly. "Come, we must be moving," he urged; "if they do not see us it is possible they will not find out that we were aboard; in any case we shall be marooned."

Cautiously retreating for a few paces and skirting a little hillock which arose to the left, they presently came upon the outer entrance to the cavern, which the Huguenots had left wide open on the day of their departure. Without a moment's hesitation Goujet darted into the place. "Come," he said impatiently, "we can fasten this door."

"Hold, my friend!" said Baillot, looking thoughtfully about him. "Let us first conceal this entrance with vines and shrubs. They could force the door

377

with ease, and we do not yet know whether there be any other exit."

"True; master, I had not thought of that."

"*Morbleu*, they are looking for us!" whispered Goujet a moment later, peering through the interstices of the boughs which they had hastily arranged before the door. "There's Lock now!" and he raised his pistol, and sighted deliberately.

"Madman!" exclaimed Baillot. "What are you thinking of?"

"If I should shoot him, I could go out this minute and claim the captaincy!" said Goujet, his eyes glittering strangely. "I know the men; they would be glad to welcome me."

"Go if you will," said Baillot turning away, "but at least do not betray my hiding-place."

"I did not mean it; forgive me, master! the sight of that man angered me. But let us explore this place."

Groping their way down the narrow passage they soon came upon the curious grotto or chamber, which has already been described, where the Huguenots on the day of their escape had found the mysterious dead man seated in the great chair, and where afterward occurred the tragedy which had hastened their departure from the island.

They found various indications that the place had been recently occupied. On the rough oaken table stood the fragments of a hasty meal; ranged against the wall were the heaps of boughs and dead leaves which had served as beds, while in one corner still hung the hammocks woven for the use of the women by Winters.

"More than four people have been here of late,"

quoth Goujet, judicially examining these different objects, "and what now might this be?"

"This" was apparently nothing more than a scrap of discolored leather, but at sight of it Baillot turned pale. He took it in his hands and looked at it carefully. "It is a part of the sole of a woman's shoe," he said hoarsely.

"They at least had a secure hiding-place," commented Goujet cheerfully.

But Baillot was not to be cheered by anything that his well-meaning companion could suggest. He looked about the place with a shudder. What tortures might have taken place within these rocky walls, what humiliation, what nameless shame! The young man buried his face in his hands and groaned aloud in the agony of his soul. Goujet meanwhile continued his investigations. He looked in the window embrasures, and under the table, pulled the beds to pieces and peered into the dark corners. He found a shapeless fragment which might once have been a hat, also a dilapidated pair of men's shoes. In one place there was an ominous dark-colored patch on the stone floor, over which he shook his head. Next the hammocks came in for a share of his attention; they were empty, and he was about to turn away, when he spied a folded piece of paper pinned to one of them. "Master, see here!" he called out. But Baillot did not stir.

Goujet glanced at him compassionately as he slowly and carefully unfolded the bit of paper, then with a cry of joy he sprang across the room.

"Master, see! But you must listen! The paper— They are safe!"

"What—what is it?"

"Here—look !—read quickly !"

Baillot seized the precious bit of paper. "To M. Henri Baillot," he read, "Something tells me that you will return to this place to search for us. We have passed through great dangers, but God has mercifully preserved us, and in a way almost miraculous has given back to us my brother, with some other good friends. This morning we leave the island on the yacht, without chart or compass, but with firm faith that God will continue his loving care of us. Afterward we shall go to America." The letter was signed simply Madeline de Langres ; it was undated.

"The yacht arrived safely !" cried Goujet joyfully. "There is no doubt about it ; they are safe. But we are not," he added ruefully, "and I'm hungry enough to eat those old shoes."

"What of that !" said Baillot ; he had sprung to his feet and was pacing up and down the floor. His eyes shone brilliantly, his face was flushed, he smiled as he looked again and again at the precious bit of paper. "To America !" he murmured. "I also shall go ; I shall find her !"

"Oh yes ! that is all very well, but have you wings, my good master ? I doubt not that the lady has ; she is unquestionably an angel, yet if we don't find something to eat before long—But stay, did you read what was on the back of that letter ?"

"No," said Baillot, pausing an instant and turning the paper over. Carefully flattening it out in his hand, he read, " 'Beware of the convict.' What can that mean ?"

"The very charming sound that we heard last night on the terrace was probably a welcome from the convict.

Wonder where he keeps himself daytimes?" said Goujet, yawning disconsolately. "I am sleepy, master," he continued, "and these hammocks look very comfortable. If a man cannot eat, he can always sleep, what do you say?"

"Sleep if you will," replied Baillot, glancing about the place, "there can be nothing here to harm us."

"Beware of the convict." The words recurred to his mind almost as though a living voice had spoken them.

"Perhaps we had best look into this gallery to the left first and see whither it leads," he added.

"But we have no torch, master, and it is blacker than the pit in there," objected Goujet.

"Very well then, sleep; I cannot." And he seated himself in the great oaken chair by the table.

Goujet threw himself into one of the hammocks without further ado and was soon sound asleep. The regular sound of his heavy breathing together with the gentle monotonous tinkle of the spring as it fell into its rocky basin in the adjacent passage, blended in a soothing murmur of sound, which ascended to the vaulted ceiling and fell back in a hundred strange airy echoes. As the young man sat motionless in his chair, he could hear the low thunder of the surf on the narrow strip of beach below, and the strident shrilling of a locust in the vine whose branches drooped over the narrow windows. Now and then a bee, gorgeous in his panoply of gold and bronze, boomed heavily in, then seeing his mistake made blind frantic dashes for liberty, butting his head stupidly against the stones and buzzing angrily at his own blundering efforts. Baillot watched these struggles with dreamy intentness, and was conscious of a distinct feeling of relief each time one of these bold adventurers found his way into the sunshine again. Then his thoughts wandered back into the past, and busied themselves with all the strange things that had befallen him. When in his musings he had reached the present, he read the precious letter once more. "She has not forgotten me," he assured himself joyfully. "She knew that I would come." And this thought was perhaps more precious to him than the certainty that she was safe. He held it up before his mental vision, and looked at it on every side, as one looks upon a jewel of price.

"I shall find her," he murmured aloud, "and then—" Ah, what a fairy-land of joyful possibilities opened before his gaze! Moment by moment his thoughts became more remote, dazzling, and fantastic. His head sank back; his eyes closed. He had passed quite through the boundary land into the realm of sleep. As he slept he continued his dream of happiness. He thought that Madeline herself stood before him, her face sweet and smiling; she bent her dark eyes upon him with a look full of joy and tenderness, then an expression of ghastly fear swept across her face; she raised one hand as if in warning, her lips forming the words, "Beware of the convict!"

The dreamer started to his feet with a cry. Not three feet away crouched the figure of a man, his naked back, which was turned toward the horrified gazer, of a livid color, deeply scarred, seamed, and encrusted with blood as if from a recent and terrible scourging. This gruesome apparition moaned dismally as it frantically tore and scratched with its long talon-like fingers at the stones of the floor which were, as Baillot observed with a thrill of horror, darkly discolored as if with blood.

After a time the man arose and stretching his skeleton arms toward heaven with a long wailing cry turned as if to go away. As he did so his eyes fell upon Baillot, who stood frozen in his place. At first the gaze of the red eyeballs was wandering and vacant, but gradually there grew in them an appalling look of ferocity. He took a single step forward, clenching and unclenching his enormous hands; then suddenly with a gesture of violent repulsion he slunk back, shaking his shaggy head from side to side with a low bellow. Step by step he retreated as if impelled by some invisible but none the less potent force, till he had reached the doorway leading to the dark gallery; there he turned and darted away with a long howl of mingled rage and despair.

"*Bon dieu!* master, what is that?" cried Goujet, starting up from his hammock. "But what have you seen, that you look like that?"

Baillot regarded his questioner dully. "I have seen," he said, slowly, "what a man may become, if once the beast in him gets uppermost. There is no more frightful sight."

"You have seen—?"

"The convict."

"And he is mad?"

"Mad—yes, horrible!" He covered his face with his hands.

"This may be his lair," said Goujet, looking about him uneasily. "What was he doing, master?"

"He was scratching at yonder spot upon the floor," said Baillot with a quick shudder. "It looks like—blood."

"It does," admitted Goujet. "However—" He stopped short and looked about him once more. "We must get out of this place as quickly as possible; it is not on the whole a good place in which to sleep. Have you looked out of the windows?"

"No," said Baillot, staring gloomily at the ominous stain. "—Who did the wretch kill here?"

"Now, master, don't you think about that; it wasn't the young lady, for you see she warned you of the convict, which showed plainly enough that he'd done something or other not quite the thing; she speaks of dangers, you remember."

"True," admitted Baillot, referring once more to the comforting words on the scrap of paper. "I wish she had written more."

"She would have written more if she had supposed that you would ever see it," hazarded Goujet, with an enlivening grin, as he swung himself up to one of the windows. "*Bon!*" he exclaimed. "Our messmates have gone! But *diable!* there is the yacht making after the other! We're marooned, master, without a mouthful of food or a round of ammunition!"

CHAPTER XLVI

MAROONED

THE hapless adventurers sallied forth into the afternoon sunshine in silence; indeed there seemed very little to be said concerning their present dubious prospects. In the orchard after much searching they found a few oranges, and a little later Goujet discovered a grape-vine loaded with luscious clusters.

"This is all very well," he said, staring about him gloomily, "but we shall be having some sort of a winter before long. What are we going to do then?"

"Do?" echoed his companion, shrugging his shoulders, "we shall repair one of the huts yonder. As for food, the sea abounds in fish, and I see indications that the barnyard fowls are not all dead; at roosting-time I promise you that you shall see a dozen fat pullets in a row."

Goujet pulled another cluster. "A roasted chicken, and some of these grapes properly fermented were more to my taste," he said dismally. "But what is this? *Sacré bleu!* 'tis the Portuguese, de Miguel; they have left the scoundrel behind with a whole skin, but with an empty pocket, I'll warrant me. Now if I had only kept those pistoles——"

"Do not bring that unfortunate occurrence to my mind," said Baillot sternly. "I care not who has the pistoles so long as they are not in my possession."

Goujet shrugged his shoulders. "May you always remain as indifferent to money as you are now, master; which is equivalent to hoping that you will always have plenty of it. Hola there!" This last to the Portuguese, whose squat figure had approached within hailing distance.

"The saints be praised that you are here, honored seigniors!" cried de Miguel, hurrying towards them as fast as his legs could carry him. "I feared lest something might have befallen you!"

"Your solicitude does you credit," sneered Goujet. "Something did happen to me last night; some infernal rascal fired a pistol at me, and the ball hit me in the shoulder."

"Ah! seignior, no one can regret that little circumstance more than the unfortunate author of it," said de Miguel, rolling up his eyes. "One should be ready to forgive and forget. I am, I assure you. My spirit is fiery—ah! like the new wine in violence—but underneath is the tender heart that forgives—ah yes, forgives and forgets. Now that we are all, as it were, united in the bonds of a similar misfortune, it is not right to cherish resentment. I appeal to you, seignior, have I not spoken truly?"

"Unquestionably, sir," said Baillot gravely, to whom these last words were addressed. "But what has become of the sailor?"

"Ah, I perceive that you are aware of the sad circumstance that removed one of our number from the island last evening—to paradise, let us hope," and the speaker paused, apparently to shed tears. "Our friend here is a good shot," he continued with a ghastly grimace,—"an excellent shot, while the sailor unfortunately

386

was possessed of a pistol the priming of which should have received his previous attention. Attention to detail, honored seignior, is most important, is it not so? It actually becomes a matter of life and death with us poor frail mortals. Yes, many times it is so."

"You're getting a little mixed, aren't you?" observed Goujet. "These pious remarks of yours should have been addressed to the ghost of the sailor—that is if ghosts can profit by such excellent advice. But speaking of ghosts, I wonder if we shall be favored by a further exhibition at the castle to-night."

De Miguel glanced furtively over his shoulder. "The ruins?" he said, lowering his voice. "Ah, yes, a most unpleasant spot and very unsafe—most dangerous indeed. We will surely pass the night—ah—in some other locality? The surviving sailor—you were asking me, noble seignior—he was carried away by the miscreants, who also seized upon my vessel and my pistoles. Before heaven, yes, I have not so much as a pistareen in the whole earth! And what shall I do, once restored to my babes again, my ten—"

"Don't fret yourself about that," broke in Goujet with a grim laugh. "It may be that the ten will be all grown up and your wife married to another by the time you get back."

"But the pirates will return!" exclaimed de Miguel. "I—I—offered them money for my ransom. The brutes swore that the three hundred pistoles were not enough. Not enough? Holy Mary take pity on me! I was forced to make an order—for what do you think? Two thousand pistoles! My babes will be turned naked into the streets! But they promised to return and fetch me after they had gotten it. They said also this; you may yourselves know what to think of it, ' *The rats will have dug out the cheese by that time.*' "

Goujet swore a little under his breath; he looked at Baillot. "So that is their game!"

"So be it," said Baillot coolly. "The rats may escape them yet."

"They left me absolutely nothing to eat," groaned de Miguel, snuffling dismally. "They said that I was too fat, that it would profit me to fast. But the saints may bear me witness that the fat on the outside of a man's belly never yet served to appease the pangs that torment it within."

"Eat some grapes," advised Baillot hospitably.

"But fruit will not suffice for the pains of such hunger as mine," moaned de Miguel, laying his hand over the pit of his stomach and looking beseechingly at the young man. "Picture to yourself, seignior, I had not a mouthful of dinner, and but a crust such as one would scorn to toss to a dog for my breakfast. And this after the wretches had stolen my pistoles, and were at the moment making merry with my wine and provisions.—I say mine; you remember, seignior, that you did not pay me for the victualling of the ship."

"I have not forgotten the fact," said Baillot coldly.

"That hundred and fifty pistoles will at least keep my little ones from starving," whined de Miguel, hugging himself. "You also remember that it was the sum of one hundred—"

"You forget the conditions on which I was to pay you that sum," interrupted Baillot. "You were to spare me the infliction of your conversation. You had little enough to say when I first made your acquaintance."

388

"Shall we leave you to your repast?" said Goujet, addressing the Portuguese, who scowling with rage at the rebuff which he had received was gorging himself with the ripe grapes.

"Leave me? No, no—I beg of you, it will soon be dark ; see, the sun is already setting. I will accompany you wherever you may be pleased to go."

"We think of spending the night on the terrace of the château," said Goujet. "We slept there last night ; we heard curious sounds it is true, but ghosts seldom molest an honest man."

"The terrace of the castle!" gasped de Miguel, choking and gurgling over a half-swallowed grape. "But no, I will not remain there—"

"Hold your tongue, fellow, and come along," said Baillot impatiently. "I am going to examine the cottage."

"The cottage? Ah, yes, the cottage will be—" commenced de Miguel, then he stopped short.

"You evidently know this place," said Baillot, looking at him keenly. "I should be pleased to learn of its purpose and of those who once lived here."

"The seignior forgets that he has offered me money to be silent," said de Miguel, showing his yellow teeth in a wicked smile, "one hundred and fifty pistoles are not to be so lightly hazarded. Perhaps the seignior thinks to cheat me out of them, by cajoling me to forget the conditions. But José de Miguel knows when to speak and when to—"

"Take the hundred and fifty pistoles, dog," cried Baillot in a fury. "And know that you are speaking to the Comte de Lantenac, with whose name dishonor cannot be coupled." And flinging his purse disdainfully toward the Portuguese, the young man strode away without so much as turning his head.

But it was Goujet who caught the purse as it fell.

"Dare to mention the subject of money again in presence of my master and I will throttle you as I would throttle a dog," he hissed. "This money is not yours; it belongs to my master; I shall keep it for him, for, heaven save him, it is all he has in the world."

"Your master, as you call him—eh? the Comte de Lantenac, has a curious servant! An avowed pirate, ha, ha! For himself, he is an escaped convict; or what is the same thing, an escaped Huguenot! He is also a dirty beggar. Aha! it is so! I knew it all the time; and what now if I shall—Help—Murder!"

"No! I will not kill you; you may be useful to us," said Goujet, falling back a pace and glaring down at his victim, who, as it has been seen, was animated by a curious mixture of abject cowardice and bold insolence. "But remember what I have said." And the speaker turned and strode rapidly after the retreating figure of the Comte de Lantenac.

"Malediction!" muttered de Miguel with a murderous gleam in his eyes. "I shall be useful to you—yes! But not in the way you think. The saints spare me and I will give a silver statute of our lady to the shrine at Terciora; after that we shall see!" And he hurried after the others.

Goujet found that his master had paused at the foot of a group of enormous pine trees, and that he was examining a rope ladder which extended from the ground to the lower branches of one of the trees.

"There is something above; I think I shall go up and see what it is," he remarked without turning his head.

"I will go first," said Goujet. "I say, master," he shouted presently, "there's a capital place up here. Come up."

Baillot was by his side almost before the last words were out of his mouth. "A famous retreat, indeed!" he exclaimed, looking about. "If I am not mistaken this is some of Winters' handiwork."

"Cupboards!" cried Goujet, "and, *morbleu*, here is something to eat!" And he drew forth a box of sea-biscuit, none the worse for their sojourn in this airy storehouse. "A mighty snug place," he continued, "when we draw up the rope-ladder."

Meanwhile de Miguel had arrived at the spot, and puzzled by the sudden disappearance of his two companions began to call their names aloud. "Seigniors, good seigniors! Where are you? Do not desert a poor, helpless old man!"

Goujet looked over the side with a grin. "Let him alone," he said, "the old fox."

But de Miguel had caught the sound of his voice. He clasped his hands and stared about him. "Dear, good, generous, gracious seigniors!" he bawled, "do not conceal yourselves, I beg of you. If I am left alone in this place for the night, I shall go mad; I know I shall go mad. May the saints in heaven soften your hard hearts!"

Baillot, who thought the matter had gone quite far enough, called out, "Come up the rope-ladder, fellow, and cease that discordant braying."

"Ah, good seignior, you are aloft? Is it possible! But why? Will you not descend?"

"Come up, I tell you!" repeated Baillot.

"But it is impossible, seignior—absolutely impossi-

391

ble ! You forget my weight—my infirmities—my weakness—my old age.''

"Come up ! Come up, idiot !" shouted Goujet.

" I cannot, I tell you. I will not. What, trust my limbs to that fabric of rope ? 'Tis monstrous to ask such a thing, I refuse absolutely.''

" Very well then, remain where you are. I shall draw up the ladder presently for the night.''

" You will come down, good seignior, I beg of you ! You will not leave a helpless old man to a night of terror fit to turn his brain ?''

" The devil take the man !" cried Goujet. " What shall we do with him ? He will bellow at us so that we cannot sleep.''

" I will go down and try to persuade him to ascend,'' said Baillot. One madman about the place is quite enough, and it is true the fellow's wits are slender enough already.''

" I don't know about that,'' grumbled Goujet ; " but while you argue the case with our interesting companion, I will return to the cavern and fetch some fresh water, and also bring the hammocks along.''

"The cavern ?'' said Baillot, "I had best go along—''

" *Peste !* I am not afraid of the convict, if that is what you mean. I shall kill the brute if he attacks me.''

Accordingly the two descended the ladder, to the great joy of de Miguel, who concluded that their hearts had been touched by his persuasive eloquence.

" Heaven will reward you for your goodness, seigniors,'' he blubbered. " Though I, because of my poverty, cannot. Not a pistole—'' He checked himself suddenly and glanced apprehensively over his shoulder. But Goujet had already departed.

CHAPTER XLVII

BAILLOT looked after the retreating figure of Goujet doubtfully. "I believe I ought to go with him," he said aloud.

"Where is he going, gracious seignior?" asked de Miguel amicably. He had apparently forgotten his re-sentment, or if not forgotten had at least ticketed and laid it away for future use as occasion might serve. As he had already very sensibly and piously observed, 'the present was no time for anger; and heaven should bear him witness, that until he was safe he would live in charity with all men.'

"He has gone to the cavern for water," replied Baillot shortly.

"To the cavern!" echoed de Miguel, with a look full of astonishment. "And where might that be? I know of no cavern on the island."

"If you choose to follow you will see."

De Miguel followed without further remark, but at the entrance of the place he stopped short, saying that he preferred to wait outside. Goujet was nowhere to be seen, and Baillot strode into the dark gallery with some misgivings.

"Goujet!" he shouted aloud. There was no reply. He quickened his pace to a run and soon came upon the missing man. He was engaged in a violent struggle with the insane convict. Both were large powerful men, and Baillot who had started forward to help Goujet found himself at a loss; the two had fallen upon the floor, and were writhing, twisting and turning so rapidly that it was impossible to strike without danger of wounding the wrong man. The breath of the wrestlers came in quick gasps, while from time to time the maniac emitted a short snapping snarl like that of a rabid wolf. Goujet at length succeeded in forcing the half-naked wretch into a corner.

"Quick, master!" he shouted breathlessly, "the knife!"

"No, bind him!" cried Baillot, rushing forward with the hammock ropes.

"Take care, master; he'll tear you if he gets a chance!" yelled Goujet, "—the knife I say!"

But Baillot had already passed the rope firmly about the limbs of the madman, who suddenly yielded with a low moan and fell prostrate to the floor.

"*Sacré bleu !* master, why do you wish the beast to live?" said Goujet, rising to his feet after he had satisfied himself that the maniac's bonds were secure. "He would have killed me ! I had but just entered, and as I saw nothing I laid my knife down for an instant to unknot the ropes of the hammocks. I had unfastened one and was about to undo the other, when—*morbleu !* —as suddenly as the lightning from heaven this wretch leapt upon me from behind ! You know the rest."

Baillot thoughtfully eyed the convict, who was now whimpering and moaning like a child. "Are you much hurt?" he asked, turning to look anxiously at Goujet.

"He tore me like a tiger. *Ma foi !* but I am unlucky of late. What now will you do with him?"

394

"I wish to find out what has happened in this place," replied Baillot, glancing with a shudder at the dark stain upon the floor.

"And do you suppose that he can tell you? He has lost the power of speech by this time!"

"No, you mistake, listen!"

The maniac was chattering to himself in a low incoherent murmur, rolling his head rapidly from side to side as he did so.

"The king of the island—" were the words that Baillot caught—"the king—but she shall be queen, ay, queen—queen. And mine! When they are all dead she will love me and follow me, but I shall kill her also at my pleasure. She scorns me and hates me now, but I can wait!"

"Who are you talking about?" demanded Baillot in a suffocated voice.

The madman paid no heed. "She is dead already— ay, dead, and buried. The shadows dance every night on her grave.—The blood—'tis accursed; I cannot rub it out. They have left me alone with the shadows. Her shadow smiles at me, but I cannot seize it, it flits— flits away. If I scourge myself for a thousand nights she will come and fetch me away from this place; she has promised, and then this fire will be taken out of my head. The fire—" And he broke off into one of the long indescribable howls which had terrified the crew of the yacht on the night of their arrival at the island.

"Great heavens, master, come! We shall both be mad if we stay here and listen much longer."

"You have heard?" said Baillot, as they issued into the open air. "She is dead."

His air of conviction was so strong, and his face so ghastly that Goujet despaired of comforting him, but he said stoutly enough, "The wretch is possessed of the devil, and knows not what he says ; surely you would not allow such nonsense to disturb you?"

Baillot made no reply.

They had quite forgotten de Miguel, and Goujet started back with a cry of alarm as he stumbled over the squat figure, huddled together in a trembling heap a few paces from the entrance to the gallery.

"Those frightful sounds," gasped the Portuguese, "holy St. Michael ! what are they?"

"A gentleman," began Goujet, "who is pleased to call himself the king of—*Morbleu !* man, what do you mean by grabbing at me like that?"

"He is dead then, and you have seen his spirit?"

"Dead? No, I wish he was ; however cursedly unpleasant ghosts may be, they at least don't bite and tear one like a mad dog."

"What then have you seen ? For the love of heaven, seignior, tell me?" implored the Portuguese, wiping the great drops from his forehead, and looking fearfully over his shoulder.

"A madman—a mad convict, who has come to this place in some way as mysterious as is the place itself."

"A convict—ah !" cried de Miguel in a tone of great relief.

Nothing further was said, and presently all three arrived once more at the foot of the great trees. At the sight of Baillot half-way up the rope-ladder, the Portuguese broke out afresh into a torrent of expostulations and reproaches, in the midst of which he was interrupted by Goujet, who informed him quietly that he, Goujet,

would take the greatest pleasure in life in blowing out
his rascally brains if he did not immediately get himself up the ladder. "You need not call upon my master," he added, "for the poor gentleman is half-mad
with grief at something the convict—may the foul fiend
fly away with him—said in his ravings."

"And what did he say?" questioned de Miguel
eagerly.

"He intimated that he had put an end to the young
lady, who in company with my master was shipwrecked
on this island," replied Goujet, hoping that if the Portuguese knew anything to the contrary he would betray
his knowledge.

De Miguel, however, suddenly turned his attention to
the rope-ladder, and with better courage than might
have been expected, soon gained the top.

"Eh!" he was saying to himself cheerfully, "and so
do the saints reward the virtuous and punish the guilty.
My fine haughty young Huguenot is plunged into mourn-
ing because of the ravings of a mad convict. It is good ;
he will perchance be more civil. What now would he
give, I wonder, for the secret old José has locked up in
his breast? But he has no money ; I know that—beyond the pittance which that rascally pirate has in his
possession, and which shall yet be mine. The grand
seignior does not wish my conversation? He shall not
have it." And with such pleasant and benevolent
thoughts did the worthy gentleman comfort himself as
he climbed the swaying ladder into the dizzy heights
aloft, where he presently fell asleep, with a smile upon
his lips like a fat, elderly and altogether disreputable
cherub.

The next morning he ventured to condole with Baillot upon the probable loss which he had sustained. "I feel for you, noble seignior, I do indeed," he murmured, rolling up his little eyes till only the very yellow whites of them were visible. "To lose a loved one, and in such a horrible and heart-rending manner ; a beautiful young creature, your faithful friend—or perhaps I should say servant—tells me. To be torn in pieces by a mad—"

"What do you mean, sir?" demanded Baillot, facing him suddenly. "How dare you !" Then he turned away with a choking sound in his throat.

De Miguel rubbed his hands and smiled.

"Why did you speak to that beast about—about what we heard in the cavern?" asked Baillot of Goujet later in the day.

"I told him because I thought that he knew something to the contrary," replied Goujet. "It cannot be true, master. It is too horrible ; the man only raved— as he had doubtless always spoken—lies."

"Don't speak to me of the matter again, if you love me," said Baillot, turning away. "But I had forgotten, we left the—the man bound. Something must be done, to leave him thus would be inhuman."

"I will attend to the matter," said Goujet gruffly. And he strode away fully resolved to put the maniac to death before he should have opportunity to do further mischief. But when he arrived at the cavern he found it empty. Nor was the convict ever again seen by any of them during their sojourn on the island. He had disappeared, perhaps led by his mad fancies over the cliff into the sea.

As the weeks passed on, it became necessary to make some preparations for the approaching winter. The autumnal gales had already begun to blow, and sullen mists brooded over the island for days at a time. The deciduous trees and shrubs dropped their foliage, and yellow fields and sodden woods afforded but a scant sustenance for three hungry men.

"We must bestir ourselves," declared Goujet, "if we wish to find ourselves alive in the spring. And, *morbleu!* master, you at least are young, and life has much that is good in it still. Once away from this accursed spot you will forget."

But Baillot only shook his head. He was as fully convinced as are most young persons under similar circumstances that on no one had ever fallen such a sorrow; that no other man in the history of the world had ever loved with such intensity as he had loved, and that it was therefore little short of impertinence for anyone to suggest the possibility of future happiness. Happiness, he assured himself gloomily, had forever fled; he would gladly die and be buried in this spot, where, he was firmly convinced, reposed the remains of his beloved Madeline.

As for the third person in this strangely assorted trio, de Miguel—he spent his time in alternately gloating over the evident wretchedness of the young Huguenot, whom he hated with all the intensity of his little soul, and in bewailing the perfidy of the pirates, who had broken their word in not returning to fetch him as they had promised.

"Holy heaven!" he would cry, "did not that monster—what you call him? Lock? Yes, Lock—did he not swear by the heart of his mother, by the soul of his father, and by everything he held sacred in heaven or on earth that having once obtained the two thousand pistoles he would return and fetch me? And now he has the pistoles and I am left to perish. Ah—malediction! I could tear his eyes out!"

"I don't doubt," says Goujet with a grin, "that he made the order to read ten thousand instead of two; there's nothing easier, you know."

"*Ten* thousand! *Ten*—thousand—pistoles! Oh, seignior, you don't think such a thing could be?—Not that I have such a sum; God knows that I am a poor man—yes wretchedly poor, but such perfidy."

"Ten thousand pistoles *is* a pretty sum," pursued Goujet relentlessly. "And Lock is not a bad-looking fellow; rather than part with such a sum your wife may have concluded to console herself for your absence. Lock will make a capital father for the ten—no it must be eleven by this time."

De Miguel could only groan and tear at his greasy locks. "The man is welcome to Marthé," he would say, "I care not a fig for the woman; and as for the ten; pah, children are easily found. But ten—thousand —pistoles! there is another matter now, and I an old man. Oh, oh! Malediction!" Then he would sink upon his knees and tell his beads over and over with fervor, while the vows of candles, silver statues, and other votive offerings mounted up steadily day by day.

But notwithstanding the mental gloom and anxiety which oppressed two of the little party, all joined heartily in the work of preparing for the months of loneliness and isolation which lay before them. The smaller of the three cottages was provided with a roof from the ruins of its neighbor, which had chanced to partly escape the flames; its chimney was rebuilt, and

a semblance of comfort given its smoke-blackened
and charred interior by the fragments of rich tapestry
which the adventurers fetched from the ruins of the
château. From the same source came two or three
chairs, a table, and even a bed, which was ceded by the
others to Baillot in tacit acknowledgment of his higher
rank.

The young count seemed to derive a gloomy pleasure
from delving amid the piles of rubbish about the ruins.
And both Goujet and the Portuguese frequently accompanied him in these expeditions. De Miguel, indeed,
after awhile developed almost a mania for this employment, and could hardly be dragged away from it even
to assist Goujet in the necessary labors of fishing, cutting fuel for their fire, and carrying water from the
spring.

The reason for this infatuation became apparent to
Goujet when one day he came upon the Portuguese at
work with his pick. "Anything new?" he inquired
cheerfully. "If you could find an iron pot it would be
a blessing."

At the sound of his voice de Miguel dropped his pick,
and hastily snatching up something from the ground
thrust it into his pocket. The action did not escape
the keen eye of Goujet.

"What have you there?" he demanded; "fetch it
out."

"Nothing—nothing at all, I swear it," said de
Miguel, turning pale.

"You are lying. Show it to me and I won't take it
from you. Out with it, or I will see it anyhow, and it
will not go back into your pocket after that, I can tell
you."

Thus urged, de Miguel produced what looked at first sight like a shapeless mass of lead. "Silver!" he whispered. "There must be heaps of it in the ruins, and I am a poor man now."

CHAPTER XLVIII

SHADOWS

GOUJET looked at the molten mass thoughtfully, then he handed it back to de Miguel. "Candlesticks, I should say," he commented briefly. "But why did they burn a place like this without removing the valuables?"

The Portuguese shrugged his shoulders and muttered something about lightning and earthquake.

"Who did the place belong to?"

"How should I know?"

"You're lying again; you do know."

"As you will, seignior. It is true that I could make you a great tale about the place, but what would it profit? Whatever José de Miguel says, you have one answer to make, you are lying. Is that the way to speak to a man of noble blood, I ask you?"

Goujet laughed uproariously at this.

"Laugh if you will, but later, we shall see! It will be my turn then." And de Miguel with a scowl turned to his digging again.

Goujet presently sauntered over to the spot where the young Comte de Lantenac was rambling about, stooping now and again to examine some fragment of torn canvas or bit of broken carving with a melancholy interest. The cold wind shrilled dismally through the ruined arches above their heads, and from the lowering clouds there fell an occasional dash of rain.

403

"Ugh, master! this is a dismal place," observed Goujet with a shiver. "Come, let us leave yonder mole to grub for his treasure, while we seek the shelter of the cottage, where I have a glorious bright fire."

"This place accords better with my temper than the cheerfulest fireside," said Baillot gloomily. "But I have found something to-day which I would fain examine at my leisure, so I will go."

De Miguel dropped his pick with a muttered curse and scuttled after them. He was afraid to be left alone, though he grudged every moment spared from his self-imposed task of examining the ruin.

"What is it that you have found, master?" asked Goujet as they walked along toward the hut.

"Nothing of value," replied the young man. "It seems to be a record or diary kept by some former inhabitant of the place. It is much injured by damp and mould, besides being partly burned, but the fragments of it may throw some light on the mystery of this strange place."

"What is this that you say, seignior?" asked de Miguel eagerly, joining them at this point in the conversation.

"I have found an old manuscript of some sort," replied Baillot shortly. It was impossible for him to disguise the dislike which he felt for de Miguel, though he always treated him with forbearance and even kindness, considering himself responsible in a measure for the undeniable misfortunes which had befallen the man.

"May I look at it, noble seignior?" asked de Miguel politely enough.

"You may, certainly, when we shall have arrived at the cottage. It is raining quite too fast for further comfort out of doors," said Baillot, quickening his steps.

Their frugal supper over and a couple of the resinous torches—of which Goujet had laid in a store for use in the long dismal evenings—lighted, the young count produced his find; he had wrapped it in his cloak for greater protection against the damp.

"I have your permission to examine this writing, noble seignior," said de Miguel, reaching out his hand confidently.

"I have not yet had opportunity to examine it myself," returned Baillot.

It was, as he had seen on his first casual examination of it, a manuscript, written on yellowish paper, and bound between heavy covers of leather, richly stamped and gilded. These covers were now sadly warped and shrunken, and the pages within scorched and charred at their edges, while damp and mildew had almost obliterated the characters upon many of them. Here and there a page could be deciphered with tolerable ease. The young Huguenot turned over the leaves for a long time in silence, while de Miguel watched his face with eager attention.

"What is it all about, master, if I may make so bold as to ask?" inquired Goujet with a yawn.

"I will read a little from it, if you would like to hear," replied Baillot.

"I should like nothing better."

De Miguel said nothing, but his black eyes gleamed with anxiety.

"It is, as I have said, a sort of diary or journal," said Baillot slowly, "and seems, at least in its earlier portions, to have been written by a child, or by one

little used to expressing himself in writing. The dates
have all been destroyed, since the upper edge of the
volume appears to have suffered more from the fire than
other portions of it."

" '—a pretty book, and a large. I may have it, I
have asked leave of monsieur, my father. I mean to
write all that I see and do in it ; it will then be a history such as I have seen of those who have now disappeared from the earth. I do many things each day. I
study and learn my tasks which I recite to monsieur, my
father, in the library. My mother is very sad, often I
find her in tears when I have done reciting. I say to
her, What, are you not pleased that I so well know my
Latin verses ? But she only weeps the more, then my
father falls into a great rage and stamps his foot, and
tells her that she is no better than a baby and that she
may take her tears and herself away. For myself I
know not why she weeps. My father is not often unkind to her, and she possesses many wonderful and
beautiful gowns, jewels, and trinkets. Sometimes I
have said this to her, and she tells me that I am but a
child ; that I do not understand, and that I will drive
her mad with my talk. Why—'

"But here," said Baillot, "I come upon a page
which is entirely obliterated. On the next page I can
read but a sentence or two ; here is one '—tells me that
this is impossible, and was so stern when he said it that
I was frightened. I am beginning to think—'

"Further down the page occurs this, 'A most beautiful suite of rooms has been furnished for me. My
father says that I am older now, and that I can no
longer occupy the little room next my mother. I do
not know whether I am glad or sorry. My mother

wept again and embraced me, and called me her poor
child; at which father again rebuked her severely.
I am making much progress in all of my studies, and
have, besides, plenty of time for recreation. I am not
permitted to go abroad alone, which I much regret,
as I should dearly love to play with the gardener's
children. I asked my mother if I might have Pierre,
the gardener's oldest son to play with me at the château; she consented and was about to send for him;
but my father, coming in at that moment and hearing
of the matter, forbade it. What are you thinking of,
madame, he said; you assuredly forget yourself? But
my mother answered—very sadly, I thought—No, I do
not forget; how can I? I only thought—'

"'You only thought—you only thought! thundered
my father. You are always thinking, and things that
you ought not. And with that he took her by the arm
and led her out of the room. I could hear her sobbing in the next room.'"

The reader paused and turned over another page;
then coming to a place where several leaves were fastened together by the damp, he carefully loosened
them, but shook his head as he glanced them over.
"There is nothing here which is legible," he said
thoughtfully.

"Malediction! this is of no interest at all," broke
out de Miguel loudly, "—the tattle of a brainless lad,
who should have been in better business. You will read
no more of it, seignior."

Baillot looked up in surprise; the man's swarthy face
was quite flushed—but that might be the effect of the
fire, which was roaring merrily up the great chimney;
his fingers were twisting themselves uneasily, and he had

the appearance of a man who with great difficulty controls himself.

"You will now graciously permit me to examine the book for myself," he continued. The last words were sufficiently courteous, but the look with which he laid hold of the book was both threatening and insolent.

Baillot quietly withdrew the volume from his grasp. "You do not, for some reason, wish to hear more of what is written here," he said, "or possibly you do not wish me to read it. If the first reason be true you are at liberty to retire to your hammock, but I beg that you will not so forget yourself in the future as to lay hands upon something which is quite as much my property as are those trinkets, which you so diligently search for at every opportunity, yours."

At this reference to his newly-gotten treasures de Miguel turned pale. He mumbled some inarticulate words, then arose and threw himself into his hammock.

"Go on, master, if you will," said Goujet, who was busily engaged in carving spoons, forks, and other homely utensils for use in their modest menage. "I think the lad's journal is likely to throw some light on this place; and, *morbleu!* as long as we are here there is nothing else to think about."

"Where next I am able to decipher the writing," observed Baillot, who seemed deeply interested in his discovery, "the writer has apparently grown older and wiser, also more impatient with his quiet life. It begins thus, 'I should like to have been born a Greek, or a Roman, though they are now all dead and gone—monsieur, my father, tells me—and their cities in ruins. I can think of nothing more splendid than to be such a man as Julius Cæsar, leading forth great armies, and compelling savage nations to submit to his rule. I should like to see Rome as it was then ; father says that too is completely destroyed. I mean shortly to get away from this place and see for myself. Even if father and mother have some secret which chains them down to this miserable island, I see no reason why I should stay here forever. When I was a child I was told that there was no other place where men could exist; but although I have said nothing I have concluded that this is not true, for where do all the things come from which appear from time to time for our use here, the satins, velvets, laces, and jewels which I wear, and which my mother wears—though she does not care for them, and weeps more than ever, so much indeed that her eyes are red all the time. It is quite spoiling her beauty. I told her this the other day and she stopped crying at once.'

" 'What do you know of beauty ? She asked with a strange look. Have I not read of Helen of Troy, I made answer, and of how the warriors and kings fought for her ? If I had lived in those days I should also have fought and I should have conquered. One should have seen how my mother looked when I said this; but she answered quietly enough, Do not speak of these things before your father, he will be ill-pleased.'

" 'I am at present learning a new art, that of painting. I like it exceedingly. It is most wonderful how one can imitate such a thing as the bloom on a peach, or the dashing foam of the sea with a few pigments, composed, I find, for the most part of earths. I am so infatuated with this new employment that I care for nothing else. Father looks very gloomy and sad, whatever I do. And my mother is not more cheerful than usual.'"

"Poor lad," observed Goujet, "whatever crimes his parents may have been guilty of, he seems innocent enough."

"From this point I can make nothing of what follows for fully a third of the volume," said Baillot; "the writing begins to be legible again with these words '—plan; I mean to bribe one of these men to take me away. I am heartily weary of this place and of my life here. I have learned enough to be sure that it is unnatural, and that there is a world of men and women beyond this hateful rim of ocean. Into this world I am determined to make my way at whatever cost. I said something of the sort to my mother yesterday evening while we were walking on the terrace; we had been looking at the roses which are just in their glory and of which she is extravagantly fond. She had seemed almost happy as we walked up and down, she leaning upon my arm. What I said to her was this. I am not happy here, madame; what can a strong young man, like me, do in a place like this? Why do we stay here? For my part I should rather be a bare-legged fisher boy, or one of the men who come here from time to time on the little black lugger.'

"'At this she started violently; What do you know of the lugger? she asked in a strange voice.'

"'I know more than you think, I answered with a laugh. What would you say if I should slip away some fine day to try my fortune in the world? She turned pale, and would, I believe, have fallen but that I passed one arm about her and held her up.'

"'Do you love me at all? she finally gasped, looking at me with her great frightened eyes. Assuredly I do, dearest mother, I answered. You do not doubt it?'

" 'No, no, child, she said, but I solemnly tell you that if you attempt to do what you have said that it will be my death. Promise—*promise* that you will not attempt it! And she actually sank down upon her knees before me, and kissed my hands as she begged and prayed and wept.'

" ' I think I should have promised her, though I should have been sorely grieved to do so, but at that moment my father stepped from the window, and upon seeing him, my mother sprang to her feet quite frightened; luckily he did not observe her attitude. He had come to bring us some very strange news. The seneschal of the castle has disappeared from our midst. It is most strange and unaccountable. Both my father and madame, my mother, seemed very much frightened and disturbed by this intelligence.'

" 'I do not see why you should care, I said very coolly; he was a bad man, and not over-straight in his dealings. He stole mother's diamonds I firmly believe, and you know how many times I have caught him prowling about my rooms. It was only yesterday that I discovered him in the act of opening my private desk, which stands in my bedchamber. How now, sirrah! I exclaimed, how dare you make free with my property in such a fashion. On my word, sir, you should be soundly dealt with were I master here! The rascal turned pale as he looked at me; I do not doubt but that I frightened him, for I was more angry than I often am. He bowed very low, and backed out of the room in such an absurd fashion that I laughed aloud.'

" 'Neither my father nor my mother interrupted me

411

by a single word while I was speaking, but when I had finished, my father said in a strange excited voice, It may be the providence of the Most High ; may the saints give me wisdom to act aright ! As for my mother she smiled as I have not seen her in many a long day. I can see plainly that secretly they are very glad to be rid of this man. I think that for some reason, which I am at a loss to understand, they were afraid of him.' "

At this point in the reading the young count paused and passed his hand across his eyes. "Your torches, Goujet, give a most uncertain light,'' he remarked. "And interesting as this chronicle is, I must leave its further perusal till daylight." He closed the volume and placing it under his pillow, threw himself down upon his bed. Goujet followed his example, and soon silence and sleep reigned in the place.

By degrees the fire died away, till at length only a bed of red coals remained, which winked and purred gently amid the gathering grey of the ashes, while the shadows which lurked in the corners and about the rafters of the room grew gradually darker and heavier. After a time a shadow blacker than the others took shape to itself and darted boldly out from among the rest; in form it resembled a man, and it thrust something deep down into the bed of sleepy coals. They licked the something gently with their red tongues, then finding it to their liking leapt up suddenly with a merry and fierce light, which roared up the great chimney. Then the dancing flames fell back as suddenly as they had sprung up, and the sleepers, who had turned uneasily as the bright light fell upon their closed eyelids, breathed softly again. As for the shadow, it slept with the rest.

CHAPTER XLIX

A NICHE IN THE WALL

IT was still raining heavily when Baillot awoke the next morning. He could hear the wind as it tore hungrily about the cottage, shrieking down the chimney as it passed, then roaring away into the tops of the great pine trees, which it lashed in a very fury of sullen rage.

Goujet was already astir, and a fresh fire crackled merrily on the hearth. "An ill day, master," he said cheerfully, seeing that Baillot's eyes were open and that he was staring thoughtfully about the room. "Little as I love this island of ours, I am not sorry for a bit of solid ground under my feet this morning; the stanchest ship ever built would be but a bubble in the grasp of such a storm. I thought of that book of yours, master, and I said to myself, not a bad thing to pass away the time a day like this. I want to find out if the lad ever made out to get away."

Thus reminded Baillot thrust his hand under the pillow. Then he sat up, turned it over and shook it, next he sprang out of bed looking rather anxious.

"Where did I put that book last night, Goujet?" he asked, "I thought I thrust it under my pillow; I remember to have had a notion that perhaps—Where is the Portuguese? I don't see him."

"In his hammock; he's a lazy dog and sleeps late,"

replied Goujet,—"But no, he isn't there. Where can the fellow have gone?"

At this moment the door flew open and de Miguel came in dripping with wet. "I have been for fresh water," he said, setting down a brimming bucket upon the floor and turning to secure the door against the blast, a task which he finally accomplished with difficulty.

"The devil you have?" exclaimed Goujet in amazement. "What has gotten you on a sudden, Monsieur de Miguel? Such a fit of usefulness is surprising."

"I was thirsty and there was nothing to drink."

"And so you went as far as the cavern alone to quench your thirst. The bucket was half full last night, but that was not fresh enough, eh?"

"Can you tell me, sir, the whereabouts of the volume from which I was reading last night, and which you were so anxious to examine?" said Baillot, who had been continuing the search for his find of the day before.

"No, seignior, I cannot," replied de Miguel doggedly, throwing himself down into a chair before the fire and stretching out his legs to the genial blaze.

"It is very strange what can have become of it," said Goujet, "I remember to have seen my master place it beneath his pillow last night. Have you not seen it?"

"I saw it last night in the hands of the noble Comte de Lantenac," replied de Miguel with an insolent wag of the head; "he refused me permission to take it in my hands."

"You have destroyed it—or hidden it!" exclaimed Baillot. De Miguel made no reply.

"Answer me, fellow; what have you done with my book?"

"What have I done with *your book*, seignior? And how pray, did it come to be *your* book? Is this island then *your* property? Was the château *yours* ? By what right did you make free with what you knew to be the private journal of another man? You prate about honor! Pah, I spit upon such honor!"

Baillot turned pale and fell back a few paces, and de Miguel perceiving his advantage sprang to his feet. "Suppose that to protect those who once lived here from your insolent curiosity I burnt the book; I say that I had the right to do so!"

"This is infamous!" cried Goujet. "I will teach you, dog, to—"

"Nay! Let him be, what he has said is true," groaned Baillot, "though God knows that I never thought of it in that light. Speak no more of the matter; it is finished," and without another word he wrapped himself in his cloak and strode out into the storm.

The smile of haughty derision and noble contempt, which de Miguel's face had worn as he thus metaphorically ground the young count under his boot-heels, now faded to a sickly, imploring grin when he perceived that he was to be left alone with Goujet. He sidled toward the door.

"You would follow my master, would you?—to insult him further perhaps. You—you dirty scoundrel, you!" roared Goujet, choking with wrath. "Try to do it and observe what follows!" And he caught the unfortunate de Miguel by the scruff of his neck, and bestowed sundry hearty kicks on that portion of his anatomy designed by nature for chastisement.

"Oh—oh! You villain, you unspeakable pig!"
bawled de Miguel. "How dare you? the seignior told
you not to touch me! He would not permit this! Help!
Mercy! You are killing me."

"Killing you, no! though you deserve it," said
Goujet, shaking his victim till the teeth rattled in his
head, then setting him down with a smart cuff on each
ear as a sort of finish to the performance. "How does
your honor feel now? Such a fine delicate sense of
honor that you can instruct and reprove the head of one
of the oldest families in France."

De Miguel whimpered dolorously, caressing meanwhile the injured portions of his frame with a fat pudgy
hand.

"You burnt that book, you scoundrel, because you
feared that it would relate some villainy in which you
have had a share. Perhaps you know more about the
disappearance of these people, and the destruction of
this place than you would like to have discovered."

"I have not—I swear I have not! Holy St. Michael
and all the saints bear me witness! I am as innocent as
a babe of any crime!"

"Of course I shall believe you, now that you have
said that," sneered Goujet. "Your sense of honor is
so great that you could not perjure yourself. Now listen,
I am going in search of my master. You need not follow."

De Miguel made no reply, and Goujet, hastily wrapping himself in his cloak, beneath which he sheltered a
bundle of torches, left the cottage. He made directly
for the cavern, some instinct telling him that there he
should find his young master. He was not mistaken;
in the great oaken chair before the table sat the young

Huguenot, his head bowed upon his arms, the water dripping off his clothing onto the stone floor, where it had formed a little pool, which was already stretching forth a long crawling finger toward the ill-omened stain as if to wash it away.

"I thought I should find you here!" exclaimed Goujet cheerfully, affecting not to notice his master's manifest abandonment to his grief. "Since we cannot read your book—which the rascal finally acknowledged that he destroyed because of his fear lest you should discover in it something against himself—we can explore this place. I have brought torches."

"He acknowledged that?" asked Baillot, without changing his attitude.

"He certainly did," said Goujet without a qualm. "I took him in hand a little after you left."

"I thought I forbade you to touch him," said Baillot, but with no anger in his voice.

"So he said," quoth Goujet. "I didn't remember anything of the sort. I didn't hurt him seriously. Come, master, don't sit there in your wet clothes. I have some torches, and we will do what we have often spoken of—explore this place thoroughly."

Baillot shuddered, then he arose as if with a sudden resolution, and taking a lighted torch began to look carefully into all the dark corners of the place; he had a lurking hope that he might find some further message from Madeline. Before many minutes had elapsed, he called to Goujet, who was examining the long gallery leading to the château.

"Hold my torch," he said. "There is something here which looks like a sliding panel, or door."

"How can that be in the solid rock?" asked Goujet.

"But yes! *Morbleu!* There is something of the kind there, and a recess back of it."

A portion, apparently of the stone itself, but upon closer examination turning out to be a panel of wood cunningly carved and colored to imitate the surrounding stone had slid back into a niche evidently made to receive it, revealing a narrow recess cut in the solid rock.

"What is in there?" cried Goujet excitedly. "*Mon dieu!* Nothing but a barrel! What now could be the reason for contriving such a cunning hiding-place for a common cask?"

"But it is not a common cask," said Baillot, removing the article in question from its niche and setting it down with a thump upon the floor. "It is monstrous heavy; look too at the curious brasswork upon it, and the wrought-iron hoops."

Goujet handed the torch to Baillot, and lifting the cask from the ground shook it violently. "There is no liquor in it, that is certain, and I am sure that I heard something rattle inside. But how to get the thing open, there's the question!" Both men stood off and looked at the newly-discovered object. It was, as has been already said, a cask; to all appearances such a cask as might be used for storing some choice and heady wine, but upon closer examination exhibiting several marked differences. It was made of some rich wood blackened with age, and solidly bound with hoops of wrought-iron, while upon either end it was still further defended from too curious investigation by heavy clampings of brasswork, now quite green with the damp of this underground place.

"The green upon the end-pieces there reminds

418

me of mouldy cheese," quoth Goujet, his head on one
side. "And speaking of cheese puts me in mind of
the remark of our former messmates, 'By that time the
rats will have found the cheese.' They had better call
for us now, for in my opinion yonder's the cheese they
had in mind."

"You think it is treasure then?"

"I've seen the outside—mind I don't say the inside—of such cases before; and I've heard tell that
the gentry sometimes keep their valuables in things of
the sort. But they're devilish hard to get into."

Baillot glanced quickly at his companion; he wore a
cunning smile and his black eyes glistened covetously.
All the pirate was awake in him at sight of this ugly
cask. "If I had no right to read the book," he said
slowly, "—and whatever the man's motive in destroy-
ing it, I see plainly that he was right—what possible
excuse can I have for appropriating another man's
treasure."

Goujet looked at the young count with an impatient
scowl. "It is not easy for us to pull in the same boat,"
he growled. "Who knows where the man is who concealed that cask; he may be dead and buried for
aught either of us know. We have as much right to
it as to anything else we find here. At any rate, before we discuss the matter further let us find out what
the cask contains." And he lifted the article in question and carried it out into the daylight. "I see no
sign of a key-hole," he observed, "but an axe will
soon open it."

The words were scarcely out of his mouth when a
figure which had been standing unobserved in the entrance, darted forward with a cry.

"Do not take an axe to it, blockhead !" he screamed, embracing the cask with both arms.

"Ah, you are here ! Did I not tell you to remain behind ?"

"And who are you that I should obey you ?" said de Miguel. "Where did you find this casket ?"

"That is my business," replied Goujet, advancing with the uplifted pickaxe. "Out of the way while I see what is in it !"

"Don't break it, fool ! I can open it. But I tell you beforehand that whatever it contains is mine. I will defend it with my life."

"How is that ?" inquired Baillot. "You did not even know of the existence of this place."

"It was stolen from me," said de Miguel. He had seated himself upon the cask with the air of a man who means to defend his rights against all comers. "It was stolen from me. To prove it, I will tell you what this cask should contain before I open it. It should, in the first place, contain certain bags of coin ; also jewels of price, diamonds, rubies, ropes of pearl, and pieces of gold plate. Now I will open it—you perceive that I know the secret of its lock—and we shall see."

Arising from his seat he closely examined the uppermost end. "It is the other end," he muttered, then aloud, "Turn it over for me."

Goujet complied ; de Miguel quickly slid aside a portion of the brasswork, pressed a concealed spring, and the top flew open. "I will remove the contents of the cask," he continued gravely, "that you may both see that I am speaking the tiuth. I rely upon your honor, seignior, to see that my property is untouched." Baillot made an impatient gesture of assent, while his face flushed darkly.

"These bags, as I have said, should contain gold coin, pistoles and double pistoles," continued de Miguel with an unctuous dignity of tone and mien, which increased as he proceeded with his congenial employment. "And now for the jewels!"

"*Mon dieu!*" cried Goujet, involuntarily stepping forward a pace, and opening and shutting his fingers longingly. Diamonds—in rings, in bracelets, set in curious watches, and glittering royally in pendants and stars, rubies burning with a scarlet flame, the milky lustre of pearls, and glistening sparks of green splendor, where an emerald caught the light, all these and more, in the shape of some curious jewels of wrought gold, the Portuguese removed from the interior of the cask and piled upon the ground.

"You behold these things," he observed, waving his hand comprehensively. "They are all mine, and I have proved it."

"Not to my satisfaction," growled Goujet. "Any knave might have known the secret of the fastening; and as for the contents, I could have made a decent guess at that myself. You'll have to be older than you are now and a better liar before you'll keep that property."

CHAPTER L

"This cask and its contents are mine," said Baillot, "mine by right of discovery."

"Ah, master, you are coming to your senses at last!" cried Goujet delightedly. "You hear that, scoundrel?"

Baillot checked him with an imperative gesture. "It is my will that the valuables be restored to the cask; I shall then restore the cask to its hiding-place. There it shall remain, until the lawful owner shall return for it; if that never happens, then there it shall remain till the day of doom. I have said it, and I will at this moment shoot anyone who dares to dispute the matter." And he drew the pistol from his belt and advanced with an air that caused de Miguel to fall back in alarm.

"The saints defend us!" he cried, "and is that the way you would deprive an honest man of his property? What accursed folly—but I comply, oh, yes—immediately! Everything shall go back into the cask; but I alone know the secret of its lock," and he smiled cunningly to himself.

"And I alone can lift it," remarked Goujet.

"You are mistaken," returned Baillot coolly. "I can lift it with ease, and I alone know the secret of its hiding-place. I shall put it back alone."

De Miguel and Goujet looked at one another. For the moment there was actually a bond of sympathy betwixt them.

"Leave me at once!" commanded the young count. And the two after a moment's hesitation sullenly obeyed.

"*Morbleu*, what folly! but I shall find it;" exclaimed Goujet.

"*We* will find it, and you shall share with me," whispered de Miguel.

"It belongs to my master. He can do what he likes with his own," replied Goujet with a look of cold dislike.

They were shortly joined by Baillot and all three strode along toward the cottage. Nothing further was said of the hidden treasure, but none the less two of the three thought of it unceasingly.

"I will have it," declared de Miguel to himself, "if I have to kill both the others to get it."

"I will have it," resolved Goujet, "if I have to tear down the whole cavern; I already know about where it was."

That evening after de Miguel had thrown himself into his hammock and his heavy breathing betrayed the fact that he was sleeping, Baillot turned to Goujet who was working at his carving in sullen silence. "You thought me very hard to-day, did you not? Almost savage, when I drove you out of the cavern at the mouth of my pistol. It is not the thing to threaten with death a man who has twice saved one's life," he added thoughtfully. "But what could I do?"

"You did not mean it then?" said Goujet brightening up.

"Mean it? No. I could never hurt a hair of your head, man," said Baillot with feeling.

"*Sacré bleu!* Do you suppose I cared about the

pistol? I mean"—and he lowered his voice to a whisper—"the treasure. You only said what you did to frighten away yonder wretch, who has no rightful claim on it."

"I agree with you there," said Baillot gently, "but I certainly did mean what I said about leaving the treasure where I found it."

"But you are a poor man, master," urged Goujet. "Did the king hesitate to confiscate your property? And is your honor more binding than his?"

"I disobeyed the king. He took my estates to punish that disobedience. To this treasure I have no shadow of right."

"Oh, folly—folly!" groaned Goujet, then as Baillot said nothing, he added: "Yonder dog will not cease to search for it."

"Let him search; he will not find it," replied the young count. "But look you, my man! I want you to pledge me your word of honor that you will not speak to him of the matter, and that you will not yourself search for it."

"The first I promise willingly. I want no words with the man, but, *diable!* You ask too much when you ask the other. I must search for it—if you will not tell me where it is, and, *morbleu*, I shall find it!"

Baillot made no comment on this speech, he continued to watch the flames which were dancing up the chimney. "I do not want it for myself," continued Goujet, looking at him uneasily. "What do I want with such a treasure? But for you, surely in a new country now—"

"You will not be with me there," said Baillot quietly, without turning his head.

"I shall not? And why? I have sworn never to leave you."

"I shall not want a—thief in my company."

Goujet started to his feet with a great oath, and half drew his knife. Baillot did not move. "Master, master, not that—don't say that! I have been everything that is wicked, but I swear to you that I shall be so no longer. I promise you that I will not look for this accursed treasure. I will be faithful!" and with a genuine sob the man dropped on his knees before the young count, and covered his hand with kisses.

"I believe you, my good Goujet, and such service as you will render will be more to me than treasure. Nay, a heart of love is treasure, and the best the world contains."

The next morning Goujet took occasion to speak aside with de Miguel. "Here is the purse my master gave you," he said; "take it, I will only keep back what is not due you. There is in it the sum of two hundred pistoles; of these one hundred and fifty he promised you for the victualling of the ship. Liar and wretch that you are, take it! The other fifty pistoles I shall keep for my master—for heaven save him, he has not another livre in the whole world."

"But why do you give it back to me?" said de Miguel, staring at him curiously. "Ah, I know! You do not care now for money; you think you will have the treasure. Viper! You shall not, you nor your miserable sneaking master. I hate you both with my whole heart, and but that I have sworn to the saints to leave you unharmed till I am safely out of this place, I would kill you now."

Goujet stood looking at the little man, who had

worked himself up into quite a white heat of anger, then he burst into an immoderate fit of laughter. "Thank you kindly, monsieur, for your forbearance," he said, and without another word turned away.

De Miguel kept the oath which he had sworn to himself. Not a day passed that he did not visit the cavern to search for the hidden treasure. He forgot his fears, and his old occupation of digging in the ruins for bits of melted silver was wholly abandoned. He rarely spoke to his two companions, returning from his self-imposed labors only to eat ravenously of the food provided by Goujet, then throwing himself sullenly into his hammock to sleep off his fatigue. Each day of unsuccessful searching added a little to the measure of hate and revenge that threatened to boil over its narrow limits.

"Curse him! I hate him!" he howled, shaking his tremulous hands toward heaven, as he paused one day exhausted after hours of fruitless toil. And the airy echoes showered back upon his head, Hate—hate—hate!

Half-mad with the dark passions which filled his breast, the unhappy wretch flew at the rocky walls, and beat against them, clawing at them fiercely with his hands, still screaming curses and imprecations. As if there was some black magic in his fearful words the hidden panel suddenly flew open revealing the cask.

"My God, I have found it! Yes—I have found it! Quick, let me open and see! Ah—the gold, the diamonds! Ha, ha, ha! And all mine—all mine— all mine!" With an almost superhuman effort he lifted the cask, and frantic with joy kissed the jewels and hugged the bags of gold to his breast.

"Ah! My diamonds—my rubies—my gold! All mine! All mine!" And the stones glittered hotly beneath his gaze as though kindled with sparks of the hell of greed that flamed within his soul.

"But what shall I do with them? They will find them! He will take them away from me, curse him—curse him!" And with a quick revulsion from his mad rapture to the haunting misery of fear, the wretch looked fearfully over his shoulder, as he stealthily and hurriedly returned the jewels to the cask.

"I must hide it—but where? He knows of this place; besides I cannot lift the cask. Where—where can I hide it?"

An hour later he emerged from the cavern with a satisfied and cunning smile upon his lips.

"He cannot find it now," he muttered. But in the middle of the night the terror came upon him again. "They will find it—they will find it! He will laugh when he sees it! Ah, I could kill them, but I dare not stay here alone," and in his anguish he bit and tore at his own flesh.

The next day he hid the cask in a new place, only to have the terror come upon him afresh. And so every day and many times in the day he hid the treasure anew, his fear growing greater and the hatred in his soul stronger till his appearance was frightful. His cheeks hung down in flabby folds; his eyes glared like those of a hunted wolf; while his fingers, which had become curved like those of a bird of prey, trembled perpetually.

Baillot felt a great compassion arise within his soul as he looked upon this wretched being, and he spoke to him more kindly than had been his wont. "You are ill," he said. "Think no more of that accursed treasure—would God I had never found it !"

"You have found it? Then I will kill you! It is mine—mine—mine !" and the wretch flew fiercely at the young count.

So sudden was the attack, and so surprised was the victim of it, that powerful as he was he could scarcely shake off the enraged creature that clung to him, snarling and foaming.

Goujet had hastened to his master's assistance, and between them they forced the man to relinquish his hold. He suddenly became limp in their grasp and fell to weeping weakly.

"Don't take it away from me—it will kill me. I did not mean what I said ; I am an old man, and poor —yes poor, I have not a pistole in the world, I swear it—I swear—" Then he fell back in strong convulsions.

"Poor wretch !" said Baillot. "It was an unlucky day for him when I found that treasure. God only knows the misery those innocent glittering stones have already wrought, what tears, what anguish, what blood !"

The convulsions ceased presently and de Miguel lay quiet. After a time he arose again and walked about, but something was vanished. "I have forgotten," he would say plaintively, passing his hand across his eyes. "What is it that I am looking for?—You will not take it from me, will you? May the saints bless you, for I am a poor old man."

Sometimes he would start up in the middle of the night with a shriek. "They will find it ! I must hide it again !" only to sink back again weakly, muttering to himself. Even Goujet was kind to him now, giving him the warmest seat by the fireside, and covering him at night with his own cloak. What he had so often said of himself had come true at last, he was nothing but a poor old man.

And so the winter wore heavily away. The rains wept themselves into the ocean ; and the ocean ceased to roar on its shingly beach, and fell to crooning softly of the long, warm, moonlit nights that were to come. The trees and shrubs budded anew, and the roses burst once more into a carnival of bloom, wreathing themselves about stone balustrades, covering the broken statues with living robes of beauty, and breaking high up on the ruined walls of the desolate château in a foam of many-colored blossoms.

The Comte de Lantenac saw in all this that it was just a year since he had first set foot on the mysterious island.

CHAPTER LI

" MASTER," said Goujet one day, "we have stayed on this island for a matter of six months or more, and I see nothing to prevent our remaining for as many years ; we are far out of the track of vessels."

" I have found a boat," replied his companion abruptly. The two were in the lookout, which had been built by Winters. At the foot of the tree crouched de Miguel ; he was chattering unintelligibly to himself, but now they could hear his voice rising to a fretful wail ; he had missed them, and was vaguely troubled by his loneliness.

" Could we reach the islands in a small boat with yonder imbecile to look after ?"

" Ay ! that is the question. The boat is not much better than a skiff, and badly knocked up."

" And we have no tools."

A little silence fell between the two. The stricken man at the foot of the tree wailed louder.

" Can't you find it for me ? Don't let him see it— he will take it away from me."

Goujet shook his shoulders angrily. " A pest on the man !" he said. " What does he mean by such chatter ?"

" The unlucky wretch found the cask, and the possession of it drove him mad."

" Do you know where it is now ?"

" No ; he has hidden it."

" Hidden it ! *Mon dieu*—and he is mad ! Then it is lost indeed."

Baillot laughed aloud, a short, bitter laugh. He glanced down at his clothing which hung in rags about him.

" Should the owner ever return, he will find no treasure," continued Goujet in an aggrieved voice. " Surely you will not hold me longer to my promise?"

" Can we clothe ourselves in gold, man ? Can we eat diamonds? Can we navigate with ropes of pearl ?"

" But we shall escape—we shall surely escape."

" Then let us preserve our reason. Suppose yonder wretch could remember where he hid the treasure, what use would it be to him now ?"

" All the better for us if we find it."

Baillot made no reply, but fell once more to studying the distant horizon. After awhile he spoke again. " What make you of yonder white fleck ?"

Goujet who had been sulkily leaning over the railing listening to the senile ravings of the man below, straightened up at this. He looked long and earnestly in the direction to which Baillot pointed.

" It is a sail !" he said at length. " Shall we fire our beacon ?"

" It can do no harm," said Baillot thoughtfully, " even should the vessel chance to be that of the pirates."

" Ha—I had almost forgotten our friends ! They will not forget us so easily. Should it be the pirates it would be better to make no sign."

As the hours wore away it became evident that the vessel which they had sighted was headed directly for

431

the island. Goujet was in a fever of impatience, he was up and down between the lookout and the cottage half a hundred times.

"We must not let it be seen that we are here," he said, as he hastily concealed various articles in the bushes, and endeavored otherwise to efface the signs of recent occupancy about their dwelling.

"What shall we do with him?" said Baillot, indicating de Miguel with a gesture.

"Let us leave him ; they will take care of him."

"He must accompany us."

"We might gag him," suggested Goujet, knowing that there was no use in combating this decision.

"I had thought of that. We had best conceal ourselves in the cavern till we find out how things are going."

They soon finished their preparations, and accompanied by de Miguel took refuge in the rock-hewn gallery leading to the cavern.

"We shall have trouble with the fellow yet," said Goujet looking anxiously at the unfortunate Portuguese. "Look at him !"

Upon entering the place, the poor wretch had at first taken no notice of his surroundings, but chancing to raise his dull eyes, something in the aspect of the place seemed to stimulate his deadened brain ; he stared about him with more of intelligence in his gaze than they had noticed for months, then, muttering something to himself, darted forward into the cavern.

The others followed. De Miguel was bending over some object which he had rolled out from under a pile of rubbish in one corner. He looked up with a childish smile as they approached. "They would never think to look here," he said, sitting flat upon the floor and hugging the object with both arms. "But I shall watch it, and never leave it again. It hurts me here to leave it," and he touched his forehead.

Baillot looked at him undecidedly for a moment.

"You will not take it away from a poor old man?" said de Miguel with a piteous smile, hugging the cask closer to his breast.

"Best let him alone for the present, master," whispered Goujet. "He would surely take to raving if we took the thing from him now. Let us get up in the window and watch. It is the yacht, sure enough," he continued, peering out anxiously.

Baillot made no reply; he was clenching his hands in an agony of impatience. Life seemed sweet to him on a sudden; he was conscious of a fierce desire to escape that filled him with astonishment and almost remorse. The rattle of the chains and the splash of the heavy anchors as they fell into the water was music in his ears.

"Two, four, six, eight!" Goujet was counting the men as they swung themselves over the side into the boat which they had lost no time in lowering. "The rascals are afraid of us! And two on the deck—yes three."

After this neither spoke for a long time; Baillot paced up and down, his head bent, his eyes burning like live coals beneath his black brows. Goujet remained in the window, staring at the yacht. De Miguel had opened the cask and was playing with the jewels, laughing delightedly as the light sparkled in their brilliant depths. After a time he began to deck himself with them, winding the pearls about his shaggy head, fastening the diamonds among his fluttering rags, and dancing with gingerly steps about the bags of gold, which he eyed jealously as if fearing that they might suddenly disappear. Then his mood changed; he replaced everything in the cask and with a darkly lowering brow began to scratch about amid the rubbish.

"I must hide it," he muttered. "I am hungry; it is growing dark. He cannot find it here." Then he stood up and began to tiptoe stealthily toward the door, looking back over his shoulder with a cunning smile.

"Where are you going?" said Baillot gently, stepping in front of him.

De Miguel stopped and stared at him. "How did you come here?" he asked. "You—you—have not—"

"No, I have not found it. It is safe."

"I must see. I must watch it. You know it is mine. You would not take it?"

"No, but you had best watch it for awhile longer. Here is food."

"Ah, then I shall not be forced to leave it!" And snatching greedily at the proffered food the wretched madman slunk back again to his rubbish-heap and began once more to claw it over, crooning and muttering to himself.

Baillot stared at him thoughtfully.

"I don't see how we can get him away," said Goujet, who had descended from his perch.

"We must get him away—even if we have to take the cask."

Goujet carefully suppressed his satisfaction at this remark. "It is quite possible that he has as much claim to the treasure as anyone," he said carelessly. "But the cask is another problem."

"Do not suppose for a moment," said Baillot
sternly, "that I have changed my mind in regard to
that unfortunate discovery; but I have not forgotten
that yonder wretch can justly lay all of his misfortunes
at my door. The loss of his home, his money and his
reason all came about through his connection with my
accursed fortunes. His life shall be sacred even at the
cost of my own."

Goujet made no reply, he had clambered back to his
post of observation in the window. Presently a sharp
cry of disappointment broke from him. "*Sacré bleu!*
the wretches have returned to the yacht. It cannot be
that they abandon the search so quickly."

"There are only four in the boat, man," said Baillot
reassuringly. "They have returned for something, liquor
probably."

"The triple fools!" exclaimed Goujet excitedly.
"There are five of them about to return; they leave
the vessel almost unguarded. It will soon be dark
enough for us to venture; luckily there is no moon."

An hour later two dark figures stole cautiously out
into the open and slid noiselessly down among the
rocks that lined the shore.

"I will return for the chest and the man," whispered
Goujet, "whilst you guard the boat."

"Remain here," said his companion shortly.

"He does not trust me!" growled the man who was
left. Away among the trees he could see the cheerful
glimmer of camp-fires. "The rascals will put in a
merry night of it," he muttered to himself. "Suppose
now I walk into their midst and tell them that I alone
know the whereabouts of a treasure worth a million of
livres! Who then would be chief of the band? And

435

why after all should I be bound for life to a Huguenot nobleman? Did I not swear that I would call no man master while the breath remained in my body? Bah—he does not care for me any more than for the dust under his feet! He has spurned me like a dog a score of times when I did not fall in with his ill humors."

Wrapped in these dark thoughts he did not hear the steps of two men who were coming toward him along the shore till they were within ten paces.

"If we must make this round again to-night," one of them was saying, "sink me if I don't bring a lantern. My eyes are so blinded by the firelight that I am as blundering as a bat."

"The whole business is accursed folly," grumbled his companion. "That pestiferous Portuguese lied to us; he is probably dead long before this, and his money-bags are already squeezed as dry as an orange."

"Then you don't believe in the treasure?"

"Believe in it? No! that was another lie concocted between old Barebones and his new swab, though I misdoubt me—" and the voices died away as the speakers passed on.

The effect of this conversation on the listener was worth remarking. He had forgotten all that he was thinking about when first he heard the steps approaching.

"A lantern and we are lost," he muttered. "But why does he not come? They will return within half an hour and our boat will be discovered." He waited for an instant longer, straining his ears for some sound from the direction of the cavern, then darted away into the darkness.

Baillot had found the wretched de Miguel asleep, his

436

head pillowed on the cask, his arms wound tightly about it. This he saw by the light of a pine splinter which he ventured to kindle, notwithstanding the imminent risk of its being observed aboard the yacht. He leaned over the man and shook him gently.

"Come, my friend," he said in his ear. "The treasure is in danger."

The sleeper opened his eyes, they were dull and heavy. He muttered something under his breath, then turned and flung himself at full length upon the floor. He seemed to have forgotten the cask.

The young man hesitated for a moment; then he tore a long strip from among his rags, and securely gagged the sleeper, who only struggled and moaned feebly without opening his eyes.

"So far good! Now if I can carry him." Again he stooped and lifted the limp figure from the floor to his shoulders. But this time he had reckoned without his host; he had not taken half a dozen steps when the burden on his back began to writhe and kick so violently that he was forced to drop it.

With what would have been a yell had he not been securely gagged, the Portuguese sprang back to the cask and fell upon it, hugging it tightly with both arms.

"Well then, I must take the cask, perhaps he will follow," said his perplexed guardian with a shrug. But no sooner did he attempt to touch the cask than the Portuguese flew at him like a tiger. The young man handled him as gently as possible, and at length succeeded in holding him down long enough to secure his arms and legs.

437

CHAPTER LII

At this moment Goujet burst into the cave. "Master!" he whispered hoarsely, "they will be upon us with a lantern directly!" His quick eye had grasped the significance of the scene before him. "I will take the man," he added. "See that his gag is secure first. Do you bring the cask. No use leaving it here for the pirates; they will have seen the light from the windows and will lose no time in finding this place."

Baillot picked up the heavy cask, and presently the two were stumbling along in the thick darkness without. They reached the shore in safety, but so exhausted that they could scarcely breathe. Goujet dropped his burden into the bottom of the boat with scant ceremony; Baillot followed with his and they shoved off. Goujet dipped the oars noiselessly with one or two long powerful pulls which sent them well out from the shore, then he paused and remained motionless; the twinkle of a lantern was approaching around the bend, the voices of the men who carried it floating distinctly across the little space of water to those in the boat. They were grumbling as before.

"Let Lock turn out himself and see what he can find," cried one. "There is nothing about the place but accursed rocks to break one's shins over," and the speaker stopped to groan and rub his legs ruefully.

"Come on, you devil's spawn!" said the other gruffly. "You are always whining; nothing suits you.

438

Now that we've made the cruise, why it stands to reason that—Hallo! what's that?''

The sentries had reached the narrow strip of beach at the base of the cliff, within whose rocky entrails was the cavern. Its narrow windows, quite indistinguishable by day amid the general irregularities of the surface, now shone out brilliantly with the expiring flame of the pine splinter, which in his haste Baillot had forgotten to extinguish. He cursed himself silently for his carelessness.

"That was a happy thought of yours, master," whispered Goujet. "It will give the rascals something to look for."

"But the whole crew will be about the place in a minute more, and—"

"Hist!"

There was a hasty splash of oars and the sound of voices. A moment more and something passed them swiftly; in the darkness they caught a few words spoken in a low anxious voice.

"—ship's all right—sea as calm as a milkpan, and she's anchored at stem and stern, but they must know about that light; the rascals—"

"They have left the ship alone!" whispered Goujet in an ecstasy. "What luck!" He again began to dip his oars quietly but in a way that sent their little craft skimming along toward a single light, which rising and falling at regular intervals betrayed the location of the schooner.

"I will reconnoitre a bit," said Baillot, as the skiff rubbed her nose softly against the hull of the yacht. As stealthily and swiftly as a cat he stole over the low rail and disappeared in the darkness.

"All's clear," he whispered a moment later, "hand up the man "—and the unfortunate de Miguel like a bale of merchandise was passed up to the deck. Goujet had thoughtfully fastened a rope onto the precious cask, which he had determined not to lose sight of. "Haul her up, quick!" he whispered to Baillot, tossing him an end of the tackle. "Now for it!" he said, as he sprang upon the deck. "Hold, I'll douse that lantern at her bow!"

Working with the desperate speed and strength of men in mortal peril, the two swiftly raised and set the sails then as noiselessly as possible slipped the anchors. Luckily there was a light breeze off shore, the canvas filled quickly, and the gentle ripple of water under the vessel's bow showed that she had begun to draw away from the perilous neighborhood of the island.

"Thank God!" murmured the young Huguenot fervently, pausing a moment to listen to the delightful sound.

For the first time he turned to look toward the shore. It was alive with the glimmer of torches, and the sound of loud angry voices engaged in violent altercation floated across the water.

"Ha, ha! A neater bit of work I never saw!" chuckled Goujet, who had grasped the tiller. "They'll have time to cool off at their leisure before they get off that place. Good luck to you, messmates!"

This last he shouted at the top of his voice. At the same moment de Miguel who had been choking and spluttering over his gag, managed in some way to rid himself of it and emitted a series of weird howls, which rang out over the water in a most startling fashion.

That the sounds were heard by those on shore was

evidenced by the behavior of the distant sparks of light, every one of which represented a man. These lights had been flitting about at the base of the cliff, one or two even appearing like enormous fire-flies half-way up its surface, showing that some of the more adventurous spirits were endeavoring in this way to discover the source of the mysterious vanished light. Now all quickly converged toward a single point, the united glare of the torches extending a long, threatening, blood-red finger toward the flying refugees. A chorus of hoarse shouts, and a shower of shot spattering the water like hailstones, showed that the pirates guessed their plight; then all the sparks of light began to flit away in irregular groups.

"They are going for their boats," quoth Goujet in a tone of the deepest satisfaction. "Much good may it do them!"

As the little vessel gathered more and more headway, in a spirit of bravado he touched a spark to the breech of the cannon which the pirates had mounted in the stern. The dull roar of the discharge had scarcely died away, when it was answered by a second report which seemed to come out of the darkness on their starboard port. They had cleared the island by this time and were standing well out under a stiff breeze.

"And what might that mean?" he exclaimed, staring fixedly into the darkness.

"It means," replied Baillot composedly, "that you have given our friends on the island a farewell salute, and at the same time have signaled their consort, the *Rouge et Noir*, that the yacht has left the island."

Goujet swore a great oath under his breath. "You are right!" he said, grasping Baillot's arm; "yonder are her lights!"

"Luckily she cannot see us," observed the young man. "We shall draw away from her rapidly in this breeze."

"*Morbleu!* I should hope so!" said Goujet. "We need half a dozen more hands to sail a race with that brigantine." He seemed much depressed, and indulged in considerable profanity of a polyglot variety, which need not be set down here.

In the meantime the other vessel proceeded to set off a number of rockets; after which she displayed in rapid succession two green lights followed by two red ones and a single white light.

"'Lay to, till we can speak you,'" growled Goujet. "I think not, my friends, to-night. We can't stop." Then as two blue lights twinkled for an instant in the darkness, "No, no! You are not mistaken in your craft. It's the men that's aboard of her you're wrong about," and he burst into a loud laugh.

De Miguel's howls had by this time quieted into a feeble moaning pitiful to hear. "I must take him below, and make him as comfortable as possible," said Baillot, with a remorseful glance at the wretched heap upon the deck. "But first we must determine upon our course."

"If we put for the islands, we walk straight into the teeth of the brigantine," said Goujet. "Let us go to America!"

"To America!" exclaimed Baillot. "We do not know whether the vessel is provisioned for such a cruise. Then too—" and he pointed to the moaning bundle of rags—"he must be taken home."

"He can be taken home afterwards; he will never see home if we go the other way. Our chances aren't worth a livre unless we throw them off our track before daylight."

"So be it," said Baillot, drawing a deep breath.

Daylight found the little vessel bowling briskly along before a steady wind, while as far as the eye could reach over the expanse of long green rollers there appeared no token of human presence.

"The weather is set fair; the season is favorable; and the vessel is staunch," said Baillot, as he emerged from the companion-way after a thorough inspection of the ship's stores; "but we have a bare larder."

"Bad news that," said Goujet. "I am as hungry as a wolf. You don't mean to say that the fellows have no victuals aboard?"

"Very little," said Baillot shaking his head ruefully. "I found one small cask of pickled meat and two of biscuit, part of the stores we left aboard I should judge, for they are none of the freshest. Worst of all there is no water to speak of."

"The rascals depended upon the brigantine," said Goujet, drawing his grizzled brows together thoughtfully. "We are in bad trim for the cruise," he added, looking down at his rags with a short laugh, "and no mistake; but there's fish in the sea for the taking, and water in the clouds; some of it will come our way before long I'm thinking. I have no mind to go back, master, what do you say?"

Baillot looked steadily out to sea. "We will continue," he said slowly, "on this tack, till we see land over our bowsprit."

"*Bon!*" cried Goujet with a great laugh. "We will! and *le bon dieu* help us to pull through on short rations and to keep warm in the skins with which he provided us, for *morbleu !* we shall soon have no other cover."

"Oh—as to that," answered his companion, "I found a couple of good jackets below ; and I believe there is something else there also in the way of clothing. I did not stop to see."

"Capital !" cried Goujet with enthusiasm. "We shall do famously ! And here comes the first of our water supply,"—as one or two great drops spattered on the deck at their feet. "Let us spread some canvas to catch it and run it off into our butts."

It soon appeared that the small crew had laid out for themselves a great task ; and what with short rations and little sleep, the two sailors were soon as gaunt and hollow-eyed as ghosts. But with wind and weather in their favor, every sail drawing, and league after league of blue water spinning away behind them, neither minded the hardships. The mysterious desolation of the island well out of sight, Baillot felt more and more hope springing up in his heart. Vague promises of joy and comfort lurked in the following breeze, and in the radiant glories of the western horizon he read glad prophecies for the future.

As for de Miguel he gave very little trouble beyond a ravenous appetite, which threatened to demolish their slender store of provisions long before they should reach the promised land. He would whine like a child and hold out a feeble shaking hand for more, and Baillot more than once fasted that he might gratify him. "I have brought it upon him," he said to himself remorsefully. At the end of the second week they found that the supplies had dwindled alarmingly in spite of their utmost care.

"We must lay it out into rations," declared Goujet, "and stick to 'em, no matter how hungry we are. And mind you, don't give that old lunatic more than his share at your own expense. You must keep up your strength and so must I; as for him, he does nothing, and therefore is the least in need of food."

"That is true enough," said Baillot, "but I cannot bear to see him cry when I refuse him."

"I'll look to his rations from now on," said Goujet gruffly.

Baillot suddenly stepped into the rigging and whipped out his glass. "I say, Goujet!" he cried. "Put her down hard; there's something yonder that looks like a number of casks lashed together! And, by heavens, there's a man atop of it!"

CHAPTER LIII

HALF a minute later *L'Espérance* was running swiftly toward the object which Baillot had described as a number of casks with a man atop.

"Raft ahoy!" shouted Goujet as they approached within hailing distance. But there was no reply, and the figure—which they could see distinctly now—did not raise its head from its knees. The casks rose and fell on the long green waves, the creaming crests breaking over them now and then in a burst of sunlit spray, and the wind gently lifting the long gray hair which lay about the shoulders of the solitary voyager. The two men turned and looked each other in the eyes.

"He is dead," said Baillot.

Goujet said nothing ; he was making ready to lay to. They presently drifted alongside of the strange craft, and Goujet, fastening a coil of rope to the railing of the yacht, jumped overboard. In another instant he had secured the raft.

"I want to look into the matter of these casks," he shouted. "It may be that there is food here, though it isn't likely."

"The man first," cried Baillot.

"He is dead," replied Goujet, after a hasty examination, "but not long dead. Shall I pass him up to you, or shall I tumble him over the side?"

446

"Pass him up—pass him up, man ! We can at least give the poor fellow a decent burial."

It was no easy matter to lift the heavy body over the side of the vessel from the uncertain standpoint afforded by the raft, but it was accomplished without accident. And Goujet who had grumbled much during the process, again turned his attention to the casks.

"Now if this gentleman has died out of pure good-will and left us his victuals," he was saying to himself, when he was startled by a loud exclamation from the deck. Baillot had torn open the shirt of the stranger and was listening at his heart. "The man is not dead !" he cried, "but he is dying of thirst. Quick, fetch me water !"

Leaving the casks still lashed to the side of the vessel, Goujet hastened to do the young man's bidding. Together they laid the castaway in an easy position, then Baillot began to wet his parched and swollen tongue with water slightly tempered with rum. At the same time Goujet instituted a vigorous rubbing of the cold limbs. After nearly an hour of this treatment the stranger gasped slightly once or twice, then opened his eyes, albeit with a dull and unseeing gaze.

"Another mouth to feed," quoth Goujet surveying him dejectedly. "We have water enough now, but we are like to starve before we sight land."

At this the castaway essayed to speak, but his stiffened tongue refused its office, a hoarse unintelligible murmur issued from his blackened lips, as he feebly raised one hand.

"He means that there is food on the raft," said Baillot quickly. "Go and see."

"The saints be praised !" shouted Goujet presently.

"I find here a cask of biscuit; but the poor fellow had no water. Now we'll cut this tackle adrift, and get under way again; every minute counts."

Before many hours the unknown had so far recovered himself as to be able to speak. He had been aboard the brig *Constance* bound to America, he said. When about two weeks out the ship had collided with an iceberg; her people and the passengers had gone away in the ship's boats; he had remained behind with the captain, since there was no room for them in the boats. Together they had constructed the raft of casks, on which they embarked with sufficient food and water for two weeks, just in time to escape being dragged down by the sinking vessel. Unfortunately on the third day their water-cask was swept away. Two days afterward the captain went mad with thirst and jumped into the sea. All this they learned little by little from the fragmentary statements which fell from the stranger's lips. Of his name and identity he made no mention, and they forbore to question him. He on his part showed no surprise at finding two men alone on such a small vessel in the midst of the ocean.

As the days passed by and his strength came back to him the castaway passed long hours pacing up and down the deck, his hands clasped behind his back, his head bent upon his breast. He did not offer to help in the labor of sailing the vessel, spoke to no one, and ate what was given him without question or comment. In short he was as one who walks in his sleep, moving, animate, yet with a strange remoteness in the glance of his dull eyes. Once only did he rouse from his apathetic silence. He had paused in his monotonous tramping and was looking out over the ocean toward the sunset

with his strange vacant stare. Baillot, after observing
him for a moment in silence, said, "The weather holds
fine, monsieur; another day or two of this and we shall
sight land."

The man dropped his eyes slowly and opened his lips
as if about to reply, then so strange an expression swept
over his features that Baillot was startled. He followed
the stranger's gaze, but could see nothing more alarming
than his own lean fingers which grasped the tiller.

"What—what!" gasped the old man. "Where—"

"But what, friend? I do not understand you."
Then he perceived that the unknown was pointing one
trembling finger at a certain curious ring which he had
picked up among the ruins of the château one day and
which he still wore.

"*That—I mean that!*" said the man, still staring at
the ring with a ghastly look. The last word was almost
a shriek; then as if for the first time, he looked keenly
about him, at the vessel, her masts, her sails, the inlaid
brasswork about her bulwarks. "I am mad," he muttered, shaking his head. "I am mad—and I dream it
all."

"I found this ring," said Baillot, almost as agitated
as the stranger, "on a strange island, where I was shipwrecked with several companions; this vessel is—"

"*L'Espérance,*" said the stranger, relapsing into his
former dull tone. "I knew it—ah!" And with a long
sobbing breath he turned away.

The castaway did not speak again. And Baillot, although he longed to question him respected the silence
in which the unknown had wrapped himself as in a garment. He said nothing to Goujet of what had taken
place, and that worthy was too fully occupied with his

multitudinous duties to take much notice of the eccentricities of their new passenger.

"A lunatic more or less makes very little difference with a man's peace of mind—once you are used to their little ways," he said sagely.

But Baillot knew that the stranger was not mad.

As for de Miguel, he remained below in the quarters assigned to him quietly enough. He hugged his cask by day, and pillowed his head upon it by night. Sometimes he played for hours with the gems, laughing and crooning to himself.

"Let him be," said Baillot, when Goujet had expressed a fear lest he should lose or throw away the treasure. "The lust of that wretched cask has deprived him of heaven's best gift to man, his reason; if he is happy in the possession of it, it is but some poor compensation meted out to him in mercy."

What blind instinct led the Portuguese to suddenly abandon his treasure one day during the latter end of the voyage will never be known. Goujet had sighted land that morning, and was jubilant in consequence. He was trolling out some piratical ditty at the top of his voice as he hauled down the topsails; Baillot was at the helm, and the strange old man, their passenger, was pacing up and down as was his wont, his head bent before the merry gale, his long white beard streaming out upon the wind. There was a good bit of sea on, the long dark green rollers crisping and breaking in clouds of tingling spray over the bow of the little vessel.

"Sing aloud, my brave lad, while we follow like thee,
By bank, shoal, and quicksand, the spoils of the sea!"

shouted Goujet. And the creaking of the taut ropes

and the dashing of the waves made a brave accompaniment.

No one observed the flabby, wax-like countenance that peered cautiously out from the companion-way, nor heard the words muttered in a low hoarse voice.

"It is *you* then! You have found me at last, and you think that now you will be revenged! You will take my jewels—my gold; mine—mine! But we shall see; José de Miguel is a cunning fox, I shall—escape." And he crept stealthily away, laughing and muttering to himself.

That night the moon was at her full, and sailing high in the cloudless heavens made of the foaming water that swept away from under the keel of the flying yacht a pathway of pure silver, winding away into the mysterious blue of the night. To the dazed eyes of the man who watched it, it seemed to promise safety. "By that road," he muttered to himself, "I shall be able to escape him. He can never find me, and my treasure shall be mine—mine—mine." The moonlight struck sparks of fiery splendor from something which the man held hugged to his breast. He kissed the something passionately. "I shall escape him by that road," he repeated, glancing behind him with a cunning smile. Then he stepped over the rail onto the shining pathway and was gone.

The next morning when Baillot visited the cabin where de Miguel slept, carrying with him the man's breakfast, he saw that the cask had been opened, and the gold and jewels lay scattered about the floor. De Miguel himself was missing. The yacht was hastily searched from stem to stern.

"Poor wretch, he must have fallen overboard in the night," said Baillot sorrowfully.

"A good riddance," commented Goujet with a shrug.

Neither óf them guessed that the cunning fellow had selected with unerring instinct the most precious jewels of them all, and had made good his escape by a road of pure silver. It is a fact that neither he nor his treasure was ever seen again. He went doubtless to a place from which he did not care to return.

CHAPTER LIV

A RICH and populous town was Boston toward the
end of the seventeenth century; as many as three
meeting-houses graced its streets, and there was even
talk of a fourth. The public buildings were fair and
handsome, and there were many stately dwellings, stores
and shops also in abundance, where the matrons and
maids could obtain that wherewith to make yet more
convincing the charms with which nature had so plentifully endowed them.

"Boston," writes an Englishman of discrimination,
who visited the place about this time, "has buildings
like to its women, neat and handsome. Its streets are
paved with pebbles—like the hearts of its men."

These paved streets all led, albeit in the wandering
and crooked paths trod a century ago by the cattle and
the Indians, down toward the harbor, where were com-
modious warehouses and busy wharves, the arteries
through which pulsed the wealth of other countries, a
life-blood destined to make of the sturdy babe, as yet
unconscious of its future, the strong and helpful guardian
of the world.

Near one of these wharves there lounged on a bright
day in early spring a couple of sailors, just on shore
perhaps from one of the tall brigs which lay at anchor
in the harbor.

"I ain't decided what I will do," said one of them

453

slowly, removing his tarpaulin that he might scratch his grizzled head. This process having been accomplished gravely and meditatively and to the apparent enlightenment of his mind, the speaker proceeded more briskly. "You see it's jest this way, I've had dealin's in the past what's determined me to live a God-fearin' life from now on. Cap'n Hornby of the brig *Sally* is a blowed good cap'n, he knows his biz; but for vi'lent and bloody talk there ain't his ekal afloat. 'Tain't edifyin', an' that's a fact."

"Ho, ho!" roared his companion, shifting a huge quid of tobacco in his capacious jaws. "You're turned religious swab, be ye? 'Sa'm singin'—Bible readin'—prayin'—preachin' an' whinin'—Ho, ho!"

"Look-a-here, mate, you'd best jam her down hard, and shift yer tack, or, b' thunder, I'll polish down that jaw of yourn in a way you won't forgit in a hurry! Nobody's agoin' to make light o' religion while Jack Winters is afloat. You hear *me!*"

"I hear ye fast enough; I ain't deaf," rejoined the other sulkily.

"I've a tarnal good mind to ship on the *Christopher Columbus*," pursued the first speaker tranquilly. "Though I ain't a mite of assurance that there's any more Godliness aboard of her—" He paused, his mouth still open, his eyes fixed on a small vessel, which with canvas half-set was slipping quietly into the bay. "Shiver my timbers!" he ejaculated violently; then he whipped out his glass and studied the vessel carefully for a full minute.

His companion stared at him in amazement. "What in perdition," he began. But Winters was gone, pushing and elbowing his way among the various persons

454

and objects that intervened between himself and the end of the wharf. "That old swab is a dummed ijit!" muttered his companion. "Kinder lost his wits overboard 'n his last cruise, I reckon." With which conclusive remark, this excellent seafaring man, with whom we have no further concern, wended his way toward the sign of *The Blue Dolphin*, where he proceeded to get gloriously drunk, though it was only ten o'clock in the morning.

In the meantime his companion had reached his goal, and from the coign of vantage afforded him by a pile of boxes, again surveyed the schooner, whose appearance in the Boston harbor had so, as he expressed it, "flabbergasted" him.

"It is—it is!" he repeated in an ecstasy. "Thar ain't no bloomin' doubt of it! But who's aboard her? how'd she come here? By the 'Sa'ms of David! won't a certain little miss I knows of open her eyes if— They're a clewin' down! Say, b' thunder! I ain't a goin' to wait for 'em to come ashore! I'm a goin' to board her." And he scrambled down from his perch with surprising alacrity, and hailing one of the boats which were plying about near the wharf, very quickly concluded a financial arrangement with its owner which sent him skimming along toward the schooner.

"Lay to along side of her!" he commanded. "Yacht ahoy!" he roared.

Now it happened that Baillot was for the moment below, securing the cask, concerning which he was greatly troubled, while Goujet was engaged in making everything snug about the sails and tackle.

"Yacht ahoy!" repeated Winters; then without waiting for an invitation, he seized a bit of rope that

455

hung over the side and quietly stepped onto the deck.

"I say, mate, can you tell me how this 'ere craft got into these parts? I've seed her before—ay, an' sailed her." He addressed this remark to a singular-looking man who stood looking shoreward. This person did not appear to have heard him, for he paid no attention to the question.

Goujet, who had caught a part of what the new arrival was saying, now descended to the deck.

"By the cut of your jib," began the old sailor judicially, "you ain't likely to be able to talk much except gibberish, an' that I don't understand and don't want to. But if you can answer an honest God-fearin' man, I'd like ye to tell me if you know anything of the whereabouts of a likely young sailor lad named Baillot?"

"What might be your business with him?" said Goujet. "—Supposing I knew any such person," he added cautiously.

"Consarn ye! what be you yawin' and tackin' about? Jack Winters ain't the man to—"

"*Winters?* Did you say your name was Winters? *Mon dieu*, what a strange thing to happen!—Stay, he is below," and without another word Goujet vanished, to reappear almost instantly followed by Baillot.

There was no need of any further explanation on the part of Goujet, who stood and looked on delightedly while the two clasped hands with many a fervent but inarticulate ejaculation.

"Now if this 'ere ain't a speshul providence—as our good parson says—then I don't know whar you'd look for one," cried Winters, blowing a violent blast with a

great red and yellow handkerchief. "I seed Miss Madeline last night, an' I sez——"

"What? She is not—dead—then?"

"Dead! Lord love ye, sir, no! Whar'd ye git such
a redic'lus notion as that. Bloomin' as a rose! My!
jest wait till you clap your eyes onto her!"

Strange to say Baillot experienced a decided qualm at
these words. "She does not care for me," he thought
dejectedly.

"Who's yonder old party?" pursued Winters in a loud
whisper, glancing at the stranger, who had begun to
walk up and down the deck after his custom, his eyes
still fixed on the busy docks.

"I don't know his name," began Baillot, suddenly
realizing the situation of the unfortunate man, old and
alone, a stranger in a strange land, and destitute of
everything save the wretched rags with which he was
clothed. Then he glanced down at his own person and
groaned aloud. "I am a ragged beggar," he thought
bitterly. "I cannot see her after all."

"Here are fifty pistoles that belong to you, master,"
said Goujet in a low tone. He had been watching the
young man's face and guessed shrewdly at his thoughts.

"Thar ain't no manner of doubt in my mind as to
what you're goin' to do," quoth Winters, slapping his
leg violently. "You'll git tidied up a bit—for it might
scare the women-folks to see ye, the way ye be now—
after that we'll crack on all sail and make for a port
where you can drop anchor for a spell. Why, Lord love
ye, lad! I wouldn't dare show my face thar an' tell
'em I'd found ye, but that you was off a cruisin' around
promiscuous like. They'd never forgive me! These
'ere gentlemen 'll come along in course. The craft we

can leave in charge of a friend of mine till we make up our minds what to do with her."

"She belongs, I suppose, to the heirs of de Miguel, since the unfortunate man is no more," said Baillot thoughtfully.

"De Miguel! that fat, black fellow at Terciora? Did ye git in with him? The consarndest scoundrel afloat! Wall, wall! I see we've got a power of talkin' to do; but the rest of 'em 'll want to hear it, so come on!"

The house of Madame de Langres, situated in the outskirts of Boston, was a sufficiently roomy and comfortable structure. Built of rough-hewn stone in a framework of wood, and surrounded by grass-plots and garden spaces, it was shut off from the highway by a low paling, which gleamed in a coat of fresh whitewash against its background of greenery. By day the spotless windows with their fresh muslin curtains and the pots of scarlet geranium on their sills presented an attractive picture to the passer-by, by night the same clear panes sent forth long beams of ruddy fire and candle-light cheerful to behold.

Madame de Langres was already well and favorably known in the community. Not only was she a discreet and personable lady, and most devout in matters of religion, but she was also reported to have a very pretty hand at concocting divers medicaments and cordials which she dispensed among the needy with an open hand. Of her worldly estate no more need be said, since it had transpired that the title-deeds, which were beyond a doubt lawfully executed, gave her possession of certain lands in the vicinity of Boston, already of great value. As to her nationality, a French Papist was one thing and an abomination ; but a Huguenot exiled from home on account of religious purism was quite another. The nationality might well be looked over.

Certain grave and thrifty youths of Puritan stock had been seen to cast glances of fervent admiration on the beautiful Madeline, who bloomed amid her new surroundings, as Winters had declared, like a rose. One of these excellent young men had actually made proposals for the hand of the maiden in marriage, and on this very evening the question was being gravely and delicately discussed ; Madame de Langres, her son, and the excellent Constantin Dinant being gathered before the genial glow of the fireside in the roomy " keeping-room " of the house.

"This youth, John Winthrop, is a godly and sober young man, well-reputed in all things, and of high standing in the community," quoth the good pastor, smiling and rubbing his hands together genially. "It is a right and a good thing that our youths and maidens should unite themselves in the holy bonds of wedlock with the excellent folk we find here. Surely we cannot hope—nor indeed would it be desirable—to keep ourselves a separate people in the land."

"Our pastor has spoken, daughter," said Madame de Langres, glancing tenderly at Madeline, who with downcast eyes was rapidly plying her knitting-needles. "I also think well of the matter ; what say you, my child ?"

"I cannot listen to it, dear mother," said the young girl, rising quickly and laying down her work with fingers which trembled visibly. "I cannot—" and with a sound suspiciously like a sob, she turned and fled away.

"What ails the maiden?" asked Constantin Dinant in astonishment. "Surely we have no wish to force her inclinations, but it is a pity that she cannot look reasonably at this marriage. Do you know of any reason why she should decline the honor of this alliance?"

"The honor would not be all on one side," quoth Madame de Langres statelily.

Oblivious to the consternation which her words had caused, the young girl had escaped to the chilly freshness of the moonlit night; clad in her long scarlet mantle, she paced rapidly up and down the garden paths. An apple tree in full bloom stood shivering in the cold wind that blew from off the water, shedding its odorous blossoms in showers upon the damp grass; a gust of the rosy petals, soft and chill as snow-flakes, drifted into the young girl's face. She brushed them away with an impatient gesture.

"How dare he?" she murmured with an angry blush. "But I will never marry him—never!"

Somewhere down the road she could hear the sound of footsteps, and presently the dark figures of four men tramping along in the moonlight came into view. They approached the gate, paused a moment, then entered.

The young girl drew back into the shadow of some flowering shrubs. She had no mind to return to the brightly-lighted room; she feared lest this might be the Puritan, John Winthrop, come for his answer. She did not look out from her hiding-place as the new-comers passed, and wandered away again into the garden closes as soon as the great door had shut behind them. Half an hour later it opened and the figure of a man came out alone.   He hesitated a moment, then walked slowly down the path to where a tall slender figure stood quietly in the brilliant white .light.

"It will be John Winthrop," thought the girl, hardening her heart.   "Well, and he shall have his answer." She turned resolutely toward the approaching figure.

"Yes—it is I," said Baillot, in his deep grave voice. "You did not expect to see me !"   Something in the lovely appealing face of the maiden spoke to his heart more certainly than words.   "Madeline !"

—But surely it would be unkind if we stop longer. For all the long months of parting and loneliness and fear, this one hour in the moonlit garden will more than suffice.   If there be those who would fain hide behind the blossoming lilac bushes and listen to every word the two lovers are saying, I must tell you that you will be far better off inside by the cheerful hearth, where a brisk fire of questioning, explanation and congratulation is in progress.

"A curiouser lot of happenin's it 'ud be hard to hear tell on," declared Winters; "but I don't see as thar's any light on the matter after all.   I'd like mighty well to know who put up all them fine buildin's on that island."

"I should rather know who lived there," said Madame de Langres, "and what became of them."

"Yes, and who carried off the Comte de Lantenac, and why?" added St. André meditatively ;   "that is one of the things that I cannot understand."

"And what that infernal rascal, de Miguel, had to do with it all?" said Goujet, who felt quite at his ease in this genial atmosphere.

"For my part I have thought much concerning the

strange sight which we saw in that underground chamber," put in Constantin Dinant. "The vision of the
dead man sitting alone in that great chair, the breeze
stirring his locks to a ghastly semblance of life has often
recurred to me since, and never without a strong desire
to know his past history."

"And I," said Madeline, who had entered unperceived followed by the young Comte de Lantenac,
"would like to know to whom mother and I were in-
debted for all the gowns and plenishings we were forced
to make so free with during our sojourn on the island."
Then feeling her lover's fingers close upon her's with a
warning pressure she glanced up at him quickly. His
eyes were fixed upon the strange old man who had accompanied them hither. Up to the present moment
this personage had sat almost unnoticed in the great
arm-chair which Madame de Langres had hospitably
placed for him. Amid all the joyful talk, conjecture
and wonderment he had sat gloomily silent, but now on
a sudden he sat upright and raised one tremulous hand
imperatively.

"I pray you of your kindness to listen to what I shall
say. I am an old man ; my days are almost spent and
before I go hence I would fain speak once more of the
strange happenings of my life. Of all that has been
meted out to me in the providence of the Most High
I think there has been nothing more marvellous than
that I should find myself surrounded by those to whom
my very existence is unknown, and yet who have been
unwittingly entangled in the same strange web of
fate."

Every eye was fixed upon the speaker in intense curiosity commingled with awe. A deep silence followed

his words, broken only by the singing of the flames in the chimney, and the slight rustling of the robes of the women as they leant forward toward the strange figure in the great chair.

CHAPTER LV

THE silence had at length grown almost painful, when the unknown again raised his hand. "My strength is failing me," he said feebly, "I must speak briefly of what is a long tale—yes, and sorrowful above most; a tale of terror, of injustice, of misery, and ending, I fear me, in the black night of oblivion. You will not wish to bruit abroad what I shall say; there is no need that I ask you to keep my bitter secret—the bitterest and the blackest of all the century; but I desire that the matter be briefly set forth in order, as I shall tell it, and that the writing be hidden away and preserved till such time as it can safely be made known. 'There is nothing hidden that shall not be made known,' even in this earth; and those who are yet to live shall know what it were death to breathe in any other air save this of the new world.

"It once made my heart beat high to think that I was the friend of a king; not a slave, not a political favorite, scarcely a courtier, but a friend.

"'Heaven has sent me many things,' my royal master would sometimes say to me with a sigh, when we chanced to be alone, 'and has set me in a high place—too high I sometimes think for my good—and after all what does it profit; I can be sure of nothing that I see; even my mother does not love me. I am the loneliest soul in all France.'

464

" This was only at odd moments, at other times Louis
XIII. was the king, greedy of pleasure, haughty, false,
vain.   Yes, I saw all of his faults plainly enough, but I
also saw—what he revealed to no one else in all the
world—his naked soul, the soul of an unhappy, lonely
man.   I loved him ; and what is more he knew that I
loved him.   He offered me many honors, much gold,
and dazzling preferments.   But I did not care for such
things ; I had witnessed the rise and fall of de Luynes,
the fate of Marshal d'Ancre and his heroic wife, the
assassination of Concini, and I said to my royal master,
'If I accept these things at your hands, you will afterward fear me ; and from fear to hate there is but a
single step.   I love you, sire, and you honor me with
your confidence—'

" 'Nay, nay,' he would say, 'more than that, I love
thee ; thou art my friend—my one friend.'   And this
was enough for me.   I held the post of private gentleman in waiting to the king, and my relations to him
.were quite unnoticed by the courtiers in their mad
scramble for the uppermost places in the king's favor.

"The queen, the lovely Anne of Austria, treated
me haughtily enough ; she suspected me of an enmity
of which, heaven knows, I was entirely innocent.
As for the great Cardinal Richelieu, he once thought to
make me his tool because of my access to the king's
ear.   But after an hour's interview he exclaimed, 'Thou
art a stupid dolt ; an' hast wit enough to brush the king's
habit 'tis a marvel !'   He never troubled me again, nor
I him ; I feared him.   But he was a great man—a great
man, and one who had the best interests of the kingdom at heart.   I saw that even then.   But the king also
feared him, and he hated him as much as he feared.

"I remember me well of the scene between Mary de Medici, the queen-mother, and Richelieu in presence of the king. The king could not conceal his pleasure in the abuse which the infuriated woman heaped upon the cardinal. It was thought that his fall was inevitable; the courtiers were mad with joy. But Louis hesitated. 'Wouldst thou down him?' he said to me, biting his nails savagely, as he walked up and down his cabinet at Versailles.

"'Who could take his place?' I asked.

"'Ay, that is the question. The man is hateful to me, but I fear—I fear—' That very night he sent for the cardinal, and it was all made up betwixt them, to the discomfiture of the queen-mother, who was soon afterward made a sort of prisoner of state at Compiègne.

"All these things are known to you, for they are matters of history; but what I have to tell you has not to do with history as it is written down by the court chronicler, but rather as it is recorded in those books which shall one day be opened before the great white throne of the King of kings, where all secrets shall be laid open.

"It was some years after this 'Day of Dupes,' as it has since been called, when the king was walking, according to his pleasure and custom, in the park at Versailles. Through the mediation of Richelieu the queen had become reconciled to her husband, and the court and the nation were rejoicing in the marvellous news that after twenty years of childless union there was at length prospect of an heir to the throne. Louis was in unusually good spirits and talked and laughed freely with his courtiers, but it chanced that after a time he

and I were for the moment separated from the others.
The king turned to me with a laugh.

"'I am like a honey-pot, plagued with a swarm of
flies,' quoth he. 'Let us give them the slip, for I am
weary of their idle chatter.' As he said this he was
hurrying down one of the close-clipped alleys of
greenery, still laughing to himself.

"I followed closely at his heels, for although I was
loath to cross his humor, I knew that the thing was
scarcely right. After threading two or three of the
hedge-grown walks the king stopped under a great
chestnut tree, which spread its green branches above
our heads all crowned with spires of snowy blossoms,
like a chandelier set with waxlights—for this was in
May, as I well remember. He drew a long breath of
pleasure as he looked up, then threw himself down on
the green sward. 'Look not so solemn, I pray thee,
good friend!' he said, laughing at my sober face. 'I
am but a sorry monarch if I cannot rid myself of the
irksome observance of court at my pleasure.' With
that he began to hum a little air under his breath,
pulling up the tiny flowers that nestled in the turf
and looking at them as if they were something new to
his eyes.

"I still stood gazing down at him, feeling somewhat
troubled by his unwonted freak, and yet sympathizing
heartily with his weariness of the courtiers and their
perpetual flatteries, when suddenly the branches of the
hedge parted and a strange figure broke through. I
started forward with a cry, but stopped, when I saw
that it was only a woman—and a very diminutive one
at that. As for the king he sprang to his feet, and laid
his hand on the hilt of his sword.

" ' Do not draw on a poor defenseless body who has not strength to harm a fly,' said the woman, in a strange low voice that somehow had a ring of authority in it. 'I have a word for you, sire, and you will do well to heed it. On the fifth day of September there will be born to you a son, on whose breast shall appear the likeness of a blood-red hand. Blood for blood. Ay—and a sorry day shall it be for the father of that child when he shall proclaim it heir to the throne of France ; few and troubled shall be his days. The prince of the bloody hand shall bring death into life.' With that she drew back into the shrubbery and was gone.

"I stood as if struck dumb ; but the king fell into a great trembling, and yet withal he raged with anger as I had never before heard him. 'The hag shall die for that word,' he said in a smothered voice ; 'and they that taught her that vile saying shall perish with her !' He would have dashed into the wood after the woman, but that I held him back.

"The whole domain of Versailles was presently searched from one end to the other, and the town and the country side for miles around, and that without delay ; but the woman was not found, nor was she ever again heard of.

"The king called me to him that night in private, and said, 'The thing that the woman said to me shall not become public ; it would come to the ears of the queen and cause a great mischief. Swear to me that you will not tell it.' I swore right gladly, kissing the king's hand which he graciously held out to me.

"The subject was not again mentioned between us, and I had all but forgotten the circumstance, when one evening it was announced that the queen's time had come. By the command of Louis, very few were in attendance, the court being assembled in the anteroom, awaiting with what anxiety may be imagined, the royal announcement. I remained alone in a small side-chamber, at the special request of my master. The queen's favorite woman was with her mistress. Before many hours had passed the king came to me in a state of uncontrollable agitation. 'The curse has come upon me,' he muttered hoarsely; 'but there is a way out, and I shall take it.'

"Half an hour later Louis XIII. presented to the court an heir to the throne of France, the Dauphin, afterward Louis XIV. There was great rejoicing, ringing of bells, firing of cannon and thanksgivings in all the churches. The infant prince was a strong and healthy child, a wonderful babe, a true heaven-sent prince!

"Amid the general excitement no one noticed that the private gentleman in waiting to the king had suddenly disappeared from his post, nor yet that the queen's favorite woman—whom very few liked and many envied—was also missing. Or if any questions were asked they were easily enough answered. The man had had the misfortune to offend, and was therefore relegated to the darkness outside the court. The court shrugged its shoulders and straightway—forgot. As for the woman, it was time she was put out of the way; she was a mischief-maker, a spy, a hypocrite.

"What then had befallen the king's friend and the queen's waiting-woman? They had been suddenly and secretly removed in the dead of night to a stronghold belonging to the king. The man was silent; the woman wept with fear. She carried moreover in her arms, something that stirred feebly in its wrappings and wailed fitfully. The man looked upon the child by the light of a taper, and behold, it bore upon its breast the likeness of a blood-red hand! The woman shook as if with palsy. 'There were two,' she whispered, 'but this one came first; I swear that it did. What does it all mean?'

"She knew the next day when the king visited the pair in private. He glanced at the child, sleeping quietly enough in the arms of the queen's waiting-woman, and a strong convulsion swept over his features. The woman looked up at him boldly. 'What does this mean, sire?' she said. '*This* is the heir; it came into the world a full five minutes before the other. I can swear to it.'

"'For all that, this is not the heir,' said the king harshly. 'I have said it, and so it shall be. And after all what harm?'—relapsing into his usual easy humor, and pacing up and down the room, his hands clasped behind his back—'The other is the stronger child, the better favored. Why should a paltry five minutes make one the king, the other a mere nobody? Assuredly I have the right to say which shall be my successor, and I have chosen. This shall be your charge. You two shall have this child; I give him to you. And the better to bind you to your duty a priest shall make you one.—Nay, no protests, no denials; it shall be as I have said.'

"With that he flung open the door and a dark figure, clad in the habit of a Jesuit priest, glided into the room. At a gesture from the king we two stood up mechanically—the woman still holding the unconscious babe in her arms, and we were wed; assuredly the strangest

bridal that ever took place on earth. The brief ceremony concluded the priest at once withdrew. The king
looked on us as we stood there dumb in his presence,
and his face hardened visibly.

" 'Why do you not thank me for your bride?' he
cried with a harsh laugh. 'It is not to every low-born
page and waiting-woman that the king does such honor.'
Then as we made him no answer—which indeed he
could hardly have expected—he went on, bringing his
closed fist down into his open hand. 'Your maintenance
shall be suited to your rank and the rank of your child.
It is not necessary for me to tell you that the blood-red
hand upon the breast of the child must forever lie upon
your mouths. Prate of this matter and such a vengeance
shall descend upon your heads as shall effectually silence
you.'

"He turned as if to leave the room. Seeing this I
recovered my wits a little and flung myself down at his
feet. I know not what wild words I cried out. I reminded him of my long devotion, of my love for him,
of the injustice to the helpless babe. She that was now
my wife knelt beside me, weeping and holding up the
child, which awakening, added its feeble wail.

" 'I have forgotten nothing,' the king made answer.
'—Nay, rather I have remembered ; but so it must be,
the interests of the kingdom demand the sacrifice.
Should the child die—but no, he must live out his allotted time.' And throwing out his hand in a gesture
of loathing toward the innocent cause of all this trouble,
he turned and left the room. Nor did we ever see him
more.

"We were kept close prisoners in the place where we
were for more than a year, being never allowed speech

with any one outside—nor inside for that matter. The time passed wearily enough; though after awhile our mutual society, which at first was very distasteful to us both, became less irksome. Nay, perhaps because of the dreadful bond which united us, we became more than ordinarily fond of one another."

The speaker paused, as if lost in painful retrospect. No one of the group assembled about the fire ventured to disturb him. Indeed to more than one of them the mystery was a mystery no longer, though there were still many things to be explained.

At length the stranger sighed heavily, and rousing himself with a visible effort looked about the circle of faces, a kindly light shining in his deep eyes. "It hath warmed my heart to speak of these matters to you," he said slowly. Then his face darkened again with pain "—If only I knew what had become of him !" he murmured. "Ah, well ! in God's good time, he shall come into his kingdom." As if comforted by this thought, he went on with his narrative.

"For more than a year, as I have said, we were kept close prisoners in the tower, the name and exact location of which we were still ignorant of. My wife often implored me with tears to devise some way of escaping; this was manifestly impossible, as she very well knew, still none the less did she urge me with all unreason, and with upbraidings hard to be borne.

" ' Thou art afraid !' she would cry with bitter scorn. ' A man ? Pah ! thou are as nerveless as this babe !' Then she would fall to weeping over the infant, kissing his tiny hands and murmuring fond foolish words in his tiny ear; and the child, by this time being grown a lusty babe, would crow and laugh and caress her in turn.

"What with the knowledge of his wrongs, and the beauty and intelligence of the child, with his innocent, unknowing joy in life, unfolding so strangely and darkly before him, there grew up in our hearts a mighty love for him, such as I believe fathers and mothers in the happy outside world never know. Yet was this love commingled with such fear for his future, and such hopeless anger at his fate, that it was more like bitter pain than like joy; it caused me to fall into strange fits of gloom and anger, and my wife to weep womanwise, at which the child marveled and was often sad as he grew older, being at a loss to understand the temper of our affections.

"But all this was after we came to live on the island. We were removed thither early in the second year of our imprisonment, with the same precautions and secrecy to which in a measure we had now grown accustomed. Of our life there I need not speak in detail, you have all seen the place and know how quietly and monotonously, yet withal in a way happily, our days and years may have glided away. We had every comfort, every luxury that could be devised. We were safe, we were peaceful, the world troubled us not. I could have been almost content had it not been for my wife; her's was a stormy, restless spirit, and although as the years passed she became more tranquil, she never lost the hope that one day would see this great wrong righted. This the more since the child had grown almost before we were aware of it into a man. His education had been my care, and it was an alternate joy and pain to me to observe the unfolding of his brilliant mind. Ah! what a ruler he would have made, bold, brave, yet tender as a woman, and endowed with such genius as the world has rarely seen.

"As he grew older he chafed sadly at the narrow confines which encompassed him. And in a terror lest he should try to escape us to a certain destruction, I endeavored to direct his mind to architecture, to painting, to science, to sculpture, in which branches I was myself but indifferently skilled. My pupil quickly outstripped me in all, and that without apparent effort. After a time these occupations palled on him, and one day, that which we had feared so long came upon us; he attempted to escape from the island. He failed, and was brought back unhurt,—would God he had perished then!

"After this he seemed on a sudden to grow old; and indeed the years had fled away so softly, albeit slowly, that it was hard for us to realize that he was no longer a child, but a man, on whom the sun of life had already begun to go down. He brooded much alone and in silence. What he thought he unfolded to no one. It was during this time that he caused the marble tomb to be built; he himself sculptured the angel which stands guardian over it.

"'Here I shall lie at rest,' he said to me. 'And the fever will have burned itself into ashes—God grant that it be soon, for why should I live?'

"I did not answer him. How could I?

"After a little he turned to me and spoke again. 'I have only known one name in all my life,' he said,—my wife had always called him Louis, as was indeed his right,—'but here I would fain write my father's name.' And he looked at me beseechingly.

"Words failed me; I could only groan aloud. The next day I stole again to the place in secret, and there I saw cut deep into the marble by his own hand the single word *Eheu*. I found that my wife had also seen

474

it, for when we were alone, she told me that she had determined to tell him all, and that come what might she would have no further hand in deceiving him. I endeavored to dissuade her, but without success. That night she told him; I came upon them just as she was kneeling before him kissing his hand. I could not help kneeling also. He was the king. One could see it.

"He was very gentle with us both, saying little for several days; then he asked me a number of questions which showed that he had gotten information from some source to which I myself had not access. He finally told me that he had bribed the Portuguese, José de Miguel, to whom had been intrusted the bringing of supplies to the island. I feared the man, but my wife was persuaded that we had found a useful tool ready to our hand. All the money, jewels and plate, left us by our thieving seneschal—who had strangely disappeared a number of years since—I had myself always secretly suspected this de Miguel of a hand in the matter—everything of value, as I have said, was passed over to the man de Miguel. In return he furnished us with the yacht *L'Espérance*, which has played so wonderful a part in your adventures. It was christened by the king, as we now chose to call him between ourselves. We had planned to escape in her to England, where we hoped to find asylum and redress. This at least was the plan which the king and my wife made with de Miguel. He was to furnish sailors for the ship and all needful provisions. I myself, as I have said, distrusted the man, and after much thought I managed to send a dispatch to England, by the hand of a common sailor on board the lugger in which de Miguel used to visit the island. I had little hope that my message would ever fall into the hands of those to whom it was addressed. It did; but alas, too late!

"De Miguel betrayed us to the French government just as our plans were ripe—for I know not how much gold, and one dreadful day saw a French frigate anchored to our leeward. We were seized without an instant's warning, every soul on the island, great and small, and carried aboard the vessel. All were gagged and bound, but upon the face of the king was forced a mask of black velvet, secured behind by a band and lock of iron. At sight of this outrage on the sacred person of him whom she loved with all the intensity of a mother, my wife fell down in strong convulsions; when they lifted her it was found that she was dead. I was glad when I saw it. If only it might have been for us all!

"I never saw the king again. I was confined closely on board ship, being never permitted to speak, and upon landing I was thrust into a foul dungeon of the Bastile, where I languished for many months. How it happened that I was ever again suffered to see the light of the sun I do not know, but certain it is that I was one day taken out and placed aboard a vessel bound for America. I have since thought that it was some strange blunder on the part of my jailors. Be that as it may, our vessel was shipwrecked, and after days of suffering during which I prayed in vain for death, I was rescued in the manner which is already known to you. Heaven willed that this tale must be told. But now my soul can pass in peace."

The speaker's voice died away into silence; his head sank upon his breast. Baillot sprang forward in alarm, thinking that life had indeed fled, but the old man was still breathing feebly. They raised him tenderly and laid him upon a couch, while Madame de Langres hastened to administer a restorative. After a little he opened his eyes; they were bright with the light of another world.

"I am going," he said, in a stronger voice than before, "and something tells my spirit that all will yet be well. My king shall be happy in that place where are gathered together all the kingdoms of the world and the glory of them. And I—shall be with him. But I have yet one word for you who shall remain behind. The treasure, which the seneschal had hidden away, and which he continued to guard in death, was mine. I leave it to be divided equally between the men who saved my life." And having thus made his peace with the world, the weary sufferer lay back upon his pillows, content and tranquil to await the end.

It did not come for several days, and those who watched him, had begun to hope that perhaps he might yet recover, so peaceful was he, and so bright a light shone in his strange eyes. But it was not to be. As he slept one day he ceased breathing, so quietly that Baillot who was watching by his bed did not know when the last sigh left his smiling lips.

Not long after the old man's burial, Madeline de Langres and Henri Baillot, Comte de Lantenac, were married, the Huguenot pastor performing the simple ceremony. But there was no lack of that heartfelt joy, which is, after all, heaven's peculiar benison on those who truly love.

As for that redoubtable mariner, Jack Winters, he conceived a hearty liking for the ex-pirate, Goujet.

"He's a mighty good sort," he declared, "an' a sea-farin' man after my own heart. Since the yacht *L'Es-pérance* has been giv' to me, to have and to hold from this day for'ard—an' a tighter craft you won't find high nor low—he's agreed to ship with me for tradin' be-twixt Boston an' the other colonies on the coast. It'll suit us both to anchor frequent, near them as is in port to stay."

APPENDIX

"THE Man with the Iron Mask" is the strangest figure in all history. The facts presented in the preceding narrative determine the identity of this sphinx-like apparition, and that without a shadow of doubt. The document containing these facts, as set down by the hand of Henri Baillot, Comte de Lantenac, was preserved for many years with other family papers in the very treasure-cask which figures in the story. When it lately fell into the hands of the author there seemed no longer any reason why the story should not be told.

History tells us that the unfortunate being known as "The Iron Mask" was confined in the island of Ste. Marguerite in the Mediterranean sea, for a short time previous to the year 1698. Where he lived before that time no one knows; though some authorities are of the opinion that he was at one time kept in a castle at Pignerol, Savoy. He was never seen without the mask of black velvet, nor was his identity ever disclosed, though a hundred conjectures have been risked as to who the mysterious personage could be, who was treated with such strange forbearance in an age of the world when all inconvenient persons were hurried with but scant ceremony off life's stage.

In the year 1698 we hear of him at the Bastile; where so far as is known, no man save the governor ever saw his face or heard his voice. Twice this unhappy being tried to communicate with the outside world ; once with words which he scrawled with his own blood upon a linen shirt ; and again by means of a silver plate upon which he had scratched a message, and which he threw out of the window of his dungeon. The persons who found these articles died without apparent cause immediately afterward, without having divulged their secret.

During his residence in the Bastile this mysterious personage was waited upon at table and at his toilet by the governor himself, who permitted no one to handle any article used by him. His linen was at once destroyed after being used. The mask, which became his distinguishing characteristic, was composed of black velvet, securely fastened behind with steel springs. It was never removed, even at the time of his death. He breathed his last at the Bastile, November 19, 1703, and was buried the following night with great secrecy in the cemetery of St. Paul, under the name of Machiati. His twin brother, known to the world as Louis XIV., "Le Grand Monarque," died September 1, 1715.

The island on which "The Man with the Iron Mask" passed his earlier and happier years, was evidently, like the Azores group, of volcanic origin. It remained desolate and uninhabited till the year 1811, when, during the convulsion which saw a volcano suddenly emerge from the sea to the height of three hundred feet, and, after discharging vast quantities of lava, stones and cinders, as suddenly disappear, it also sank beneath the waves of the Atlantic to be seen no more.